Language and Society

The Collected Works of M. A. K. Halliday

Volume 10 in the Collected Works of M. A. K. Halliday

Language and Society

M. A. K. Halliday

Edited by Jonathan J. Webster

continuum

Continuum

The Tower Building	80 Maiden Lane
11 York Road	Suite 704
London	New York
SE1 7NX	NY 10038

First published in paperback 2009

British Library Cataloguing-in-Publication Data
A catalogue record for this book is available from the British Library.

ISBN: HB: 0–8264–5876–9 (hardback)
9780826458766
ISBN: PB: 9781847065773 (paperback) 2009

Library of Congress Cataloguing-in-Publication Data
A catalog record for this book is available from the Library of Congress.

Typeset by Data Standards Ltd, Frome, Somerset, UK.
Printed and bound in Great Britain by MPG Books, Cornwall

CONTENTS

PREFACE

For now we see through a glass, darkly; but then face to face:
now I know in part; but then shall I know even as also I am known
(I Corinthians 13:12)

The first time I encountered the name of M. A. K. Halliday was when, as an undergraduate majoring in linguistics at SUNY Buffalo, I read 'The users and uses of language' (1964), the first paper in this volume. Back then, what I appreciated most was how helpful his work was in giving me a handle on such sociolinguistic concepts as dialect, register, accent, etc. Now some 30 years on since my days as an undergraduate, having had the privilege these past several years to serve as Editor for Professor M. A. K. Halliday's Collected Works, I appreciate so much more the depth of insight this great linguist has brought to the study of language, not just in terms of language as institution, or even as system, but as social semiotic.

When it comes to studying language, or what Professor Halliday refers to as "the single most complex phenomenon in nature", it may seem as though we only see through a glass, darkly. But then, if we approach language from a functional perspective as an interorganism phenomenon, "putting language into the context of 'language and social man'", observing exchanges of meaning in face-to-face encounters, then we begin to see more clearly and appreciate more fully its richness in meaning potential.

I close with the following poem dedicated to the teacher turned grammarian, Professor M. A. K. Halliday, whose work for over more than half a century continues to teach and inspire:

Poem for the Teacher turned Grammarian
M. A. K. Halliday

He recalls May 13 '45 when the teacher first taught the students
Chinese. Learning how to mean, exploring together. Then the sixties,
Now the grammarian developing system networks, written on laundry
cards, then in *Notes on transitivity and theme in English*, early days
in appliable linguistics.

Thinking meaning, probing logic in living logos, seeking
To know meanings, light and darkness, and the shades between,
Seen not as shadows in greyscale, but as spectrums of living
Colour. Construing meanings to explain those processes of meaning.

It seems that meaning was how the world began. In the beginning ...
The Word. There is grandeur in this view of life. And Nigel said ...
I want that. . .let's do that. . .here, I am. From so simple a beginning
Endless forms most beautiful and most wonderful have been, and
are being evolved.

Continuing discourse, encouraging dialogue, on language as theorizer
And mediator, exploring the excellence, pure function, and best power
Both of objects seen and eye that sees, shaping forms of consciousness,
Opening a window to the soul of language, as process, as semiotic
system.

Where does language live? In the works of man, and across the face
Of human life. In the Word made flesh, and dwelling among us.
Exchanging meaning in shared context of situation. No matter
How commonplace or highly valued, whether sacred or secular,
There is no semiotic act that leaves the world exactly as it was before.

Since setting foot in that classroom some sixty years ago, the Teacher
Turned grammarian has continued to advance our understanding
Of what is perhaps the single most complex phenomenon in nature,
Inspiring new perspectives on language as system rich in unending
meaning potential.

ACKNOWLEDGEMENTS

We are grateful to the original publishers for permission to reprint the articles and chapters in this volume. Original publication details are provided below, and also at the beginning of each chapter.

Chapter 1
'The Users and Uses of Language', from M A K Halliday, Angus McIntosh and Peter Strevens, *The Linguistic Sciences and Language Teaching,* London: Longman, 1964. Copyright © Pearson Education Limited.

Chapter 2
'Language in a Social Perspective', from *Educational Review,* 23.3, pp.165–188, (1971). Copyright © Taylor and Francis Ltd. www.tandf.co.uk/journals/titles/00131911.asp

Chapter 3
Language and Social Man, Schools Council Programme in Linguistics and English Teaching: Papers, Series II, Vol. 3, London: Longman, 1974. Copyright © Pearson Education Limited.

Chapter 4
'Sociological Aspects of Semantic Chang', from Luigi Heilmann (ed.), *Proceedings of the Eleventh International Congress of Linguists,* 853–879, (1975). Originally published Bologna: Il Mulino, 1974. **[Rights reverted to author so no copyright line]**

Chapter 5
'Language as Social Semiotics: Towards a General Sociolinguistic Theory', from Adam Makkai and Valerie Becker Makkai (eds.), *The First LACUS Forum*, 17–46, (1975). Copyright © Hornbeam Press, California. **[Acknowledgement for chapter: 'The paper was first published in LACUS Forum I, 1975, published by the Linguistics Association of Canada and the United States].**

Chapter 6
'Some Aspects of Sociolinguistics', from *Interactions between Linguistics and Mathematical Education,* Report on a Symposium Sponsored by UNESCO – CEDO – ICMI, Nairobi, September 1974, ED-74/CONF. 808 (64-73). Reproduced by permission of UNESCO.

Chapter 7
'Foreword', from Basil Bernstein (ed.), *Class, Codes and Control Vol. II: Applied Studies towards a Sociology of Lanugage,* London: Routledge and Kegan Paul, 1973, pp.ix–xvi. Copyright © Taylor and Francis Ltd.

Chapter 8
'Language and the Theory of Codes', from Alan Sadovnik (ed.), *Knowledge and Pedagogy: The Sociology of Basil Bernstein,* Westport: Greenwood Publishing Group, 1995. Copyright © 1995 by Alan Sadovnik and contributors. Reproduced with permission of Greenwood Publishing Group, Inc., Westport, CT.

Chapter 9
'An Interpretation of the Functional Relationship between Language and Social Structure', from Uta Quasthoff (ed.), *Sprachstruktur – Sozialstruktur: Zur Linguistischen Theorienbildung,* 3-42. Copyright © Scriptor, Konigstein.

Chapter 10
'Anti-languages', from *American Anthropologist,* 78.3, 570-584, (1976). Copyright © 1976 by the American Anthropological Association.

PART ONE

USERS AND USES

EDITOR'S INTRODUCTION

This first section consists of the paper "The users and uses of language" (1964), which first appeared in the book *The Linguistic Sciences and Language Teaching* (London: Longman, 1964). In this groundbreaking work on the relation between a language and the people who use it, Professor Halliday focuses attention on the following four major topics, which he groups under the heading of institutional linguistics: (i) languages in contact, i.e. what happens when one language community impinges on another; (ii) dialects, i.e. varieties distinguished by user; (iii) registers, i.e. varieties distinguished according to use; and (iv) the attitudes of members of a language community towards their language and its varieties.

Since this paper first appeared, readers have continued to benefit from Professor Halliday's explanation of such core sociolinguistic concepts as idiolect, dialect, standard language, accent and register. Readers come away with a better grasp of the fundamental sociolinguistic notions concerning variation in language. One notes, for example, that while individuals each possess their own **idiolect**, nevertheless people tend to group themselves according to their perceived sense of identity with a particular language and dialect. The **dialect** used by an L1 speaker belonging to a particular language community, i.e. people who regard themselves as speaking the same language, may vary "at any or all levels" from the dialects of other L1 speakers of the same language. Typically, one dialect emerges as the **standard language**, serving as a **lingua franca** among speakers of the various dialects within the same language community. Most speakers of this standard language, however, continue to speak with the phonetics of their native dialect, i.e. **accent**, without loss in intelligibility.

3

The concept of *register*, on the other hand, is needed to account for what people do with their language. "The study of registers", maintains Professor Halliday, "is crucial both to our understanding of how language works and in application to literary analysis, machine translation and native and foreign language teaching." The term 'register', as used here, does not just refer to marginal or special varieties of language, but rather covers the total range of our language activity in various situations and situation types. Registers are distinguishable on the basis of a classification along the three dimensions of *field of discourse*, i.e. the area of operation of the language activity (e.g. shopping and games-playing as well as medicine and linguistics); *tenor* or *style of discourse*, i.e. the relations among the participants (e.g. 'casual', 'intimate', 'deferential'); and *mode of discourse*, i.e. the medium or mode of the language activity (e.g. spoken and written language).

The approach presented here represents a significant step forward in efforts at achieving a better understanding of change and variation in language, which is no small task considering "the complex and deep-rooted attitudes of the members of a language community towards their language".

Chapter One

THE USERS AND USES OF LANGUAGE (1964)

Description is not the only approach to the study of language. There are other branches of linguistics: one may for example treat language historically, showing how it persists and modifies through time. In application to language teaching, it is descriptive linguistics that is the most important. Even for this purpose, however, description is not the only type of linguistic study which is relevant.

In this section we are concerned with the branch of linguistics which deals, to put it in the most general terms, with the relation between a language and the people who use it. This includes the study of language communities, singly and in contact, of varieties of language and of attitudes to language. The various special subjects involved here are grouped together under the name of "institutional linguistics".

There is no clear line dividing institutional from descriptive linguistics; the two, though distinct enough as a whole, merge into one another. The study of context leads on to the analysis of situation types and of the uses of language. The descriptive distinction into spoken and written language naturally involves us in a consideration of the different varieties of language they represent. In institutional linguistics we are looking at the same data, language events, but from a different standpoint. The attention is now on the users of language, and the uses they make of it.

There are many ways of finding patterns among people. Some patterns are obvious: everyone is either male or female, with a fairly

'The Users and Uses of Language', from M A K Halliday, Angus McIntosh and Peter Strevens, *The Linguistic Sciences and Language Teaching*, London: Longman, 1964. Copyright © Pearson Education Limited.

clear line between the two. Some, equally obvious, are less clearly demarcated: people are either children or adults, but we may not be sure of the assignment of a particular individual. Humorously, we may recognize all sorts of *ad hoc* patterns, like W. S. Gilbert's classification of babies into "little liberals" and "little conservatives". The human sciences all introduce their own patterning: people are introverts or extroverts; negriform, mongoliform, caucasiform or australiform; employed, self-employed, non-employed or unemployed. No clear boundaries here, though the categories, statistically defined and, sometimes, arbitrarily delimited, are useful enough. Other patterns, such as national citizenship, are thrust upon us, often with conflicting criteria: each state tends to have its own definition of its citizens.

In linguistics, people are grouped according to the language or languages they use. This dimension of patterning is sometimes applied outside linguistics: a nation, in one view, is defined by language as well as by other factors. On the other hand, the category of "nation" defined politically has sometimes been used in linguistics to give an institutional definition of "a language": in this view "a language" is a continuum of dialects spoken within the borders of one state. On such a criterion, British English and American English are two languages, though mutually intelligible; Chinese is one language, though Pekingese and Cantonese are not mutually intelligible; and Flemish, Dutch, German, Austrian German and Swiss German are five languages, though the pairing of mutually intelligible and mutually unintelligible dialects does not by any means follow the various national boundaries.

This is not the only way of defining "a language"; there are as many definitions as there are possible criteria. Even within institutional linguistics various criteria are involved, each yielding a definition that is useful for some specific purpose. The concept of 'a language' is too important to be taken for granted; nor is it made any less powerful by the existence of multiple criteria for defining it. But we have to be careful to specify the nature of this category when we use it.

In institutional linguistics it is useful to start with the notion of a **language community**, and then to ask certain questions about it. The language community is a group of people who regard themselves as using the same language. In this sense there is a language community 'the Chinese', since they consider themselves as speaking Chinese, and not Pekingese, Cantonese and so on. There is no language community 'the Scandinavians'; Norwegians speak Norwegian, Danes Danish and Swedes Swedish, and these are not regarded as dialects of the

6

'Scandinavian language', even though they are by and large all mutually intelligible. The British, Americans, Canadians, Australians and others call their language "English"; they form a single language community.

This method of recognizing a language community has the advantage that it reflects the speakers' attitude towards their language, and thus the way they use it. All speakers of English, for example, agree more or less on the way it should be written. At the same time, like all institutional linguistic categories and most of the basic categories of the human sciences, it is not clear-cut, because people do not fall into clear-cut patterns. There is a minor tendency for Americans to regard themselves as using a different language from the British, and this is again reflected in minor variations in orthography. But it is a mistake to exaggerate this distinction, or to conclude therefrom that there is no unified English-speaking language community.

Some of the questions that can be asked about a language community and its language are these. First, what happens when it impinges on other language communities? Second, what varieties of its language are there? Under the second question come these subdivisions: varieties according to users (that is, varieties in the sense that each speaker uses one variety and uses it all the time) and varieties according to use (that is, in the sense that each speaker has a range of varieties and chooses between them at different times). The variety according to users is a **dialect**; the variety according to use is a **register**. Third, what attitudes do the speakers display towards their language and any or all of its varieties?

2

Situations in which one language community impinges on another have been called "language contact" situations. Such situations are characterized by varying degrees of bilingualism. Bilingualism is recognized wherever a native speaker of one language makes use of a second language, however partially or imperfectly. It is thus a cline, ranging in terms of the individual speaker, from the completely monolingual person at one end, who never uses anything but his own native language or "L1", through bilingual speakers who make use in varying degree of a second language or "L2", to the endpoint where a speaker has complete mastery of two languages and makes use of both in all uses to which he puts either. Such a speaker is an "ambilingual".

True ambilingual speakers are rare. Most people whom we think of as bilingual restrict at least one of their languages to certain uses: and in

7

any given use, one or the other languages tends to predominate. There are probably millions of L2 English speakers throughout the world with a high degree of bilingualism, but who could neither make love or do the washing up in English nor discuss medicine or space travel in their L1. Even those who have learnt two languages from birth rarely perform all language activities in both; more often than not a certain amount of specialization takes place.

This distinction between an L1 and an L2, a native and a non-native or learnt language, is of course not clear-cut. Moreover it cuts across the degree of bilingualism. Some bilingual speakers, including some who are ambilingual, can be said to have two (occasionally more) native languages. There is no exact criterion for this; but one could say arbitrarily that any language learnt by the child before the age of instruction, from parents, from others, such as a nurse, looking after it, or from other children, is an L1. It is clear, however, that only a small proportion of those who learn two or more languages in this way become ambilingual speakers; and conversely, not all ambilinguals have two L1s.

A point that has often been observed about native bilingual, including ambilingual, speakers is that they are unable to translate between their L1s. This does not mean of course that they cannot learn to translate between them. But translation has to be learnt by them as a distinct operation; it does not follow automatically from the possession of two sets of native language habits. This has been linked with the fact that those with two L1s are usually not true ambilinguals: that they have usually specialized their two or more native languages into different uses. But this cannot be the only reason, since even those who approach or attain true ambilingualism are still usually unable to translate without instruction. It appears that it is a characteristic of an L1, defined in the way suggested above, to operate as a distinct set of self-sufficient patterns in those situations in which language activity is involved. However ambilingual the speaker is, in the sense that there is no recognizable class of situation in which he could not use either of his languages, there is always some difference between the actual situations in which he uses the one and those in which he uses the other, namely that each of the two is associated with a different group of participants.

This raises the question: how unique is or are the native language or languages in the life of the speaker? No sure answer can yet be given to this question. It is clear that for the great majority of bilingual speakers the L2 never replaces the L1 as a way of living; nor is it intended to do so. We may want to attain a high degree of competence in one or more foreign languages, but we usually do not expect thereby to disturb the part played in our lives by the native one. On the other hand, those who move permanently to a new language community may, if they move as individuals and not as whole families, abandon at least the active use of their native language and replace it throughout by an L2.

This in itself is not enough to guarantee a particular degree of attainment in the L2. Some speakers are more easily content: they may, for example, not try to adopt the phonetic patterns of the L2 beyond the point where they become comprehensible to its native speakers. Others may simply fail to achieve the standard of performance that they themselves regard as desirable. In this way they cut down the role played by language in their lives. On the other hand, there is clearly no upper limit to attainment in an L2. The L2 speaker may live a normal, full life in his adopted language community, absorb its literature and even use the language for his own creative writing, as Conrad and Nabokov have done so successfully with English. Whether the learnt language will ever be so "infinitely docile", in Nabokov's words, as the native language, it is hard to say. Certainly the user of an L2 may learn to exploit its resources as widely as do its native speakers; and though he is more conscious of these resources than the majority of native speakers, in this he merely resembles that minority who have learnt to be conscious of how their native language works: principally the creative writers, literary analysts and linguists. But while one can set no limit to the possible degree of mastery of an L2, it remains true that such a level of attainment is rarely aimed at and still more rarely achieved.

The individual speaker, in contact with a new language community, may react by developing any degree and kind of bilingualism within this very wide range. Over language communities as a whole, in contact situations, certain patterns tend to emerge. Sometimes the solution adopted, at least in the long term, is not one of bilingualism. What happens in these instances is either that one language community abandons its own language and adopts that of the other – here there will be a transitional period of bilingualism, but it may be very short; or that a mixed language develops which incorporates some features of both.

Such mixed languages have usually had either English or French as one of their components; less frequently Dutch or Portuguese. Those that remain restricted to certain uses, as many have done, without ever attaining the full resources of a language, are called **pidgins**. Some mixtures, however, have developed into full languages; these are known as **creoles**. In some areas, for example in language communities in Sierra Leone, Haiti, Mauritius and Melanesia, creoles are acquired by children as their L1. Here they have full status as community languages, and there is not necessarily any bilingualism at all. The fact that in most of these areas children are expected to acquire a second language as L2 at school reflects the social status of the mixed languages, but is entirely without prejudice to their linguistic status as full community languages.

In other instances the long-term solution has been one of as it were institutionalized bilingualism. This frequently takes the form of a *lingua franca*. One language comes to be adopted as the medium of some activity or activities which the different language communities perform in common. It may be a common language for commerce, learning, administration, religion or any or all of a variety of purposes: the use determines which members of each language community are the ones who learn it.

Latin was such a lingua franca for a long period in the history of Europe; in certain countries it retains this status to the present day, though to a much restricted extent, as the lingua franca of religion. Among other languages which have been lingua franca at certain times, over certain areas and for certain uses, are Arabic, Malay, Hausa, Classical and Mandarin (Pekingese) Chinese, Swahili, Sanskrit, French, Russian and English. Since the lingua franca normally operates for certain specific purposes, it is often a more or less clearly definable part of the language that is learnt as L2. There may even develop a special variety for use as a lingua franca, as with Hindustani and "bazaar Malay". These are distinct in practice from the mixed pidgins and creoles, in that each has clearly remained a variety of its original language; but it is difficult to draw an exact theoretical distinction.

Languages such as English and Russian, which are widely learnt as second languages in the world today, are a type of lingua franca. They are a special case only in the sense that they are being learnt by unprecedented large numbers of people and for a very wide range of purposes, some of which are new. In any serious study of the problems and methods of teaching English as a second language it is important to find out what these purposes are, and how they differ in different areas and according to the needs of different individuals. Possibly the major aim that is common to all areas where English is taught as L2 is that of its use in the study of science and technology. But there are numerous other aims, educational, administrative, legal, commercial and so on, variously weighted and pursued in different countries.

The task of becoming a bilingual with English as L2 is not the same in all these different circumstances; and it is unfair to those who are struggling with the language, whether struggling to learn it or to teach it, to pretend that it is. English is 'a language' in the sense that it is not Russian or Hindi; any two events in English are events in 'the same' language. But if we want to teach what we call "a language", whether English or any other, as a second or indeed also as a first language, we must look a little more closely at the nature of the varieties within it.

3

In one dimension, which variety of a language you use is determined by who you are. Each speaker has learnt, as his L1, a particular variety of the language of this language community, and this variety may differ at any or all levels from other varieties of the same language learnt by other speakers as their L1. Such a variety, identified along this dimension, is called a "dialect".

In general, 'who you are' for this purpose means 'where you come from'. In most language communities in the world it is the region of origin which determines which dialectal variety of the language a speaker uses. In China you speak Cantonese if you come from Canton, Pekingese if you come from Peking and Yunnanese if you come from Yunnan.

Regional dialects are usually grouped by the community into major dialect areas; there may, of course, be considerable differentiation within each area. The dialects spoken in Canton, Toishan, Chungshan and Seiyap, all in Kwangtung province, are clearly distinct from one another; but they are all grouped under the general name of "Cantonese".

Within Cantonese, the local varieties form a continuum: each will resemble its neighbours on either side more closely than it resembles those further away. Among major dialect areas, there is usually also a continuum. There may be a more or less clear dialect boundary, where the occurrence of a bundle of *isoglosses* (lines separating a region displaying one grammatical, lexical, phonological or phonetic feature from a region having a different feature at the same place in the language) shows that there are a number of features in which the dialects on either side differ from each other: but the continuum is not entirely broken. Thus there is a fairly clear distinction between Cantonese and Mandarin in the area where the two meet in Kwangsi, and there is indeed a strip of country where the two coexist, many villages having some families speaking Cantonese and some speaking Mandarin. Nevertheless the variety of Cantonese spoken in this dialect border region is closer to Mandarin than are other varieties of

11

Cantonese, and the Mandarin is closer to Cantonese than are other varieties of Mandarin.

This situation represents a kind of median between two extremes: an unbroken continuum on the one hand, as between Mandarin and the Wu or lower Yangtsze dialect region, and a sharp break on the other, as between Cantonese and Hakka in Kwangtung. In this case the reason for the break is that the Hakka speakers arrived by migration from the north roughly a thousand years after the original settlement of Kwangtung by the ancestors of the modern Cantonese speakers.

This general dialect pattern turns up in one form or another all over the world. An instance of wide dialectal variety in modern Europe is provided by German. Here we have to recognize three, and possibly four, different language communities. The Flemings, in Belgium, speak Flemish, though this is now officially regarded as a variety of Dutch; the Dutch speak Dutch; Germanic speakers in Switzerland regard themselves, in general, as speaking a distinct "Swiss-German". The Germans and the Austrians, and the Swiss in certain circumstances, regard themselves as speaking German. But over the whole of this area there is one unbroken dialect continuum, with very few instances of a clear dialect boundary; ranging from the High German of Switzerland, Austria and Bavaria to the Low German of Northwest Germany, Holland and Belgium.

The normal condition of language is to change, and at times and in places where there is little mobility between dialect communities there is nothing to cause the various dialects of a language to change in the same direction. Under these conditions dialects tend to diverge from each other at all levels, perhaps most of all in phonology and phonetics. It may happen that mutual intelligibility is lost; that the language community is as it were broken up into dialect regions such that there are many pairs of regions whose speakers cannot understand one another. This happened in China. There are six major dialects in modern China: Mandarin, Cantonese, Wu, North Min, South Min and Hakka; each of which is mutually unintelligible with all the others.

This situation tends to be resolved by the emergence of one dialect as a lingua franca. In China, the spoken lingua franca has traditionally been the Pekingese form of the Mandarin dialect. But under the empire very few people from outside the Mandarin-speaking area ever learnt Mandarin unless they were government officials. Mandarin was the language of administration and some literature; but classical Chinese remained the lingua franca for most written purposes, being supplemented as an educational medium, since it could no longer function as a spoken language, by the regional dialects. In nationalist China some progress was made towards introducing Mandarin as a 'second language' in schools, and the process has continued in communist China, where with the expansion of educational facilities Mandarin is now regularly taught at some stage in the school career. It is in fact becoming a "standard" or "national" language.

A similar process took place in Germany. "Standard German" of course is 'standard' only for the language community that considers itself as speaking German (not, however, limited to Germany itself). The concept of a standard is defined in relation to the language community: to a Dutchman "standard" could only mean standard Dutch, not standard German.

In Germany, and similarly in China, there is no suggestion that the dialect chosen as the 'standard' language is any better than any other dialect. A modern state needs a lingua franca for its citizens, and there are historical reasons leading to the choice of one dialect rather than another. It may have been the one first written down, or the language of the capital; or it may, as in Germany, include a somewhat artificial mixture of features from different dialects. Nor is there any suggestion that those who learn the standard language should speak it exactly alike. The aim is intelligibility for all purposes of communication, and if a Cantonese speaks Mandarin, as most do, with a Cantonese accent, provided this does not affect his intelligibility nobody will try to stop him or suggest that his performance is inferior or that he himself is a less worthy person.

In the history of the English language, dialects followed the familiar pattern. In the fifteenth century England was a continuum of regional dialects with, almost certainly, some mutual unintelligibility. With the rise of urbanism and the modern state, a standard language emerged; this was basically the London form of the southeast Midlands dialect, but with some features from neighbouring areas, especially from the south-central Midlands. The orthography, which in Middle English had varied region by region, became more and more standardized according to the conventions associated with this dialect. As in other countries, for ease of communication, the notion of a 'correct' orthography grew up: by the late seventeenth century educated people were expected to spell alike, although in earlier times individuality had been tolerated in spelling just as it had been (and still was) in pronunciation.

The emergence of a standard language gives rise to the phenomenon of "accent", which is quite distinct from "dialect". When we learn a foreign language, we normally transfer patterns from our native language on to the language we are learning. These may be patterns at any level. Those of form, however, and most of those of phonology and orthography, tend to be progressively eliminated. This is because they may seriously impair intelligibility; they are less directly interrelated, thus reinforcing each other less; and they are easier to correct once observed, because they are not patterns of muscular activity. With phonetic patterns, on the other hand, there is greater intelligibility tolerance, more reinforcement and much greater difficulty in correction even when they are observed. Transference of phonetic habits, in other words, is easier to tolerate and harder to avoid than transference at other levels. So we usually speak with a 'foreign accent', even when our grammar and lexis are in general conformity with the native patterns of the learnt language.

So also when a speaker learns a second dialect. He generally speaks it with 'an accent': that is, with the phonetic features of his native dialect. The learning of a standard language is simply the learning of a second dialect, the dialect that happens to have been 'standardized'. Most speakers, learning the standard language of their community, continue to speak with the phonetics of their native dialect, and there is usually no loss in intelligibility.

It is quite normal for members of a language community which has a standard language to continue to use both the native and the learnt (standard) dialect in different situations throughout their lives. This happens regularly in China and even in Germany. But while in a rural community, where there is less movement of people, the native dialect is appropriate to most situations, in an urban community the relative demands on native and standard dialect are reversed. The population is probably made up of speakers of various different dialects, so that the standard language becomes a lingua franca among them; in addition there is greater mobility within and between towns.

As a consequence, many speakers drop their native dialect altogether, having very few situations in which to use it, and replace it with the standard language. In so doing, they transfer to the standard language the phonetics of the native dialect, speaking it with a regional 'accent'. In time, this form of the standard language with regional accent comes to be regarded itself as a dialect. Today, for example, people use the term "Yorkshire dialect" equally to refer both to the speech of Leeds, which is standard English with generalized West Riding phonetics, and to the speech of Upper Wharfedale, which is an 'original' West Riding dialect. Since urban speech forms expand outwards at the expense of rural ones, the longer established dialects of England are disappearing and being replaced by the standard spoken with the various regional accents.

This process is liable to happen anywhere where there is a high degree of industrialization and consequent growth of cities. What is peculiar to England, however, is the extent to which, concurrently with this process, a new dimension of dialect differentiation has come into operation. In most countries, even those highly industrialized like Germany, the way a person speaks is determined by the place he comes from: he speaks either the regional dialect or the standard language with a regional accent. In England, however, and to a lesser extent in France, Scotland, Australia and the United States, a person's speech is determined not only by the region he comes from but also by the class he comes from, or the class he is trying to move into. Our dialects and accents are no longer simply regional: they are regional and social, or "socio-regional". Nowhere else in the world is the feature found in the extreme form it has reached in England. It is a feature of English life which constantly amazes the Germans and others into whose national mythology the facts, or some version of them, have penetrated.

The dialect structure of England today can be represented by a pyramid. The vertical plane represents class, the horizontal one region. At the base, there is wide regional differentiation, widest among the agricultural workers and the lower-paid industrial workers. As one moves along the socio-economic scale, dialectal variety according to region diminishes. Finally at the apex there is no regional differentiation at all, except perhaps for the delicate shades which separate Cambridge and Oxford from each other and from the rest.

This regionally neutral variety of English, often known as "RP", standing for "received (that is, generally accepted) pronunciation", carries prestige and may be acquired at any stage in life. It tends to be taught by example rather than by instruction. Certain institutions, notably the preparatory and public schools, create, as part of their function, conditions in which it can be learnt. The speaker of this form of English has, as is well known, many social and economic advantages. There are, for example, many posts for which he will automatically be preferred over a candidate who does not speak it. If there are any posts for which the opposite is true, as is sometimes claimed, these are posts which are not likely to arouse serious competition.

When a speaker states what language he regards himself as speaking, he is defining a language community. By implication a language community may be delimited regionally, although national frontiers may enter into the definition of the region. When he states what dialect he speaks, he is defining a dialect community. Here again the delimitation that is implied is normally regional; but there are some countries, notably England, in which it is socio-regional. If the community has a standard language, there may be not only dialects but also accents: in other words 'new dialects', varieties of the standard language with regional or socio-regional phonetic patterns. The line dividing dialect and accent is often not clear-cut, and the speaker may well conflate the two. All his observations, but especially those on dialect and accent, may be coloured by value judgements; but the discussion of these we leave to the final section of this chapter.

4

A dialect is a variety of a language distinguished according to the user: different groups of people within the language community speak different dialects. It is possible also to recognize varieties of a language along another dimension, distinguished according to use. Language varies as its function varies; it differs in different situations. The name given to a variety of a language distinguished according to use is "register".

The category of "register" is needed when we want to account for what people do with their language. When we observe language activity in the various contexts in which it takes place, we find differences in the type of language selected as appropriate to different types of situation. There is no need to labour the point that a sports commentary, a church service and a school lesson are linguistically quite distinct. One sentence from any of these and many more such situation types would enable us to identify it correctly. We know, for example, where *an early announcement is expected* comes from and *apologies for absence were received*; these are not simply free variants of *we ought to hear soon* and *was sorry he couldn't make it*.

It is not the event or state of affairs being talked about that determines the choice, but the convention that a certain kind of language is appropriate to a certain use. We should be surprised, for example, if it was announced on the carton of our toothpaste that the product was *just right for cleaning false teeth* instead of *ideal for cleansing artificial dentures*. We can often guess the source of a piece of English from familiarity with its use: *mix well* probably comes from a recipe, although the action of mixing is by no means limited to cookery – and *mixes well* is more likely to be found in a testimonial.

The choice of items from the wrong register, and the mixing of items from different registers, are among the most frequent mistakes made by non-native speakers of a language. If an L2 English speaker uses, in conversation, a dependent clause with modal *should*, such as *should you like another pint of beer*, where a native speaker would use a dependent clause with *if*, he is selecting from the wrong register. Transference of this kind is not limited to foreigners; the native schoolboy may transfer in the opposite direction, writing in his Shakespeare essay *it was all up with Lear, who couldn't take any more of it.*

Linguistic humour often depends on the inappropriate choice and the mixing of registers: P. G. Wodehouse exploits this device very effectively. Fifty years ago the late George Robey used to recite a version of "The house that Jack built" which ended as follows: ... *that disturbed the equanimity of the domesticated feline mammal that exterminated the noxious rodent that masticated the farinaceous produce deposited in the domiciliary edifice erected by Master John.*

Dialects tend to differ primarily, and always to some extent, in substance. Registers, on the other hand, differ primarily in form. Some registers, it is true, have distinctive features at other levels, such as the voice quality associated with the register of church services. But the crucial criteria of any given register are to be found in its grammar and its lexis. Probably lexical features are the most obvious. Some lexical items suffice almost by themselves to identify a certain register: *cleanse* puts us in the language of advertising, *probe* of newspapers, especially headlines, *tablespoonful* of recipes or prescriptions, *neckline* of fashion reporting or dressmaking instructions. The clearest signals of a particular register are scientific technical terms, except those that belong to more than one science, like *morphology* in biology and linguistics.

Often it is not the lexical item alone but the collocation of two or more lexical items that is specific to one register. *Kick* is presumably neutral, but *free kick* is from the language of football. Compare the disc jockey's *top twenty*; *thinned right down* at the hairdresser's (but *thinned out* in the garden); and the collocation of *heart* and *bid* by contrast with *heart* and *beat*.

Purely grammatical distinctions between the different registers are less striking, yet there can be considerable variation in grammar also. Extreme cases are newspaper headlines and church services; but many other registers, such as sports commentaries and popular songs, exhibit specific grammatical characteristics. Sometimes, for example in the language of advertising, it is the combination of grammatical and lexical features that is distinctive. *Pioneers in self-drive car hire* is an instance of a

17

fairly restricted grammatical structure. The collocation of the last four lexical items is normal enough in other structures, as in *why don't you hire a car and drive yourself?*; but their occurrence in this structure, and in collocation with an item like *pioneer* or *specialist*, is readily identifiable as an advertising slogan.

Registers are not marginal or special varieties of language. Between them they cover the total range of our language activity. It is only by reference to the various situations and situation types in which language is used that we can understand its functioning and its effectiveness. Language is not realized in the abstract: it is realized as the activity of people in situations, as linguistic events which are manifested in a particular dialect and register.

No one suggests, of course, that the various registers characteristic of different types of situation have nothing in common. On the contrary, a great deal of grammatical and lexical material is common to many of the registers of a given language, and some perhaps to all. If this was not so we could not speak of 'a language' in this sense at all, just as we should not be able to speak of 'a language' in the sense of a dialect continuum if there was not a great deal in common among the different dialects.

But there tends to be more difference between events in different registers than between different events in one register. If we failed to note these differences of register, we should be ignoring an important aspect of the nature and functioning of language. Our descriptions of languages would be inaccurate and our attempts to teach them to foreigners made vastly more difficult.

It is by their formal properties that registers are defined. If two samples of language activity from what, on non-linguistic grounds, could be considered different situation-types show no differences in grammar or lexis, they are assigned to one and the same register: for the purpose of the description of the language there is only one situation-type here, not two. For this reason a large amount of linguistic analysis is required before registers can be identified and described. It is one thing to make a general description of English, accounting, to a given degree of delicacy, for all the features found in some or other variety of the language. Most native speakers will agree on what is and what is not possible, and the areas of disagreement are marginal. It is quite another thing to find out the special characteristics of a given register: to describe for example the language of consultations between doctor and patient in the surgery.

For such a purpose very large samples of textual material are needed. Moreover much of the language activity that needs to be studied takes place in situations where it is practically impossible to make tape recordings. It is not surprising, therefore, that up to now we know very little about the various registers of spoken English. Even studies of the written language have only recently begun to be made from this point of view. For this reason we are not yet in a position to talk accurately about register; there is much work to be done before the concept is capable of detailed application.

While we still lack a detailed description of the registers of a language on the basis of their formal properties, it is nevertheless useful to refer to this type of language variety from the point of view of institutional linguistics. There is enough evidence for us to be able to recognize the major situation types to which formally distinct registers correspond; others can be predicted and defined from outside language. A number of different lines of demarcation have been suggested for this purpose. It seems most useful to introduce a classification along three dimensions, each representing an aspect of the situation in which language operates and the part played by language in them. Registers, in this view, may be distinguished according to *field of discourse*, *mode of discourse* and *style of discourse*.

"Field of discourse" refers to what is going on: to the area of operation of the language activity. Under this heading, registers are classified according to the nature of the whole event of which the language activity forms a part. In the type of situation in which the language activity accounts for practically the whole of the relevant activity, such as an essay, a discussion or an academic seminar, the field of discourse is the subject-matter. On this dimension of classification, we can recognize registers such as politics and personal relations, and technical registers like biology and mathematics.

There are on the other hand situations in which the language activity rarely plays more than a minor part: here the field of discourse refers to the whole event. In this sense there is, for example, a register of domestic chores: 'hoovering the carpets' may involve language activity which, though marginal, is contributory to the total event. At the same time the language activity in a situation may be unrelated to the other activities. It may even delay rather than advance them, if two people discuss politics while doing the washing up. Here the language activity does not form part of the washing up event, and the field of discourse is that of politics.

Registers classified according to field of discourse thus include both the technical and the non-technical: shopping and games-playing as well as medicine and linguistics. Neither is confined to one type of situation. It may be that the more technical registers lend themselves especially to language activity of the discussion type, where there are few, if any, related non-language events; and the non-technical registers to functional or operational language activity, in which we can observe language in use as a means of achievement. But in the last resort there is no field of activity which cannot be discussed; and equally there is none in which language cannot play some part in getting things done. Perhaps our most purely operational language activity is "phatic communion", the language of the establishment and maintenance of social relations. This includes utterances like *how do you do*! and *see you*!, and is certainly non-technical, except perhaps in British English where it overlaps with the register of meteorology. But the language activity of the patient consulting the doctor in the surgery, or of research scientists in the performance of a laboratory experiment, however technical it may be, is very clearly functioning as a means of operation and control.

This leads to "mode of discourse", since this refers to the medium or mode of the language activity, and it is this that determines, or rather correlates with, the role played by the language activity in the situation. The primary distinction on this dimension is that into spoken and written language, the two having, by and large, different situational roles. In this connection, reading aloud is a special case of written rather than of spoken language.

The extent of formal differentiation between spoken and written language has varied very greatly among different language communities and at different periods. It reached its widest when, as in medieval Europe, the normal written medium of a community was a classical language which was unintelligible unless learnt by instruction. Latin, Classical Arabic, Sanskrit and Classical Chinese have all been used in this way. By comparison, spoken and written varieties of most modern languages are extremely close. The two varieties of French probably differ more than those of English; even popular fiction in French uses the simple past (preterite) tense in narrative. But spoken and written English are by no means formally identical. They differ both in grammar and in lexis, as anyone by recording and transcribing conversation can find out.

Within these primary modes, and cutting across them to a certain extent, we can recognize further registers such as the language of newspapers, of advertising, of conversation and of sports commentary. Like other dimensions of classification in linguistics, both descriptive and institutional, the classification of modes of discourse is variable in delicacy. We may first identify 'the language of literature' as a single register; but at the next step we would separate the various genres, such as prose fiction and light verse, as distinct registers within it. What is first recognized as the register of journalism is then subclassified into reportage, editorial comment, feature writing and so on.

Some modes of discourse are such that the language activity tends to be self-sufficient, in the sense that it accounts for most or all of the activity relevant to the situation. This is particularly true of the various forms of the written mode, but applies also to radio talks, academic discussions and sermons. In literature particularly the language activity is as it were self-sufficient. On the other hand, in the various spoken modes, and in some of the written, the utterances often integrate with other non-language activity into a single event. Clear instances of this are instructions and sets of commands. The grammatical and lexical distinction between the various modes of discourse can often be related to the variable situational role assigned to language by the medium.

Third and last of the dimensions of register classification is "style of discourse", which refers to the relations among the participants. To the extent that these affect and determine features of the language, they suggest a primary distinction into colloquial and polite ("formal", which is sometimes used for the latter, is here avoided because of its technical sense in description). This dimension is unlikely ever to yield clearly defined, discrete registers. It is best treated as a cline, and various more delicate cuts have been suggested, with categories such as 'casual', 'intimate' and 'deferential'. But until we know more about how the formal properties of language vary with style, such categories are arbitrary and provisional.

The participant relations that determine the style of discourse range through varying degrees of permanence. Most temporary are those which are a feature of the immediate situation, as when the participants are at a party or have met on the train. At the opposite extreme are relations such as that between parents and children. Various socially defined relations, as between teacher and pupil or labour and management, lie somewhere intermediately. Some such registers may show more specific formal properties than others: it is probably easier to identify on linguistic evidence a situation in which one participant is serving the others in a shop than one involving lecturer and students in a university classroom.

Which participant relations are linguistically relevant, and how far these are distinctively reflected in the grammar and lexis, depends on the language concerned. Japanese, for example, tends to vary along this dimension very much more than English or Chinese. There is even some formal difference in Japanese between the speech of men and the speech of women, nor is this merely a difference in the probabilities of occurrence. In most languages, some lexical items tend to be used more by one sex than the other; but in Japanese there are grammatical features which are restricted to the speech of one sex only.

It is as the product of these three dimensions of classification that we can best define and identify register. The criteria are not absolute or independent; they are all variable in delicacy, and the more delicate the classification the more the three overlap. The formal properties of any given language event will be those associated with the intersection of the appropriate field, mode and style. A lecture on biology in a technical college, for example, will be in the scientific field, lecturing mode and polite style; more delicately, in the biological field, academic lecturing mode and teacher to student style.

The same lecturer, five minutes later in the staff common room, may switch to the field of cinema, conversational mode, in the style of a man among colleagues. As each situation is replaced by another, so the speaker readily shifts from one register to the next. The linguistic differences may be slight; but they may be considerable, if the **use** of language in the new situation differs sharply from that in the old. We cannot list the total range of uses. Institutional categories, unlike descriptive ones, do not resolve into closed systems of discrete terms. Every speaker has at his disposal a continuous scale of patterns and items, from which he selects for each situation type the appropriate stock of available harmonies in the appropriate key. He speaks, in other words, in many registers.

He does not, normally, speak in many dialects, since a dialect represents the total range of patterns used by his section of the language community. But he may, as a citizen of a nation, learn a second dialect for certain uses, and even a third and a fourth. In Britain, choice of dialect is bound up with choice of register in a way that is unique among the language communities of the world: it is a linguistic error to give a radio commentary on cricket in cockney or sing popular songs in the Queen's English. Many of the languages of older nations show some such mutual dependence between dialect and register.

In the newer nations, this is less apparent; instead there is often a tendency for the register to determine not the choice of dialect, but the choice of language. Machine translation will in time make it possible for each community to use its own language for all purposes. Meanwhile, in many parts of the world, it is necessary to learn a second language in order to be equipped with a full range of registers; and foreign language teaching has become one of the world's major industries. By the time when it is no longer necessary for anyone to learn a foreign language in order to be a full citizen of his own community, it may well be recognized as desirable for everyone to do so in order to be a citizen of the world.

5

It is the individual who speaks and writes; and in his language activity dialect and register combine. In the dialect range, the finer the distinctions that are recognized, the smaller, in terms of number of speakers, the unit which we postulate as the dialect community becomes. Eventually we reach the individual. The individual is, so to speak, the smallest dialect unit: each speaker has his own *idiolect*.

Even the homogeneity of the idiolect is a fiction, tenable only so long as we continue to treat language *synchronically*, in abstraction from time. As soon as we consider *diachronic* varieties of language, taking in the dimension of persistence and change in time, we have to recognize that changes take place not only in the transmission of language from one generation to the next but also in the speech habits of the individual in the course of his life.

Literacy retards linguistic change. But even in a community with a high literacy rate we can usually observe some differences in speech between successive generations. The individual member of the dialect community may retain his own idiolect unchanged; or he may adopt some features of the dialect of the next generation, even consciously adjusting his language performance to incorporate the neologisms of the young. At the least these will enter into his receptive use of language. In this sense the smallest dialectal unit is not the individual but the individual at a certain period in his life. Here we are approaching the theoretical limit of delicacy on the dialect dimension.

In the register range, the countless situations in which language activity takes place can be grouped into situation types, to which correspond the various uses of language. A corpus of language text in a given use is marked off by its formal properties as a register. Registers, like dialects, can be more and more finely differentiated; here again we can approach a theoretical limit of delicacy, at least in imagination, by progressive sub-classification of features of field, mode and style.

Ultimately, register and dialect meet in the single speech event. Here we have reached the *utterance*, the smallest institutional unit of language activity. In arriving through dialect and register at the 'piece of activity', we have completed the circuit which led from this in the first place, via the description of substance and form, through context, to language in use. Viewed descriptively, the speech event was the occurrence of a formal item 'expounded' in substance. Viewed institutionally, it is an utterance in a situation, identifiable by dialect and register.

In the last resort, since each speaker and each situation is unique, each single utterance is also itself unique. But, as we saw at the beginning, the uniqueness of events is irrelevant to their scientific description, which can only begin when different events are seen to be partially alike. We become interested in one piece of language activity when we can show that it has something in common with another.

It is possible to group together a limited number of utterances according to what they have in common in dialect and register. One way of so delimiting a language variety is to retrace our steps a little up these two scales, to where we meet the individual as a participant in numerous situations. We can then define a set of language events as the language activity of one individual in one register. This intersection of idiolect and register provides an institutional definition of individual style.

Some registers are extremely restricted in purpose. They thus employ only a limited number of formal items and patterns, with the result that the language activity in these registers can accommodate little idiolectal or even dialectal variety. Such registers are known as **restricted** languages. This is by no means a clearly defined category: some restricted languages are more restricted than others. Extreme examples are the "International Language of the Air", the permitted set of wartime cable messages for those on active service, and the bidding code of contract bridge. Less restricted are the various registers of legal and official documents and regulations, weather forecasts, popular song lyrics, and verses on greeting cards. All these can still be regarded as restricted languages.

The individual may still sometimes be recognizable even under the impersonal uniformity of a restricted language. This is often due to **paralinguistic** features: these are features, such as voice quality and handwriting, which do not carry formal contrasts. (In languages in which voice quality does carry formal contrasts it is not paralinguistic but linguistic.) Such features, like the phonetic and phonological characteristics by which an individual is sometimes marked out, will appear in a restricted language just as in an unrestricted register. Occasionally we even come across individual formal patterns in a

24

restricted language: there is the bridge player who expects her partner, but not her opponent, to interpret correctly her private structural distinction between *one club* and *a club*.

Except in restricted languages, it is normally assumed that individuals will differ in their language performance. In spoken registers the individual may stand out within his own dialect community through idiosyncratic phonetic habits. That he would of course stand out in a dialect community other than his own is trivial, since it is no more relevant to his linguistic individuality than the fact that an Englishman would stand out in France by speaking English. Even phonology gives some scope to individual variety: the present authors pronounce *transparent plastic* in three phonologically different ways. Graphological practice is more uniform: we no longer tolerate individual spelling, though punctuation is allowed to vary somewhat.

Nevertheless, even in written registers the individual stands out. His language is distinctive at the level of form. A person's idiolect may be identified, through the lens of the various registers, by its grammatical and lexical characteristics. This is how we recognize the individual qualities of a particular writer. All linguistic form is either grammar or lexis, and in the first instance it is the grammatical and lexical features of the individual writer's language, together with a few features of punctuation, that constitute his "style".

Individual style, however, is linked to register. It is the writer's idiolect, especially the grammar and lexis of the idiolect, in a given register. In so far as "style" implies literary style, register here means literary, including poetic, genre and medium. Style is thus linguistic form in interrelation with literary form.

If we refer to "the style of Pope" we presumably imply that there is something in common to the language of the *Essays*, the *Satires* and other works: that they constitute in some sense a single idiolect. In fact, style, like other, related concepts, must be recognized to be variable in delicacy: each genre, and each individual work, has its style. If it is assumed from the start that two texts are alike, the differences between them may be missed or distorted. It is a sound principle of descriptive linguistics to postulate heterogeneity until homogeneity is proved, and the study of literary texts is no exception. By treating the *Satires* and the *Essays* as different registers we can display the similarities as well as the dissimilarities between them.

Literature forms only a small part of written language, but it is the part in which we are most aware of the individual and most interested in the originality of the individual's language. At the same time it is of the essence of creative writing that it calls attention to its own form, in the sense that unlike other language activity, written or spoken, it is meaningful as activity in itself and not merely as part of a larger situation: again, of course, without a clear line of demarcation. This remains true whether or not the writer is consciously aiming at creating an individual variety. Thus the linguistic uniqueness of a work of literature is of much greater significance than the individuality of a variety of language in any other use.

The language activity of one user in one use: this concept will serve as the fundamental variety of a language. Such an individual variety is a product of both dialect and register, and both are involved in its study.

Dialectology is a long-established branch of linguistic studies. In Britain, which has lagged notably behind other European countries and the United States, large scale dialect survey work did not begin until after the Second World War; but the three national surveys now being conducted at the universities of Leeds, Edinburgh and Wales have amassed a large amount of material and the first results are now in course of publication.

Serious work on registers is even more recent in origin. Very large samples of texts have to be subjected to detailed formal analysis if we wish to show which grammatical and lexical features are common to all uses of the language and which are restricted to, or more frequent in, one or more particular register. Such samples are now being collected and studied at University College London, in the Survey of English Usage under the direction of Professor Randolph Quirk; and related work is in progress at the universities of Edinburgh and Leeds. The study of registers is crucial both to our understanding of how language works and in application to literary analysis, machine translation and native and foreign-language teaching.

6

Languages in contact, dialects and registers are three of the major topics of institutional linguistics. The fourth and last to be considered is the observation of the attitudes of members of a language community towards their language and its varieties. Here we mention briefly some of the attitudes that are relevant to the present discussion, with commentary where necessary.

Most communities show some reverence for the magical powers of language. In some societies, however, this respect is mingled with, and maybe eclipsed by, a newer set of attitudes much more disdainful of the language, or of a part of it. The value judgements that underlie these attitudes may be moral or aesthetic, or they may rest on a pragmatic appeal to efficiency. The degree of social sanction they carry varies according to the language community; but whether the judgements and attitudes are social or individual, the individual expounding them frequently claims objectivity for his opinions. A typical formulation is: 'Obviously it is better (or: 'Everybody agrees that it is better') to say, or write, this than that, because' either 'it's clearer' or 'it sounds better' or 'it's more correct'. Less common, and more sophisticated, are 'because the best people do it' and 'because I prefer it'.

The most far-reaching among such value judgements are those passed on whole languages. Those who argue that it is necessary for English to remain the language of government, law, education or technology in former colonies sometimes claim, in support of their view, that the national languages are not suitable for these purposes. This reason is even put forward by the native speaker of the languages concerned.

The arguments for and against the use of English in such situations are complex; but this particular factor is irrelevant, because it is not true. This misapprehension, that some languages are intrinsically better than others, cannot just be dismissed as ignorance or prejudice; it is a view held by people who are both intelligent and serious, and can bring forward evidence to support it. Nevertheless it is wholly false and can do a great deal of harm.

Essentially, any language is as good as any other language, in the sense that every language is equally well adapted to the uses to which the community puts it. There is no such thing as a 'primitive' language. About the origins of language, nothing is known; there is merely a tangle of conflicting speculation, none of it falling within linguistics. But there is evidence that speech in some form goes back at least a hundred thousand years, and quite certainly no society found in the world today, or known to us in history, represents anything but a stage long after language had become a fully developed form of social activity. If historians or anthropologists use "primitive" as a technical term, to designate a certain stage of social development, then the term may be transferred to the language used by a community that is in that stage; but it is **not** a linguistic classification and tells us nothing whatever about the nature of the language concerned.

Among the languages in the world today, there is no recognizable dimension of **linguistic** progress. No language can be identified as representing a more highly developed state of language than any other. Worora, in Western Australia, is as well adapted to the needs of the community which developed it as English is to our own. Neither language could be transferred to the other society without some changes, because the needs and activities are different; in both cases new lexical items would have to be added. But only the lexis would be affected, and only a portion of that. There would be no need for any changes in the grammar. At most there might be a statistical tendency for certain grammatical changes to take place over a very long period; but no simple change would be predictable in any given instance, none would be bound to occur, and certainly none would be necessary to the continued efficiency of the language.

In other words, the changes that would be necessary in Worora, for it to operate as a full language in the modern world, would be those that were also necessary to English as it was before the modern period. Middle English, even Elizabethan English, was not adapted to the needs of a modern state either. One could no more describe an electronic computer in Middle English than in Worora. Different languages have different ways of expanding their lexis, determined by their own internal structure: Chinese, for example, coins scientific terminology in a very different way from Japanese, being a language of a very different type. But all languages are capable of incorporating the lexical additions they require.

Whether or not it is economically feasible for the language of a very small community to be used as a medium for all the purposes of the modern world is of course an entirely different question, which each community has the right to decide for itself. It is worth pointing out that in the next generation machine translation will probably become efficient enough, and cheap enough, to overcome the problem of translating all the material such a community would need to have translated from other languages. Whatever considerations may affect the choice of a language for science or administration in a newly independent nation, this at least can be made clear: all languages are equally capable of being developed for all purposes, and no language is any less qualified to be the vehicle of modern science and technology than were English and Russian some centuries ago.

A type of language that particularly attracts adverse value judgements is the mixed language. As long as this remains a pidgin, it can be nobody's L1 and has not the status of a language; it exists only in certain restricted varieties. But in those communities which have developed a mixed language as their L1, the new language has thereby gained full stature and become a completely effective medium of language activity.

In any case a creole is only an extreme result of a normal phenomenon in the development of language: linguistic borrowing. There is no reason why a language with such a history should be less effective than any other. They are languages in the defined sense of the word; some of them are already used as literary media, and they would be fully viable as media of education and science. At present they tend to be more discriminated against than languages with a more conventional history. But there is no justification for discriminating against any language whatever. In most parts of the world today, including Britain, there has to be some measure of linguistic policy and planning; decisions may have to be taken, for example, to establish certain languages as the national languages of a new nation. What matters is that the real issues and problems should not be allowed to become clouded by false notions that one language may be objectively inferior to another.

Many speakers from communities whose language is in some or other respect denied full status, while they would not maintain that their own L1 was in any way inferior, and might vigorously reject such a suggestion, nevertheless in their language activity, as speakers, accept and thereby help to perpetuate its diminished status. In countries where English, or some other L2, is the mark of education and social standing, conversation in the government office or college staff common room normally takes place in English. Alternatively, if the L1 is allowed into these surroundings, no sentence in it is complete without at least one item from English.

This is sometimes explained on the grounds that the speakers do not share a common L1, as indeed they may not. It often is in countries which face a really difficult national language problem that a foreign language flourishes as a lingua franca. As is well known, many speakers from minority communities, whose language is not a strong candidate for national status, so firmly oppose the claims of any other language from within the country that they prefer to assign this status to a foreign language, which at least has the merit of being neutral. Probably this is at best a temporary solution; moreover there is reason to suggest that shelving the problem makes it more difficult to solve in the future.

But the lacing of L1 utterances with L2 items is not confined to multilingual societies. It is likely to happen wherever a foreign language is a mark of social distinction and the sole medium of language activity in certain registers. English probably occupies this position more than any other language. There are of course no grounds on which the linguist, who observes and describes this phenomenon, could object to

29

it as a use of language: it works. But he may also reasonably point out that the use of English in situations for which the L1 is adequately developed, and of English items in L1 utterances where L1 items are available, tends to inhibit the progress of the L1 towards regaining its full status in the community.

7

Within our own language community, value judgements on English as a whole are relatively rare. Occasionally one hears it compared unfavourably with French, by those who subscribe to the myth, sedulously kept alive by the French themselves, that French is a 'more logical' language. What are extremely common, however, are value judgements on varieties of English: sometimes referring to registers but principally to dialects. The English language community, especially the British section of it, is almost certainly unique in the extent to which its members pass judgement on varieties of their language. One of the few other communities that at all resembles us in this respect is the French. The English attitudes are of course bound up with the socio-regional character of our dialect; as such, they are class attitudes rather than individual attitudes. Nearly all the widely accepted value judgements can be traced to this origin, though some reflect it more directly than others.

It is at the new urban dialects, the varieties of the standard language with regional accent, that the most severe criticisms are levelled. The original dialects, now confined to the rural areas, have become quaint. They are tolerated; sometimes they may be praised, as 'soft', 'pleasant' or even 'musical'. And, somewhat inconsistently, though it is the rural dialects which provide the only instances of pairs of mutually unintelligible varieties remaining in England, it is often on grounds of incomprehensibility that criticism is directed at the urban dialects.

Perhaps the most frequent complaint is that formulated in various terms implying some sort of linguistic decay. The urban dialects are said to be 'slovenly', 'careless' or 'degenerate'. Similar terms were used about English and French in the nineteenth century, by those who regarded all recent linguistic change as a process of degeneration and decay. It is implied, and sometimes stated explicitly, that in the urban dialects there has been some loss of the communicative power of language.

This is simply nonsense. All the dialects, including all forms of standard English, are subject to change, both through the normal tendency of language to change and as a result of external factors such as movement of populations. Rate of change in language varies considerably, between different languages, between dialects and at different times and places; even at different levels within the same variety of a language. English has altered rather strikingly over the last thousand years; the dialect now functioning as standard English is one of those that has changed the most, though it is difficult to measure comparative rates of change very accurately.

To the way of thinking that these attitudes represent, probably the slovenliest people in the world would be the French and the north Chinese: Parisian and Pekingese are the result of a high rate of change over long periods. There is no difference between the type of change undergone by these two languages and that which has affected the dialectal varieties of English, including the dialect that has become standardized and its modern regional derivatives.

There is actually no such thing as a slovenly dialect or accent. That the dialect of Sheffield or Birmingham has evolved in a different direction from one's own is hardly a matter for reproach, and anyone who labels it "debased" is committing two errors. First, he is assuming that one type of standard English preserves an earlier variety of the language from which others have deviated; this is not true. Second, he is claiming that there is merit in this imagined conservatism; if there was, such merit might appropriately be claimed by the Italians, the Cantonese and the Germans in reproach to their slovenly neighbours the French, the Pekingese and the English.

Traditionally, this charge of debasement rested on straightforward moral grounds: it was wrong and irresponsible to let the language fall into decay. More recently the same imputed shortcoming has come to be criticized from another point of view, that of the loss of efficiency. Since the fault is imaginary, the grounds on which it is censured might seem unimportant. But one comment at least is called for. Many people, including for a time some linguists, have been taken in by the spurious rigour of some pseudo-scientific "measurements" of the "efficiency" of language. There is no evidence whatever that one language, or one variety of a language, can be more efficient than another. Nor is there, either in our intuitive judgement or yet in mathematics or linguistics, any means of measuring whatever such efficiency might be. Information theory, which has a place in the quantitative description of a language, implies nothing about the relative efficiency of languages or the effectiveness of language activity.

31

A second accusation has been brought against the urban dialects that is somewhat different from that of slovenliness, in either its moral or its utilitarian form. This is an aesthetic criticism. The dialects are labelled 'harsh', 'grating', 'guttural' – this last probably refers to the higher frequency, in some varieties, of glottal closure unaccompanied by oral stops – or simply 'ugly'.

Here the person judging is on safer ground, if he means that he personally does not like the sound of certain varieties of English: no one can dispute that. The formulation may be a general one, but there is a broad human tendency to generalize one's prejudices, and we probably all know people who would not distinguish between 'I dislike the sound of Cardiff English' and 'Cardiff English is ugly'.

It is true that there is often a wide range of agreement in these aesthetic judgements. What is not realized, however, is that they are usually learnt. An Indian brought up in the Indian musical tradition will not agree with European judgements on European music, and a European who does not know the Chinese language and Chinese cultural values does not appreciate – that is, agree with Chinese judgements of – the sounds of Chinese poetry. Whether or not the adult ever does produce an unconditioned aesthetic response, in general what we like is as much a result of what we have learnt to like socially as of what we have grown to like individually. In language, we know already that people from different language communities respond quite differently to the aesthetic qualities of the dialects of a given language: a Persian or a Japanese not knowing English would be as likely to prefer Birmingham to RP as the other way round. The chief factor in one's evaluation of varieties of a language is social conditioning: there is no universal scale of aesthetic judgement. Those who dislike the Birmingham accent often do so because they know that their children will stand a better chance in life if they do not acquire it.

It is thus the socio-regional pattern of English dialect distribution that gives rise to both the aesthetic and the moral or pragmatic value judgements on the urban and rural dialects, in so far as these judgements are held in common by a large section of our language community. In many countries such judgements either are not passed at all or, if they are, are regarded both by those who pass them and by those who listen to them as subjective expressions of personal taste. Foreign students in Britain listen in polite wonder while their teatime hosts in Leeds or Manchester explain how important it is that they should not copy the speech of their landladies: 'everybody agrees', they are told, that this is an ugly, distorted form of English.

Not everybody does agree, in fact: such views seem to be most general among speakers of mildly regional varieties of Standard English. But when these attitudes are shared by those who themselves speak the dialect, and no other, they become rather harmful. A speaker who is made ashamed of his own language habits suffers a basic injury as a human being: to make anyone, especially a child, feel so ashamed is as indefensible as to make him feel ashamed of the colour of his skin.

Various courses of instruction are available in spoken English, under headings such as "Speech and Drama", "Elocution" and "Normal Voice and Speech". In general three different kinds of instruction take place. The first is concerned with techniques of speaking on the stage and in public; this is a form of applied phonetics, and is often very successful. The second is concerned with personal attainments such as voice quality and clarity in speech, and is often linked to aspects of social behaviour under the general heading of 'developing the personality'; these aspects lie outside the scope of application of linguistics or phonetics.

In the third type of instruction, which is again applied phonetics, the individual is taught to use some accent of English other than the one he has acquired naturally. This may be for particular professional purposes, as in the schools where dance-band leaders and pop singers can acquire the pronunciation considered appropriate to their calling, and the courses in which actors, for the purpose of character parts, may learn reasonable imitations of regional accents or at least a conventional Mummerset. It may, on the other hand, be for general social purposes; classes are held where those who speak with a regional accent can learn a pronunciation which they have found carries greater social prestige and better prospects of employment. Here the teaching is catering for social attitudes to language; but they are still recognized as social attitudes.

In the extreme forms of such accent-teaching, however, the particular accent taught is extolled by those who teach it as 'more beautiful' and 'better' than any other. This accent is generally a variety of RP with a number of special vowel qualities and lip postures. Sometimes the speech of a particular individual is held up as a model for imitation; but more often an absolute aesthetic merit is claimed for the way of speaking that is taught. Some of the teachers have themselves been taught that there is a scale of values on which vowels may be judged, ranging from 'bad and ugly' to 'good and beautiful'. The teacher is thus attempting to alter the speech of her pupils for reasons which seem to her sensible and obvious, but which are inexplicable to most of the pupils. The view that some sounds are inherently higher or lower than others on an absolute scale of aesthetic values has no evidence to support it, though it is of interest to phoneticians to know how widely it is held.

Perhaps the most uncomfortable of all the conflicts of approach between linguists and phoneticians on the one hand and teachers of 'speech' (who may invoke the authority of these disciplines) on the other, are those centring on the subject commonly known as "Normal Voice and Speech". This subject is included within the curriculum for speech therapists, in which phonetics also plays a prominent part. "Normal" here is used prescriptively; the assumption is that one particular accent of English is in some way 'normal', all others being 'abnormal', and that the 'normal' accent is RP. Such judgements, as we have seen, reflect no property of the accent itself, but merely the social standing of those who have acquired it.

If all the patients treated by speech therapists belonged to this group, the confusion would do no actual harm. But those with speech defects are a representative cross-section of the whole population, the majority of whom do not speak RP, so that the background provided by "Normal Voice and Speech" is both culturally loaded and, for many, therapeutically irrelevant. Many phoneticians continue to provide courses for students of speech therapy because they hope to give an objective training which will counterbalance the prescriptive nature of "Normal Voice and Speech"; but the harnessing of two such differently conceived subjects in a single course can only be likened to an attempt to combine astronomy with domestic science, or perhaps rather chemistry with alchemy.

8

The English tendency to linguistic intolerance is not confined to strictures on the sounds of language. Value judgements also flourish in grammar. In grammar, however, the features subjected to those judgements are on the whole not dialectal. Many dialectal grammatical patterns pass unnoticed in speech provided the speaker is using the phonetics of RP: even such a markedly regional clause structure as that exemplified by *they've never been to see us haven't the Joneses* is tolerated in spoken English if the accent is an acceptable one. It would not on the other hand be tolerated in writing.

In grammar we have a set of arbitrary prescriptions and proscriptions relating to particular patterns and items. Some are applied to written

34

English only, others to both spoken and written. Neither the prescribed nor the proscribed forms correspond to any particular regional varieties. As with the dialectal prescriptions, there are various ways of giving a bad name to the proscribed forms: they are called 'slipshod' and 'crude', sometimes simply 'wrong'. 'Incorrect', taken from a different register, is sometimes used as if it was an explanation of 'wrong'.

In this context 'slipshod' and 'crude' are meaningless, and a native speaker of English who happened not to know which of a pair of forms was approved and which censured would have no evidence whatsoever for deciding. As effective language activity, there is nothing to choose between *do it as I do* and *do it like I do*, just as soup has the same food value however it is eaten (or whether it is *eaten* or *drunk*). 'Wrong' is a social judgement: what is meant is 'the best people use this form and not that form'. These are in effect social conventions about language, and their function is that of social conventions: meaningless in themselves, they exert cohesive force within one society, or one section of a society, by marking it off from another.

As we have seen, all languages have formally distinct varieties. What is unusual about the language situation in Britain is the extent to which rules are consciously formulated for what is regarded as appropriate grammatical behaviour. Other communities have sometimes attempted to impose patterns of linguistic form, generally without much success; at the most, what is prescribed is the distinction between the spoken and the written language, some forms being rejected as inappropriate to the latter. Conventions in the spoken language are normally confined to lexical taboos: certain items are not to be used before children, strangers or members of the opposite sex. In Britain, rules are made for speech as well as for writing, and the speaker's grammar contributes, alongside his phonetics and phonology, to his identification on the social scale.

Since 'incorrect' linguistic behaviour, whether dialectal or otherwise, may be counted against one in many situations, the solution chosen by many speakers, in face of the prevalent attitudes, is to acquire a second idiolect. Indeed so strong is the feeling that there are correct and incorrect forms of linguistic behaviour that if one asks, as the present writers have asked many groups of university students, 'what is the purpose of the teaching of English in English schools?' a frequent answer is 'to teach the children to speak and write correct English'. The old observation that parents in the new dialect regions send their children to school so that they can be taught to 'talk proper' is by no means out of date. If children have to learn new speech habits, it is the social attitude to their dialect, and no fault of the dialect itself, that is forcing them to do this: at least they need not be taught that their own speech is in some way inferior or taboo.

Some voices are raised against the prevailing attitudes, and some of the rules are occasionally called into question. Priestley once wrote, in *English Journey* (1934, p. 290), "Standard English is like standard anything else – poor tasteless stuff". Hugh Sykes-Davies, in *Grammar Without Tears* (1951, pp. 131–2), suggested reversing the polarity of prescription and proscription: "the use of the indirect cases of *who* should be avoided wherever possible by putting the preposition at the end of the sentence, and making *that* the relative, or omitting the pronoun altogether. It is better to say 'the man I found the hat of' than 'the man whose hat I found'". But here the speaker is still being told how to behave; there is still a right and a wrong in language.

Serious interest in dialectal varieties of the language is fostered by such bodies as the Yorkshire Dialect Society, which publishes both literary work in, and academic studies of, the Yorkshire dialects, urban as well as rural. Detailed surveys of the dialects of England, Wales and Scotland are, as has been mentioned, now well advanced. The Linguistic Survey of Scotland takes account of urban varieties of Scots; and although the English Dialect Survey has not yet turned its attention to the new dialects in English this is because the original, now rural, dialects are fast disappearing and must be recorded first. And teachers and university students seem to be becoming increasingly aware of the artificial and arbitrary nature of the conventional notions of 'good English' and 'bad English'.

Interwoven with the highly prescriptive attitudes towards the linguistic behaviour of individuals is a strong protective feeling for the language as a whole. Unlike the selective judgements, which are rare among language communities, the defensive 'leave our language alone' attitude is very commonly found. Perhaps the most striking instance of this in Britain is the fierce resistance to any suggestions for spelling reform. So strongly is the feeling against it that it seems unlikely at present that any orthographic revision of English will be undertaken for a long time.

Not all language communities are equally conservative in this respect. The Chinese, whose traditional orthography is even more difficult to master than ours, and is a serious barrier to the learning of the standard language, have recently embarked on what is probably the most far-reaching programme of script reform ever attempted in any language community. Intense interest was aroused from the start; and

36

although this was by no means all favourable, some tens of thousands of suggestions, and over six hundred reformed scripts, were submitted to the committee which first drafted the new proposals.

It has been argued that if the English expect their language to operate as an international medium they should consider reforming the script in the interests of foreign learners. On the other hand any project for doing so would face enormous difficulties. The linguist, as a linguist, does not take sides in this issue, though as a private citizen he may; but he is qualified to act as a consultant, and to make suggestions as to how best to revise the orthography if it is once decided to do so. Apart from this, the role of linguistics at this stage is to help clear the air for rational discussion of the problem, as of all the other problems that are raised by the complex and deep-rooted attitudes of the members of a language community towards their language.

From: Halliday, M. A. K., McIntosh, Angus, and Strevens, Peter, *The Linguistic Sciences and Language Teaching* (London: Longman, 1964). Reprinted with permission.

Note: This book was co-authored. The chapter reproduced here was written by M. A. K. Halliday, with the exception of the last five paragraphs of Section 7, which were written by Peter Strevens. All authors were responsible for the final draft.

PART TWO

SOCIOLINGUISTIC THEORY

EDITOR'S INTRODUCTION

The four papers in this section outline a theory of language as social behaviour. As Professor Halliday notes in the lead chapter of this section, entitled 'Language in a social perspective' (1971), "The investigation of language as social behaviour is not only relevant to the understanding of social structure; it is also relevant to the understanding of language." Such an approach offers insight not only into the nature of language but also into the social foundations of how one behaves as a social being. The potential of language for realizing this behaviour potential is referred to as its 'meaning potential', or, put very simply, " 'can mean' is 'can do' when translated into language".

Fundamental to the formulation of this sociolinguistic theory is the distinction Professor Halliday draws in the next two chapters, 'Language and social man' (1974) and 'Sociological aspects of semantic change' (1975), between inter-organism (social) and intra-organism (psychophysiological) perspectives. The child becomes a social being as a result of social interaction. The child's behaviour potential is learned through the medium of language, not by instruction, but instead indirectly through "the countless microsemiotic processes of social interaction", or as he also puts it, "through the accumulated experience of numerous small events, insignificant in themselves, in which his behaviour is guided and controlled, and in the course of which he contracts and develops personal relationships of all kinds".

Chapter 5, 'Language as social semiotic: towards a general socio-linguistic theory' (1975), was written while Professor Halliday was at the Center for Advanced Study in the Behavioral Sciences, Stanford, California. His stated aim was "to interrelate the various components of the sociolinguistic universe, with special reference to the place of language within it". However, he acknowledges the difficulty in integrating linguistic interaction studies with other areas of socio-linguistic research, resulting from the lack of an explicit formulation of the relationship between what people mean (the text) and what they *can* mean (the system). Without such an explicit formulation, one cannot adequately engage with questions along the lines of those posed in this chapter, e.g. How are participants exploiting their semantic potential? How does this potential relate systematically to features of the context of situation?

The educational significance of our ability to predict most of what the other person is going to say, or mean, "whether or not and in whatever way he says it", is highlighted in Chapter 6, 'Aspects of sociolinguistic research' (1975). Unless a pupil can predict about 90 per cent of what a teacher is going to say, argues Professor Halliday, the pupil is unlikely to learn very much. Thus, he concludes that "one of the main problems of multilingual education is to create conditions in which at any one moment the pupil knows most of the meanings that are coming at him next, so that those which are unknown are kept down to learnable proportions".

Chapter Two

LANGUAGE IN A SOCIAL PERSPECTIVE (1971)

The studies which are described in the series of monographs entitled *Primary Socialization, Language and Education*, edited by Basil Bernstein, show how in a coherent social theory a central place is occupied by language, as the primary means of cultural transmission.

What is the nature of language, when seen from this point of view? There are two sides to this question. The first is, what aspects of language are highlighted – what do we **make** language look like, so to speak – in order to understand its function in the socialization of the child, and in the processes of education? The second is the same question in reverse: what do we learn about language – what **does** it look like, in fact – when it is approached in this way?

1. Language as social behaviour an acknowledged concern of modern linguistics, and not limited to the study of instances

It has been suggested that one of the main preoccupations of the 1970s will be a concern with social man. This implies not simply man in relation to some abstract entity such as 'society as a whole', but man in relation to other men; it is a particular facet of man in relation to his environment, only it shifts the emphasis from the physical on to the human environment – on to man in the environment of men. The individual is seen as the focus of a complex of human relationships which collectively define the content of his social behaviour.

This provides a perspective on language. A significant fact about the behaviour of human beings in relation to their social environment is that a large part of it is linguistic behaviour. The study of social man presupposes the study of language and social man.

A concern with language and social man has for a long time been one of the perspectives of modern linguistics. In 1935 J. R. Firth, introducing the term "sociological linguistics", discussed the study of language in a social perspective and outlined a programme of "describing and classifying typical contexts of situation within the context of culture ... [and] types of linguistic function in such contexts of situation" (p. 27). We tend nowadays to refer to sociolinguistics as if this was something very different from the study of language as practised in linguistics *tout court*; but in a way new 'sociolinguistics' is but old 'linguistics' writ large, and the linguist's interests have always extended to language as social behaviour.

It was Malinowski from whom Firth derived his notions of 'context of culture' and 'context of situation' (Malinowski 1923); and Malinowski's ideas about what we might call cultural and situational semantics provide an interesting starting point for the study of language and social man, since they encourage us to look at language as a form of behaviour potential. In this definition, both the 'behaviour' and the 'potential' need to be emphasized. Language, from this point of view, is a range of possibilities, an open-ended set of options in behaviour that are available to the individual in his existence as social man. The context of culture is the environment for the total set of these options, while the context of situation is the environment of any particular selection that is made from within them.

Malinowski's two types of context thus embody the distinction between the potential and the actual. The context of culture defines the potential, the range of possibilities that are open. The actual choice among these possibilities takes place within a given context of situation.

Firth, with his interest in the actual, in the text and its relation to its surroundings, developed the notion of 'context of situation' into a valuable tool for linguistic enquiry. Firth's interest, however, was not in the accidental but in the typical: not in this or that piece of discourse that happened to get recorded in the fieldworker's notebook but in repetitive patterns which could be interpreted as significant and systematizable patterns of social behaviour. Thus, what is actual is not synonymous with what is unique, or the chance product of random observations. But the significance of what is typical – in fact, the concept 'typical' itself – depends on factors which lie outside language, in the social structure. It is not the typicalness of the words and structures which concerns us, but the typicalness of the context of situation, and of the function of the words and structures within it.

Malinowski (1935) tells an interesting story of an occasion when he asked his Trobriand Island informant some questions about the Trobrianders' gardening practices. He noted down the answers, and was surprised a few days later to hear the same informant repeating what he had said word for word in conversation with his young daughter. In talking to Malinowski, the informant has as it were borrowed the text from a typical context of situation. The second occasion, the discussion with the little girl, was then an instance of this context of situation, in which the socialization of the child into the most significant aspect of the material culture – the gardening practices – was a familiar process, with familiar patterns of language behaviour associated with it.

There is not, of course, any conflict between an emphasis on the repetitive character of language behaviour and an insistence on the creativity of the language system. Considered as behaviour potential, the language system itself is open-ended, since the question whether two instances are the same or not is not determined by the system; it is determined by the underlying social theory. But in any case, as Ruqaiya Hasan (1971) has pointed out, creativeness does not consist in producing new sentences. The newness of a sentence is a quite unimportant – and unascertainable – property, and 'creativity' in language lies in the speaker's ability to create new meanings: to realize the potentiality of language for the indefinite extension of its resources to new contexts of situation. It is only in this light that we can understand the otherwise unintelligible observation made by Katz and Fodor (1963), that "almost every sentence uttered is uttered for the first time" (p. 171). Our most 'creative' acts may be precisely among those that are realized through highly repetitive forms of behaviour.

Firth did not concern himself with Malinowski's 'context of culture', since he preferred to study generalized patterns of actual behaviour, rather than attempting to characterize the potential as such. This was simply the result of his insistence on the need for accurate observations – a much-needed emphasis in the context of earlier linguistic studies – and in no way implied that the study of language could be reduced to the study of instances, which in fact he explicitly denied (1968). More to the point, Firth built his linguistic theory around the original and fundamental concept of the 'system', as used by him in a technical

45

sense; and this is precisely a means of describing the potential, and of relating the actual to it.

A 'system', as the concept was developed by Firth, can be interpreted as the set of options that is specified for a given environment. The meaning of it is 'under the conditions stated, there are the following possibilities'. By making use of this notion, we can describe language in the form of a behaviour potential. In this way the analysis of language comes within the range of a social theory, provided the underlying concepts of such a theory are such that they can be shown to be realized in social context and patterns of behaviour.

The interest in language and social man is thus no new theme in linguistics. It is also predominant in the important work of Pike (1967, first published 1954–60). Its scope is not limited to the description of individual acts of speech; more significant has been the attempt to relate grammatical and lexical features, and combinations of such features, to types of social interaction and, where possible, to generalized social concepts. From a sociological point of view it would be of no interest otherwise; a social theory could not operate with raw speech fragments as the only linguistic exponents of its fundamental ideas.

2. Language in a social perspective interpreted through the concept of 'meaning potential'

If we regard language as social behaviour, therefore, this means that we are treating it as a form of behaviour **potential**. It is what the speaker can do.

But 'can do' by itself is not a linguistic notion; it encompasses types of behaviour other than language behaviour. If we are to relate the notion of 'can do' to the sentences and words and phrases that the speaker is able to construct in his language – to what he can say, in other words – then we need an intermediate step, where the behaviour potential is as it were converted into linguistic potential. This is the concept of what the speaker 'can mean'.

The potential of language is a meaning potential. This meaning potential is the linguistic realization of the behaviour potential; 'can mean' is 'can do' when translated into language. The meaning potential is in turn realized in the language system as lexicogrammatical potential, which is what the speaker 'can say'.

Each stage can be expressed in the form of options. The options in the construction of linguistic forms – sentences, and the like – serve to realize options in meaning, which in turn realize options in behaviour that are interpretable in terms of a social theory.

We can illustrate this point by reference to Basil Bernstein's work in the area of language and social structure (Bernstein 1967, 1970). On the basis of a theory of social learning, Bernstein identifies a number of social contexts which are crucial to the socialization of the child, for example contexts in which the mother is regulating the child's behaviour or in which she is helping him in learning to carry out some kind of task. These are 'typical contexts of situation', in Firth's sense, but given significance by the theory underlying them.

For any one of these contexts Bernstein is able to specify a range of alternatives that is open to the mother in her interaction with the child. For example, in regulating the child's behaviour she may adopt one (or more) of a number of strategies, which we might characterize in general terms as reasoning, pleading, threatening and the like, but which the theory would suggest represent systematic options in the meanings that are available to her. Bernstein in fact makes use of the term "meanings" to refer to significant options in the social context; and he regards those as being "realized" in the behaviour patterns. But this is realization in exactly the linguistic sense, and the behaviour patterns are, at least partly, patterns of meaning in the linguistic sense – the mother's behaviour is largely language behaviour. So the chain of realizations extends from the social theory into the language system.

Hence the behaviour potential associated with the contexts that Bernstein identifies may be expressed linguistically as a meaning potential. Some such step is needed if we are to relate the fundamental concepts of the social theory to recognizable forms and patterns of language behaviour.

A word or two should be said here about the relation of the concept of meaning potential to the Chomskyan notion of competence, even if only very briefly. The two are somewhat different. Meaning potential is defined not in terms of the mind but in terms of the culture; not as what the speaker knows, but as what he can do – in the special sense of what he can do linguistically (what he 'can mean', as we have expressed it). The distinction is important because 'can do' is of the same order of abstraction as 'does'; the two are related simply as potential to actualized potential, and can be used to illuminate each other. But 'knows' is distinct and clearly insulated from 'does'; the relation between the two is complex and oblique, and leads to the quest for a "theory of performance" to explain the 'does'.

This is related to the question of idealization in linguistics. How does one decide what is systematic and what is irrelevant in language – or, to put the question another way, how does one decide what are different sentences, different phrases, and so on, and what are different instances of the same sentence, the same phrase? The issue is a familiar one to readers of this journal,[1] from the article by Peter Geach in the volume *The Place of Language* (Wilkinson 1969). Geach's argument is that in order to understand the logical structure of sentences we have to "iron out" a lot of the differences that occur in living speech: ". . . idealization which approximates slightly less well to what is actually said, will, by the standards of logical insight into the structures of sentences, pay off better than some analyses that try to come closer to what is actually said" (p. 23).

The philosopher's approach to language is always marked by a very high degree of idealization. In its extreme form, this approach idealizes out **all** natural language as irrelevant and unsystematic and treats only constructed logical languages; a less extreme version is one which accepts sentences of natural language but reduces them all to a "deep structure" in terms of certain fundamental logical relations. Competence, as defined by Chomsky, involves (as Geach objects) a lower degree of idealization than this. But it is still very high from other points of view, particularly that of anyone interested in language as behaviour. Many behaviourally significant variations in language are simply ironed out, and reduced to the same level as stutterings, false starts, clearings of the throat and the like.

It might be claimed at this point that linguistics is anyway an autonomous science and does not need to look outside itself for criteria of idealization. But this is not a very satisfactory argument. There is a sense in which it is autonomous, and has to be if it is to be relevant to other fields of study: the particulars of language are explained by reference to a general account of language, not by being related piecemeal to social or other non-linguistic phenomena. But this 'autonomy' is conditional and temporary; in the last analysis, we cannot insulate the subject within its own boundaries, and when we come to decide what features in language are to be ignored as unsystematic we are bound to invoke considerations from outside language itself. This problem is met by Chomsky, who regards linguistics as a branch of theoretical psychology. But one may agree with the need for a point of departure from outside language without insisting that this must be

---

1. *Education Review*

sought in one direction and no other – only in psychology, or only in logic. It may just as well be sought in a field such as sociology whose relationship with linguistics has been no less close.

Sociological theory, if it is concerned with the transmission of knowledge or with any linguistically coded type of social act, provides its own criteria for the degree and kind of idealization involved in statements about language; and Bernstein's work is a case in point. In one sense, this is what it is all about. There is always some idealization, where linguistic generalizations are made; but in a sociological context this has to be, on the whole, at a much lower level. We have, in fact, to 'come closer to what is actually said'; partly because the solution to problems may depend on studying what is actually said, but also because even when this is not the case the features that are behaviourally relevant may be just those that the idealizing process most readily irons out. An example of the latter would be features of assertion and doubt, such as *of course, I think*, and question tags like *don't they?*, which turn out to be highly significant – not the expressions themselves, but the variations in meaning which they represent, in this case variation in the degree of certainty which the speaker may attach to what he is saying (Turner and Pickvance 1969).

In order to give an account of language that satisfies the needs of a social theory, we have to be able to accommodate the degree and kind of idealization that is appropriate in that context. This is what the notion of meaning potential attempts to make possible. The meaning potential is the range of **significant** variation that is at the disposal of the speaker. The notion is not unlike Dell Hymes' (1970) "communicative competence", except that Hymes defines this in terms of 'competence' in the Chomskyan sense of what the speaker knows, whereas we are talking of a potential – what he can do, in the special linguistic sense of what he can mean – and avoiding the additional complication of a distinction between doing and knowing. This potential can then be represented as systematic options in meaning which may be varied in the degree of their specificity – in what has been called *delicacy*. That is to say, the range of variation that is being treated as significant will itself be variable, with either grosser or finer distinctions being drawn according to the type of problem that is being investigated.

49

3. Language as options

Considering language in its social context, then, we can describe it in broad terms as a behaviour potential; and more specifically as a meaning potential, where meaning is a form of behaving (and the verb *to mean* is a verb of the 'doing' class). This leads to the notion of representing language in the form of options: sets of alternative meanings which collectively account for the total meaning potential.

Each option is available in a stated environment, and this is where Firth's category of system comes in. A system is an abstract representation of a paradigm; and this, as we have noted, can be interpreted as a set of options with an entry condition – a number of possibilities out of which a choice has to be made if the stated conditions of entry to the choice are satisfied. It has the form: if *a*, then either *x* or *y* (or ...). The key to its importance in the present context is Firth's "polysystemic principle", whereby (again following this interpretation) the conditions of entry are required to be stated for each set of possibilities. That is to say, for every choice it is to be specified where, under what conditions, that choice is made. The 'where', in Firth's use of the concept of a system, was 'at what point in the structure'; but we interpret it here as 'where in the total network of options'. Each choice takes place in the environment of other choices. This is what makes it possible to vary the 'delicacy' of the description: we can stop wherever the choices are no longer significant for what we are interested in.

The options in a natural language are at various levels: phonological, grammatical (including lexical, which is simply the more specific part within the grammatical) and semantic. Here, where we are concerned with the meaning potential, the options are in the first instance semantic options. These are interpreted as the coding of options in behaviour, so that the semantics is in this sense a behavioural semantics.

The semantic options are in turn coded as options in grammar. Now there are no grammatical categories corresponding exactly to such concepts as those of reasoning, pleading or threatening referred to above. But there may be a prediction, deriving from a social theory, that these will be among the significant behavioural categories represented in the meaning potential. In that case it should be possible to identify certain options in the grammar as being systemic realizations of these categories, since presumably they are to be found somewhere in the language system. We will not expect there to be a complete one-to-one correspondence between the grammatical options and the semantic ones; but this is merely allowing for the normal phenomena of neutralization and diversification that are associated with all stages in the realization chain.

There is nothing new in the notion of associating grammatical categories with higher level categories of a 'socio-' semantic kind. This is quite natural in the case of grammatical forms concerned with the expression of social roles; particularly those systems which reflect the inherent social structure of the speech situation, which cannot be explained in any other way. The principal component of these is the system of mood. If we represent the basic options in the mood system of English in the following way:

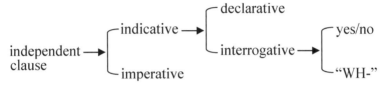

(to be read "an independent clause is either indicative or imperative; if indicative, then either declarative or interrogative", and so on), we are systematizing the set of choices whereby the speaker is enabled to assume one of a number of possible communication roles – social roles which exist only in and through language, as functions of the speech situation. The choice of interrogative, for example, means, typically, 'I am acting as questioner (seeker of information), and you are to act as listener and then as answerer (supplier of information)'. By means of this system the speaker takes on himself a role in the speech situation and allocates the complementary role – actually, rather, a particular choice of complementary ones – to the hearer, both while he is speaking and after he has finished.

These 'communication roles' belong to what we were referring to as "socio-semantics". They are a special case in that they are a property of the speech situation as such, and do not depend on any kind of a social theory. But the relationship between, say, 'question' in semantics and 'interrogative' in grammar is not really different from that between a behavioural-semantic category such as 'threat' and the categories by which it is realized grammatically. In neither instance is the relationship one to one; and while the latter may be rather more complex, a more intensive study of language as social behaviour also suggests a somewhat more complex treatment of traditional notions like those of statement and question. Part of the grammar with which we are familiar is thus a sociological grammar already, although this has usually been confined

51

to a small area where the meanings expressed are 'social' in a rather special sense, that of the social roles created by language itself.

However, the example of the mood system serves to show that, even if we are operating only with the rather oversimplified notions of statement, question, command and the like, categories like these occupy an intermediate level of 'meaning potential' which links behavioural categories to grammatical ones. We do not usually find a significant option in behaviour represented straightforwardly in the grammatical system; it is only in odd instances that what the speaker 'can do' is coded immediately as what he 'can say'. There is a level of what he 'can mean' between the two.

The relation between the levels of meaning and saying, which is one of realization, involves as we have said departures from a regular pattern of one-to-one correspondence. In any particular sociolinguistic investigation, only some of the total possible behavioural options will be under focus of attention; hence we shall be faced especially with instances of 'one-to-many', where one meaning is expressed in different forms. But in such instances we can often invoke the 'good reason' principle, by which one of the possibilities is the 'unmarked' one, that which is chosen to express the meaning in question unless there is good reason to choose otherwise. For example, a question is typically realized in the grammar as an interrogative, and there has to be a 'good reason' for it to be expressed in some other form, such as a declarative. And secondly, the implication of 'one meaning realized by many forms', namely that there is free variation among the possibilities concerned, is unlikely to be the whole truth; it nearly always signifies that there is a more subtle choice in meaning that we have not yet cottoned on to, or that is irrelevant in this particular context.

So a category like that of 'threat', assuming that such a category is identified within the meaning potential, on the basis perhaps of a theory of socialization, will be realized in the language system through a number of different grammatical options. These might include, for example, declarative clauses of a certain type, perhaps first person singular future tense with a verb from a certain lexical set (often identifiable in Roget's *Thesaurus*!), and with attached *if* clause, e.g. *if you do that again I'll smack you*; but also certain other forms, negative imperative with *or* (*don't do that again or* ...), conditioned future attributive clauses with *you* (*you'll be sorry if* ...), and so on. These may appear at first sight to be merely alternative ways of expressing threat, in free variation with each other. But it is very likely that on closer inspection they will be found to represent more delicate (though

52

perhaps still significant) options in the meaning potential. At the same time it might be the case that one of them, possibly the first one mentioned above, could be shown on some grounds to be the typical form of threat (perhaps just in this context), the others all being 'marked' variants; we are then committed to stating the conditions under which it is **not** selected but are not required to give any further explanation when it is.

4. An example

Let us consider a hypothetical example of the behaviour potential associated with a particular social context. We will keep within the general framework of Bernstein's theory of socialization, and take up the type of context already mentioned, that of parental control; within this area, we will construct a particular instance that will yield a reasonably simplified illustration. It should be said very clearly that both the pattern of options and the illustrative sentences have been invented for this purpose; they are **not** actual instances from Bernstein's work. But they are modelled closely on Bernstein's work, and draw on many of his underlying concepts. In particular I have drawn on Geoffrey Turner's studies, in which he has made use of the linguistic notion of systems representing options in meaning for the purpose of investigating the role of language in control situations (Turner 1973).

Let us imagine that the small boy has been playing with the neighbourhood children on a building site. His mother disapproves both of the locale and of the company he has been keeping, and views with particular horror the empty tin or other object he has acquired as a trophy. She wants both to express her disapproval and to prevent the same thing happening again. She might say something like 'that sort of place is not for playing in', or 'I don't like you taking other people's things', or 'they don't want children running about there', or 'just look at the state of your clothes', or 'I'm frightened you'll hurt yourself', or many other things besides.

Various means are open to the mother here for making her intentions explicit. Now, in terms of the actual sentences she might utter, the range of possibilities is pretty well unlimited. But a particular theory about the function of the regulatory context in the socialization of the child would suggest that she is actually operating within a systematic framework of very general options, any one of which (or any one combination) might be expressed through the medium of a wide range of different lexico-grammatical forms. These options represent the meaning potential lying behind the particular instances.

We will assume that the mother is using some form of appeal, as distinct from a direct injunction or a threat. She may simply enunciate a rule, based on her authority as a parent; or she may appeal to reason, and give an explanation of what she wants. Let us call this "authority or reason". Secondly, and at the same time, she may formulate her appeal in general or in particular terms, either relating this event to a wider class of situations or treating it on its own; we will say that the appeal may be "general" or "particular". And she may slant her appeal away from the persons involved towards the material environment and the objects in it ("object-oriented"); or she may concentrate on the people ("person-oriented") – in which case the focus of attention may either be on the parent (the mother herself, and perhaps the father as well) or on the child. Finally, if the orientation is towards people, there is another option available, since the appeal may be either "personal" or "positional": that is, relating to the child or herself either as individuals, or in their status in the family, the age group and so on. Thus *you* may mean 'you, Timmy'; or it may mean 'you as my offspring', 'you as a young child' or in some other defined social status.

We may now represent these possibilities in the following way as a network of alternatives:

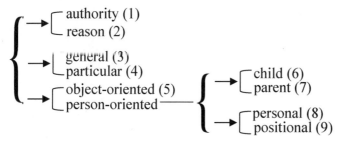

This represents the meaning potential that is open to the mother in the situation, as far as we have taken it in the present discussion.

The categories in this semantic network are not immediately recognizable as linguistic categories. There is no category of "object-oriented" or "positional" in the grammar of English, no grammatical system of 'authority/reason'. But if this network of options is a valid account of a part of the range of alternatives that are open to the mother as regards what she 'can mean' in the situation, then the implication is that these options will be found to be realized somewhere in the linguistic system, in the things that she can say.

Any one selection from within this range of options could be realized through a wide range of different grammatical categories and lexical items. Take for example the combination "authority, general, object-oriented". The mother might say *that sort of place is not for playing in*, or she might say *we don't go into places like that*, or *other people's things aren't for playing with*, or *we don't take other people's property*; all of these would be instances of the particular combination of options just mentioned. Here we have alternative forms of expression for what are, within the limits of the few distinctions recognized in our illustration, the same selections in meaning. As far as their grammar and vocabulary is concerned, there are certain things common to two or more of these examples which can be related to their common element in their meanings: for example the form ... *(is/are) not for ... ing (in/with)*, the form *we don't ...*, the reference to *place*, and so on. But in other respects they are very different, and involve categories that might not otherwise be brought together from their different places in the description of the grammar, such as *we don't X with/in Y* and *Y is not for X-ing with/in* as forms of disapproval, or the different categories represented by the words *place* and *thing* (including *property*, which can be interpreted as either). Note that *place* and *thing* are grouped together under the option "object-oriented"; no doubt if the analysis was carried through to a more delicate stage they would then be distinguished, since although both represent non-personalized forms of appeal there is a difference between the notion of territory and the notion of ownership that might be significant. Meanwhile they serve to illustrate a further point, that the analysis seeks to specify as far as possible the contribution made by each particular option to the form of the sentences used. Here, for example, the feature of "authority" is reflected in the negative and in the modal forms; that of "general" in the tense and the noun modifiers *that sort of ...*, *... like that*; that of "object-oriented" in the words *place*, *thing* and (*other people's*) *property*, coupled with the absence of individualized personal pronouns.

Even though the forms used to express any one meaning selection are very varied, they are nevertheless distinct from those realizing other selections: we must in principle be able to tell what the mother means from what she says, since we are crediting the child with the ability to do so. Here to complete the illustration is a set of possible utterances by the mother representing different selections in the meaning potential. These are not intended to cover the whole of the mother's verbal intervention; some of them would need to be (and all of them could be) accompanied by an explicit injunction such as *you're not to do that again*.

They exemplify only options in the type of appeal she is using; as such, each one could occur either alone or in combination with an appeal of one of the other types. The figures following each example indicate, by reference to the network, the options it is assumed to express.

> other people's things aren't for playing with (135)
> you know you don't play with those sorts of boys (1368)
> they don't want children running about there (1369)
> Daddy doesn't like you to play rough games (1378)
> that tin belongs to somebody else (145)
> you can go there when you're bigger (1469)
> I was worried, I didn't know where you'd got to (1478)
> you'll ruin your clothes playing in a place like that (235)
> it's not good for you to get too excited (2368)
> boys who are well brought up play nice games in the park (2369)
> we don't want people to think we don't look after you, do we? (2379)
> that glass they keep there might get broken (245)
> you might have hurt yourself on all that glass (2468)
> I'd like you to stay and help me at home (2478)

Not all the possible combinations of options have been exemplified, and some of them are unlikely in this particular instance, although probably all could occur. Let us stress again here that both the examples and the network of options, although inspired by Bernstein's work, have been invented for the present discussion, in order to keep the illustration down to a manageable size.

A system network of this kind is open-ended. It may represent only certain very gross distinctions: in the simplest case, just a choice between two possibilities, so that all the meaning potential associated with a particular social context is reduced to 'either this or that'. But it is always capable of accommodating further distinctions – of being made more and more "delicate" – when these are brought into the picture. Each new distinction that is introduced has implications both 'upwards' and 'downwards': that is, it is significant as an option in behaviour, and it is systematically (however indirectly) expressed in the language. Only in very restricted types of situation can anywhere near all the linguistic features of an utterance be derived from behaviourally significant options; but then there is no such thing as 'all the linguistic features of an utterance' considered apart from some external criteria of significance. The point is that, as further specification is added to the semantic systems, so more of the linguistic features come to be accounted for. This can be seen in Turner's work, already referred to, in which he is investigating the meaning potential associated with certain contexts of the general kind we have been illustrating.

5. Interpretation of linguistic forms determined by reference to concepts of social theory

In understanding the nature of 'social man', and in particular the processes – and they are largely linguistic processes – whereby the child becomes social man, we are likely to be deeply concerned with those aspects of his experience which centre around social contexts and settings of the kind just exemplified.

We shall not of course expect to assign anything like the whole of an individual's language behaviour to situations of this kind, which can be investigated and interpreted in the light of some significant social theory. The meaning of a poem, or a technical discussion, cannot be expressed in terms of behavioural options. (It can, on the other hand, be related to a set of generalized functions of language which define the total meaning potential of the adult language system; see the discussion in the next section.) At the same time, the social contexts and settings for which we can recognize a meaning potential in behavioural terms are not at all marginal or outlandish; and they are contexts which play a significant part in the socialization of the child. The importance of such contexts is given by the social theory from which they are derived.

Not all the distinctions in meaning that may be associated with a context of this kind can be explained by reference to behavioural options which are universally significant in that context. Within the actual words and sentences used there is bound to be much that is particular to the local situation or the shared experience of the individuals concerned. In the illustration given in the last section, the reference to breaking glass or getting hurt by it is obviously specific to a small class of instances of a control situation; and it is likely to be significant only in relation to that setting. It is possible, however, that a highly particular feature of this kind could be the local realization of an option having a general significance: there might be some symbolic value attached to broken glass in the family, having its origin in a particular incident, and we could not know this simply from inspecting the language. And there are general shifted meanings too, extended metaphors whereby, especially in the interaction of adult and child, behavioural options are encoded in highly complex, more or less

57

ritualized linguistic forms; for example the bedtime story, where the princes and the giants and the whole narrative structure collectively express patterns of socialization and interpersonal meanings. Here we are led into the realms of literary interpretation, of levels of meaning in the imaginative mode, of the significance of poetic forms and the like.

Looking to the other end of the scale, we can find settings, for example games where the language plays an essential part, like pontoon or contract bridge, for which a system of meaning potential will account for a very high proportion of the words and sentences used by the participants (Mohan 1969). These restricted settings are interesting from the point of view of sociolinguistic method, since they illustrate very well the principle of language as behaviour potential. But they may have little or no significance in themselves as social contexts, relative to any general theory of social behaviour.

What we are referring to as a "social context" is a generalized type of situation that is itself significant in terms of the categories and concepts of some social theory. The theory may focus attention on different facets of the social structure: not only on forms of socialization and cultural transmission, but also on role relationships, on the power structure and patterns of social control, on symbolic systems, systems of values, of public knowledge and the like. Our example was drawn from the socialization of the child, because that is where most work has been done; but systematic options in language behaviour are not limited to situations of this type. Any situation in which the behavioural options open to the participants are, at least in part, realizations of some general theoretical categories is relevant as a 'social context' in this sense. Hence a particular linguistic feature may have a number of different meanings according to the type of context in which it occurs: for example, *they don't want children in there* might not be any kind of appeal – it might occur in a context that had nothing to do with socialization, not being addressed to a child at all. We could not simply take the linguistic forms for granted, as having just one behavioural interpretation.

More important, perhaps, or at least less obvious, is the fact that even within the same context a linguistic form may have different meanings, since there may be sub-cultural variants in the meaning potential (different "codes", in Bernstein's sense; see Hasan 1973) typically associated with that context. In other words, assuming that the sentence above was in fact being used in a regulatory context such as the one invented for the illustration, it might still have more than one meaning, given two distinct social groups one of which typically exploited one area of meaning potential (say, "elaborated code") and the other another ("restricted code"). Within a "code" in which the typical appeal was positional and non-discretionary, this example would be interpreted as an imperative, whereas in one tending towards more personal and more challengeable appeals it could be taken as a partially explicit rule. The meaning of selecting any one particular feature would be potentially different in the two "codes", since it would be selected from within a different range of probable alternatives.

We have suggested that this use of a social context corresponds to what Firth meant by the "typical context of situation", and that it makes the link between the two Malinowskian notions of 'context of situation' and 'context of culture' referred to at the beginning of this paper. It is the social context that defines the limits of the options available; the behavioural alternatives are to this extent context-specific. But the total range of meanings that is embodied in and realized through the language system is determined by the context of culture – in other words by the social structure.

The study of language as social behaviour is in the last resort an account of semantic options deriving from the social structure. Like other hyphenated fields of language study, sociolinguistics reaches beyond the phonological and morphological indices into the more abstract areas of linguistic organization. The concept of sociolinguistics ultimately implies a 'socio-semantics' which is a genuine meeting ground of two ideologies, the social and the linguistic. And this faces both ways. The options in meaning are significant linguistically because selections in grammar and vocabulary can be explained as a realization of them. They are significant sociologically because they provide insight into patterns of behaviour that are in turn explainable as realizations of the pragmatic and symbolic acts that are the expressions of the social structure.

In principle we may expect to find some features of the social structure reflected directly in the forms of the language, even in its lower reaches, the morphology and the phonology. The phenomenon of "accent" is a direct reflection of social structure in the phonetic output. Such low level manifestations may be of little interest, although Labov's (1968) work on the New York dialects showed the potential significance of phonological variables in the social structure of an urban speech community. There is an analogy within the language system itself, where sometimes we find instances of the direct expression of meanings in sounds: voice qualities showing anger, and the like. But in general the forms of expression involve a number of levels of realization – a "stratal" system (Lamb 1966) – even within language itself; and this is all the more clear when linguistic features are seen as the expression of meanings derived from behaviour patterns outside language: we will not expect to find a direct link between social content and linguistic expression, except in odd cases. The socio-semantics is the pivotal level; it is the interface between the two. Any set of strategies can be represented as a network of options; the point is that by representing it in this way we provide a link in the chain of realizations that relates language to social structure.

6. Importance of sociolinguistic studies for understanding of the nature of language

The investigation of language as social behaviour is not only relevant to the understanding of social structure; it is also relevant to the understanding of language. A network of socio-semantic options – the representation of what we have been calling the "meaning potential" – has implications in both directions; on the one hand as the realization of patterns of behaviour and, on the other hand, as realized by the patterns of grammar. The concept of meaning potential thus provides a perspective on the nature of language. Language is as it is because of its function in the social structure, and the organization of behavioural meanings should give some insight into its social foundations.

This is the significance of functional theories of language. The essential feature of a functional theory is not that it enables us to enumerate and classify the functions of speech acts, but that it provides a basis for explaining the nature of the language system, since the system itself reflects the functions that it has evolved to serve. The organization of options in the grammar of natural languages seems to rest very clearly on a functional basis, as has emerged from the work of those linguists, particularly of the Prague school, who have been aware that the notion 'functions of language' is not to be equated merely with a theory of language use but expresses the principle behind the organization of the linguistic system.

The options in the grammar of a language derive from and are relatable to three very generalized functions of language which we have referred to elsewhere as the ideational, the interpersonal and the textual (Halliday 1970c). The specific options in meaning that are characteristic of particular social contexts and settings are expressed through the medium of grammatical and lexical selections that trace back to one or other of these three sources. The status of these terms is that they constitute a hypothesis for explaining what seems to be a fundamental fact about the grammar of languages, namely that it is possible to discern three distinct principles of organization in the structure of grammatical units, as described by Daneš (1964) and others, and that these in turn can be shown to be the structural expression of three fairly distinct and independent sets of underlying options.

Those of the first set, the ideational, are concerned with the content of language, its function as a means of the expression of our experience, both of the external world and of the inner world of our own consciousness – together with what is perhaps a separate sub-component expressing certain basic logical relations. The second, the interpersonal, is language as the mediator of role, including all that may be understood by the expression of our own personalities and personal feelings on the one hand, and forms of interaction and social interplay with other participants in the communication situation on the other hand. The third component, the textual, has an enabling function, that of creating text, which is language in operation as distinct from strings of words or isolated sentences and clauses. It is this component that enables the speaker to organize what he is saying in such a way that it makes sense in the context and fulfils its function as a message.

These three functions are the basis of the grammatical system of the adult language. The child begins by acquiring a meaning potential, a small number of distinct meanings that he can express, in two or three functional contexts: he learns to use language for satisfying his material desires ('I want an apple'), for getting others to behave as he wishes ('sing me a song'), and so on. In a paper in a previous volume of this journal I suggested a list of such contexts for an early stage in his language development (1969b; see also Wilkinson 1971). At this stage each utterance tends to have one function only; but as time goes on the typical utterance becomes functionally complex – we learn to combine various uses of language into a single speech act. It is at this point that we need a grammar: a level of organization intermediate between content and expression, which can take the various functionally distinct meaning selections and combine them into integrated structures. The components of the grammatical system are thus themselves functional; but they represent the functions of language in their most generalized form, as these underlie all the more specific contexts of language use.

The meaning potential in any one context is open-ended, in the sense that there is no limit to the distinctions in meaning that we can apprehend. When we talk of what the speaker can do, in this special sense of what he 'can mean', we imply that we can recognize significant differentiations within what he can mean, up to some point or other which will be determined by the requirements of our theory. The importance of a hypothesis about what the speaker can do in a social context is that this makes sense of what he does. If we insist on drawing a boundary between what he does and what he knows, we cannot explain what he does; what he does will appear merely as a random selection from within what he knows. But in the study of language in a social perspective we need both to pay attention to what is said and at the same time to relate it systematically to what might have been said but was not. Hence we do not make a dichotomy between knowing and doing; instead we place 'does' in the environment of 'can do', and treat language as speech potential.

The image of language as having a 'pure' form (*langue*) that becomes contaminated in the process of being translated into speech (*parole*) is of little value in a sociological context. We do not want a boundary between language and speech at all, or between pairs such as langue and parole, or competence and performance – unless these are reduced to mere synonyms of 'can do' and 'does'. A more useful concept is that of a range of behaviour potential determined by the social structure (the context of culture), which is made accessible to study through its association with significant social contexts (generalized contexts of situation), and is actualized by the participants in particular instances of these contexts or situation types.

There is no need to wait until some speaker is observed to produce a particular utterance, before one can take account of the relevant features embodied in it. Sociolinguistic studies are not bounded by the accidental frontiers of the data collected, although they do take such data rather seriously. As Bernstein's work has shown, there are many ways of investigating the language behaviour associated with a social context, ranging from hypothetico-deductive reasoning through various forms of elicitation to hopeful observation. All these are valid parts of the investigator's equipment.

The study of language in a social context tends to involve a rather lower degree of idealization than is customary in a psycho-philosophical orientation, as we have noted already. But there is always some idealization, in any systematic enquiry. It may be at a different place; the type of variation which is least significant for behavioural studies may be just that which is most faithfully preserved in another approach – variation in the ideational meaning, in the "content" as this is usually understood. We might for example be able to ignore distinctions such as that between singular and plural, or between *cat* and *dog* – if we were using the notion of competence and performance, then these distinctions would be relegated to performance – while insisting on the difference in meaning between *don't do that, you mustn't do that, you're not to do that*, and other variants which differ simply in intonation, in pausing and the like.

This overstates the position, no doubt. But it serves to underline the point made earlier: that the object of attention in linguistic studies is not, and never can be, some sort of unprocessed language event. When language is studied in a social perspective, the object of attention is what is usually referred to as "text", that is, language in a context; and the text, whether in origin it was invented, elicited or recorded, is an idealized construction. But all this means is that a linguistic item – a sentence, or whatever – is well formed if it is well formed; there must be criteria from somewhere by which to judge. It is not easy to find these criteria within language; in 'autonomous' linguistics it is in practice usually the orthography that is used to decide what the limits of relevant differentiation are, since the orthography is itself a codified form of idealization (rather as the 'text' of a piece of music is the score). Criteria are found more readily at the interfaces between language and non-language, by reference to something outside language; in a social context, the degree and kind of idealization is determined at the socio-semantic interface. In principle, what is well formed is whatever can be shown to be interpretable as a possible selection within a set of options based on some motivated hypothesis about language behaviour; and "motivated" here means extrinsically motivated by reference ultimately to (a theory about) some feature of the social structure.

The perspective is one in which there are two different but related depths of focus. The more immediate aim, from the point of view of linguistics, is the intrinsic one of explaining the nature of language. This implies an 'autonomous' view of linguistics. There is also a further, extrinsic aim, that of explaining features of the social structure, and using language to do so. This implies an 'instrumental' approach. But ultimately the nature of language is explained in terms of its function in the social structure; so the pursuit of the first aim entails the pursuit of the second. To understand language, we examine the way in which the social structure is realized through language: how values are transmitted, roles defined, and behaviour patterns made manifest.

The role of language in the educational process is a special aspect of the relation between language and social structure. Bernstein's theories concerning the linguistic basis of educational failure are part of a wider theory of language and society, which encompasses much more than

63

the explanation of the linguistic problems imposed by the educational system on the child whose socialization has taken certain forms. Bernstein's concern is with the fundamental problem of persistence and change in the social structure. Language is the principal means of cultural transmission; but if we seek to understand how it functions in this role, it is not enough just to point up odd instances of the reflection of general sociological categories in this or that invented or recorded utterance. An approach to this question presupposes not only a theory of social structure but also a theory of linguistic structure – and hence may lead to further insights into the nature of language, by virtue of the perspective which it imposes. The perspective is a 'socio-semantic' one, where the emphasis is on function rather than on structure; where no distinction is made between language and language behaviour; and where the central notion is something like that of 'meaning potential' – what the speaker 'can mean', with what he 'can say' seen as a realization of it.

Preoccupations of a sociological kind, which as was pointed out at the beginning have for a long time held a place in linguistic studies, assume a greater significance in the light of work such as Bernstein's: not only because Bernstein's social theory is based on a concern with language as the essential factor in cultural transmission, but also because it has far-reaching implications for the nature of language itself. And these, in turn, are very relevant to the educational problems from which Bernstein started. Bernstein has shown the structural relationship between language, the socialization process and education; it is to be expected, therefore, that there will be consequences, for educational theory and practice, deriving from the perspective on language that his work provides. Some concept of the social functioning of language must in any case always underlie the approach of the school towards its responsibility for the pupil's success in his mother tongue.

This paper was first prepared for the Second International Congress of Applied Linguistics, Cambridge, September 1969. A revised version of it was presented to the Oxford University Linguistic Society on 21 October 1969.

Chapter Three

LANGUAGE AND SOCIAL MAN (1974)

1. Language and the environment

If we ever come to look back on the ideology of the 1970s, as suggested by the writer of an imaginary "retrospect from 1980" published in the *Observer* in the first issue of the decade, we are likely to see one theme clearly standing out, the theme of 'social man'. Not social man in opposition to individual man, but rather the individual in his social environment. What the writer was forecasting – and he seems likely to be proved accurate – was, in effect, that while we should continue to be preoccupied with man in relation to his surroundings, as we were in the sixties, the seventies would show a change of emphasis from the purely physical environment on to the social environment. This is not a new concern, but it has tended up to now to take second place; we have been more involved over the past 20 years with town planning and urban renewal, with the flow of traffic around us and above our heads, and most recently with the pollution and destruction of our material resources. This inevitably has distracted us from thinking about the other part of our environment, that which consists of people – not people as mere quanta of humanity, so many to the square mile, but other individuals with whom we have dealings of a more or less personal kind.

The 'environment' is social as well as physical, and a state of well-being, which depends on harmony with the environment, demands

Language and Social Man, Schools Council Programme in Linguistics and English Teaching: Papers, Series II, Vol. 3, London: Longman, 1974. Copyright © Pearson Education Limited.

harmony of both kinds. The nature of this state of well-being is what environmental studies are about. Ten years ago we first came to hear of "ergonomics", the study and control of the environment in which people work; many will remember London Transport's advertising slogan "How big is a bus driver?", announcing the design of new buses "on ergonomic principles". This was characteristic of the conception of the environment at that time. Today we would find more emphasis laid on the social aspects of well-being. No one would assert that the shape of the bus driver's seat is unimportant; but it no longer seems to be the whole story. There are other aspects of environmental design which seem at least as significant, and which are considerably more difficult to adjust.

Consider for example the problem of pollution, the defensive aspect of environmental design. The rubbish creep, the contamin- ation of air and water, even the most lethal processes of physical pollution appear to be more tractable than the pollution in the social environment that is caused by prejudice and animosity of race, culture and class. These cannot be engineered away. One of the more dangerous of the terms that have been coined in this area is "social engineering"; dangerous not so much because it suggests manipulating people for evil ends – most people are alert to that danger – but because it implies that the social environment can be fashioned like the physical one, by methods of demolition and construction, if only the plans and the machines are big enough and complicated enough. Some of the unfortunate effects of this kind of thinking have been seen from time to time in the field of language and education. But social well-being is not definable, or attainable, in these terms.

"Education" may sound less exciting than social engineering, but it is an older concept and one that is more relevant to our needs. If the engineers and the town planners can mould the physical environment, it is the teachers who exert the most influence on the social environment. They do so not by manipulating the social structure (which would be the engineering approach) but by playing a major part in the process whereby a human being becomes social man. The school is the main line of defence against pollution in the human environment; and we should not perhaps dismiss the notion of 'defence' too lightly, because defensive action is often precisely what is needed. Preventive medicine, after all, is defensive medicine; and what the school has failed to prevent is left to society to cure.

In the development of the child as a social being language has the central role. Language is the main channel through which the patterns of living are transmitted to him, through which he learns to act as a member of a 'society' – in and through the various social groups, the family, the neighbourhood, and so on – and to adopt its 'culture', its modes of thought and action, its beliefs and its values. This does not happen by instruction, at least not in the pre-school years; nobody teaches him the principles on which social groups are organized, or their systems of beliefs, nor would he understand it if they tried. It happens indirectly, through the accumulated experience of numerous small events, insignificant in themselves, in which his behaviour is guided and controlled, and in the course of which he contracts and develops personal relationships of all kinds. All this takes place through the medium of language. And it is not from the language of the classroom, still less that of courts of law, of moral tracts or of textbooks of sociology, that the child learns about the culture he was born into. The striking fact is that it is the most ordinary everyday uses of language, with parents, brothers and sisters, neighbourhood children in the home, in the street and the park, in the shops and the trains and the buses, that serve to transmit, to the child, the essential qualities of society and the nature of social being.

This, in brief, is what this paper is about. It is a general discussion of the relation of language to social man, and in particular language as it impinges on the role of the teacher as a creator of social man – or at least as a midwife in the creation process. That this does not mean simply language in school is already clear. It means, rather, language in the total context of the interaction between an individual and his human environment: between one individual and others, in fact. But the point of view to be adopted will be an educational one, emphasizing those aspects of language and social man that are most relevant to the teacher in the classroom.

It might seem that one could hardly begin to consider language at all without taking account of social man, since language is the means whereby people interact. How else can one look at language **except** in a social context? In the last resort, it is true that the existence of language implies the existence of social man; but this does not by itself determine the point of vantage from which language is being approached. Let us think for a moment of an individual human being, considered as a single organism. Being human, it is also articulate: it can speak and understand language, and perhaps read and write it as well. Now the ability to speak and understand arises, and makes sense, only because there are other such organisms around, and it is natural to think of it as an interorganism phenomenon to be studied from an interorganism point of view. But it is also possible to investigate language from the standpoint of the internal make-up of that organism: the brain structure, and the cerebral processes, that are involved in its speaking and understanding and also in its learning to speak and to understand. So there is an intraorganism perspective on language as well as an interorganism one. The two standpoints are complementary; but there tend to be shifts of emphasis between them, trends and fashions in scholarship which lead to concentration on one, for a time, at the expense of the other. In the 1960s the major emphasis was on what we are calling intraorganism studies, on the investigation of language as knowledge, of 'what the speaker knows', running parallel to, and probably occasioned by, the relative neglect of man's social environment. There has now been a move back towards a greater concern with the social aspects of language, a restoring of the balance in linguistic studies, with account once more being taken of the interorganism factor – that of language as social behaviour, or language in relation to social man.

A diagrammatic representation of the nature of linguistic studies and their relation to other fields of scholarship will serve as a point of reference for the subsequent discussion. The diagram shows the domain of language study – of linguistics, to give it its subject title – by a broken line; everything within that line is an aspect or a branch of linguistic studies.

In the centre is a triangle, shown by a solid line, which marks off what is the central area of language study, that of language as a system. One way of saying what is meant by "central" here is that if a student is taking linguistics as a university subject he will have to cover this area as a compulsory part of his course, whatever other aspects he may choose to take up. There are then certain projections from the triangle, representing special sub-disciplines within this central area: phonetics, historical linguistics and dialectology – the last of these best thought of in broader terms, as the study of language varieties. These sometimes get excluded from the central region, but probably most linguists would agree in placing them within it; if one could give a three-dimensional representation they would not look like excrescences.

Then, outside this triangle, are the principal perspectives on language that take us beyond a consideration solely of language as a system and, in so doing, impinge on other disciplines. Any study of language involves some attention to other disciplines; one cannot

68

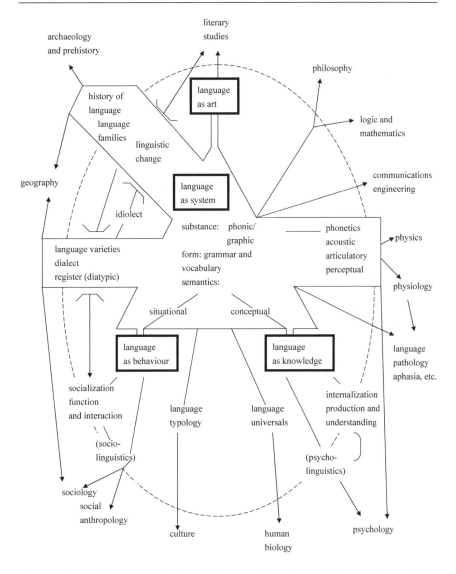

draw a boundary round the subject and insulate it from others. The question is whether the aims go beyond the elucidation of language itself; and once one goes outside the central area, one is enquiring not only into language but into language in relation to something else. The diagram summarizes these wider fields under the three headings "language as knowledge", "language as behaviour", "language as art".

The last of these takes us into the realm of literature, which is all too often treated as if it was something insulated from and even opposed to

69

language: 'we concentrate mainly on literature here – we don't do much on language', as if 'concentrating on literature' made it possible to ignore the fact that literature is made of language. Similarly the undergraduate is invited to 'choose between lang. and lit.'. In fact the distinction that is being implied is a perfectly meaningful one between two different emphases or orientations, one in which the centre of attention is the linguistic system and the other having a focus elsewhere; but it is wrongly named, and therefore, perhaps, liable to be misinterpreted. One can hardly take literature seriously without taking language seriously; but language here is being looked at from a special point of view.

The other two headings derive from the distinction we have just been drawing between the intraorganism perspective, language as knowledge, and the interorganism perspective, language as behaviour. These both lead us outward from language as a system, the former into the region of psychological studies, the latter into sociology and related fields. So in putting language into the context of 'language and social man', we are taking up one of the options that are open for the relating of language study to other fields of enquiry. This, broadly, is the sociolinguistic option; and the new subject of sociolinguistics that has come into prominence lately is a recognition of the fact that language and society – or, as we prefer to think of it, language and social man – is a unified conception, and needs to be understood and investigated as a whole. Neither of these exists without the other: there can be no social man without language, and no language without social man. To recognize this is no mere academic exercise; the whole theory and practice of education depends on it, and it is no exaggeration to suggest that much of our failure in recent years – the failure of the schools to come to grips with social pollution – can be traced to a lack of insight into the nature of the relationships between language and society: specifically, of the processes, which are very largely linguistic processes, whereby a human organism turns into a social being.

2. Interorganism and intraorganism perspectives

The diagram in Section 1 suggests a context for language study, placing it in the environment of other fields of investigation. It also suggests where 'language and social man' fits in to the total picture of language study. The discussion of the diagram will perhaps have made it clear (and this harks back to what was said at the beginning)

70

that when we talk of "social man" the contrast we are making is not that of social versus individual. The contrast is rather that of social versus psychophysiological, the distinction which we have attempted to draw in terms of interorganism and intraorganism perspectives.

When we refer to social man, we mean the individual considered as a single entity, rather than as an assemblage of parts. The distinction we are drawing here is that between the behaviour of that individual, his actions and interactions with his environment (especially that part of his environment which consists of other individuals), on the one hand, and on the other hand his biological nature, and in particular the internal structure of his brain. In the first of these perspectives we are regarding the individual as an integral whole, and looking at him from the outside; in the second we are focusing our attention on the parts, and looking on the inside, into the works. Language can be considered from either of these points of view; the first is what we called on the diagram 'language as behaviour', the second 'language as knowledge'. "Language and social man" means language as a function of the whole man; hence language man to man (interorganism), or language as human behaviour.

These are two complementary orientations. The distinction between them is not a difficult one to make; in itself it is rather obvious and simple. But it has become complicated by the fact that it is possible to embed one perspective inside the other: to treat language behaviour as if it were an aspect of our knowledge of language (and hence to see it in terms of the capacity of the human brain), and also, though in a rather different sense, to treat the individual's knowledge of language as a form of behaviour. In other words we can look at social facts from a biological point of view, or at biological facts from a social point of view. Let us try and explain this.

The study of language as knowledge is an attempt to find out what goes on inside the individual's head. The question being asked is what are the mechanisms of the brain that are involved in speaking and understanding, and what must the structure of the brain be like in order for the individual to be able to speak and understand language, and to be able to learn to do so.

Now one important fact about speaking and understanding language is that it always takes place in a context. We do not simply 'know' our mother tongue as an abstract system of vocal signals, or as if it was some sort of a grammar book with a dictionary attached. We know it in the sense of knowing how to use it; we know how to communicate with

71

other people, how to choose forms of language that are appropriate to the type of situation we find ourselves in, and so on. All this can be expressed as "know how to", as a form of knowledge: we know how to behave linguistically.

Therefore it is possible, and is in fact quite usual in what is nowadays called "sociolinguistics", to look at language behaviour as a type of knowledge; so that although one's attention is focused on the social aspects of language – on language as communication between organisms – one is still asking what is essentially an intraorganism kind of question: how does the individual **know how to** behave in this way? We might refer to this as psychosociolinguistics: it is the external behaviour of the organism looked at from the point of view of the internal mechanisms which control it.

We said above that the two perspectives were complementary and it would be reasonable to conclude that they are really inseparable one from the other. But if so the inseparability holds in both directions. It is true that the individual's potential for linguistic interaction with others implies certain things about the internal make-up of the individual himself. But the converse is also true. The fact that the brain has the capacity to store language and use it for effective communication implies that communication takes place: that the individual has a 'behaviour potential' which characterizes his interaction with other individuals of his species.

Since no doubt the human brain evolved in its present form through the process of human beings communicating with one another, the latter perspective is likely to be highly significant from an evolutionary point of view. But that is not our main point of departure here. There is a more immediate sense in which the individual, considered as one who can speak and understand and read and write, who has a 'mother tongue', needs to be seen in a social perspective. This concerns the part that language has played in his own development as an individual. Let us start with the notion of the individual human organism, the human being as a biological specimen. Like the individual in many other species, he is destined to become one of a group; but unlike those of all other species, he achieves this – not wholly, but critically – through language. It is by means of language that the 'human being' becomes one of a group of 'people'. But 'people', in turn, consist of 'persons'; by virtue of his participation in a group the individual is no longer simply a biological specimen of humanity – he is a person. Again language is the essential element in the process, since it is largely the linguistic interchange with the group

72

that determines the status of the individuals and shapes them as persons. The picture is:

INDIVIDUAL   GROUP

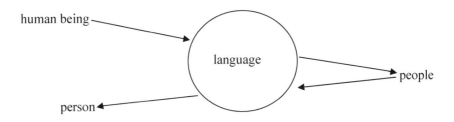

In other words, instead of looking at the group as a derivation from and extension of the biologically endowed mental powers of the individual, we explain the nature of the individual as a derivation from and extension of his participation in the group. Instead of starting inside the organism and looking outwards, we can adopt a Durkheimian perspective and start from outside the organism in order to look inwards.

But when we do adopt this perspective it becomes apparent that we can take the dialectic one stage further, and that when we do so language will still remain the crucial factor. The individual as a 'person' is now a potential 'member': he has the capacity to function within society, and once more it is through language that he achieves this status. How does a society differ from a group, as we conceive it here? A group is a simple structure, a set of participants among whom there are no special relations, only the simple coexistence that is implied by participation in the group. A society, on the other hand, does not consist of participants but of relations, and these relations define social roles. Being a member of society means occupying a social role; and it is again by means of language that a 'person' becomes potentially the occupant of a social role.

Social roles are combinable, and the individual, as a member of a society, occupies not just one role but many at a time, always through the medium of language. Language is again a necessary condition for this final element in the process of the development of the individual, from human being to person to what we may call "personality", a personality being interpreted as a role complex. Here the individual is seen as the configuration of a number of roles defined by the social relationships in which he enters; from these roles he synthesizes a personality. Our model now looks like this:

INDIVIDUAL   GROUP

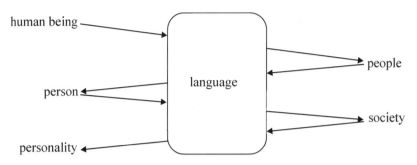

Let us now interpret this in terms of a perspective on language. We have gone some way round in order to reach this particular angle of vision, certainly oversimplifying the picture and perhaps seeming to exaggerate the importance of language in the total process. The justification for this is that we have been trying to achieve a perspective that will be most relevant in an educational context. From this point of view, language is the medium through which a human being becomes a personality, in consequence of his membership of society and his occupancy of social roles. The concept of language as behaviour, as a form of interaction between man and man, is turned around, as it were, so that it throws light on the individual: the formation of the personality is itself a social process, or a complex of social processes, and language – by virtue of its social functions – plays the key part in it. Hence just as the view of language as knowledge, which is essentially an individual orientation, can be used to direct attention outwards, through such concepts as the speech act, towards language in society, so the essentially social interpretation of language as behaviour can be used to direct attention on to the individual, placing him in the human environment, as we expressed it earlier, and explaining his linguistic potential, as speaker-hearer and writer-reader, in these terms. This does not presuppose, or preclude, any particular theory about the nature of the mental processes that are involved in his mastery of language, either in how he speaks and understands or in how he learnt to do so in the first place. There are conflicting psychological theories on these questions, as we shall see in the next section; but our present perspective is neutral in their regard.

The ability to speak and understand, and the development of this ability in the child, are essential ingredients in the life of social man. To approach these from the outside, as interorganism phenomena, is to take a functional view of language. The social aspect of language becomes the reference point for the biological aspect, rather than the other way round. In the next two sections we shall consider briefly what this means.

3. A functional approach to language and language development

In the last part of this paper we shall suggest a number of specific topics which might be explored, both inside and outside the school, as a way of finding out for oneself more about the nature of language and its place in the life of social man. These are related to the general perspective outlined in Section 2, that of the individual as seen through the lens of his membership of 'society' – that is, in the context of other individuals; with his language potential being understood as the medium by which the relationships into which he enters are established, developed and maintained. This means that we are taking a functional view of language, in the sense that we are interested in what language can do, or rather in what the speaker, child or adult, can do with it; and that we try to explain the nature of language, its internal organization and patterning, in terms of the functions that it has evolved to serve.

First of all, therefore, we should look briefly into the question of linguistic function, and say a little about it, both in regard to what language is and in regard to how it is learnt by a child. Let us take the latter point first, and consider a functional approach to the question of how the child learns his mother tongue. This process, the learning of the mother tongue, is often referred to as "language acquisition". This seems rather an unfortunate term because it suggests that language is some kind of a commodity to be acquired, and, although the metaphor is innocent enough in itself, if it is taken too literally the consequences can be rather harmful. The use of this metaphor has led to the belief in what is known as a "deficit theory" of language learning, as a means of explaining how children come to fail in school: the suggestion that certain children, perhaps because of their social background, have not acquired enough of this commodity called language, and in order to help them we must send relief supplies. The implication is that there is a gap to be filled, and from this derive various compensatory practices that may be largely irrelevant to the children's needs. Now this is a false and misleading view of language and of educational failure; and while one should not make too much of one item of terminology, we prefer to avoid the term "language acquisition" and return to the earlier and entirely appropriate designation of "language development".

75

In the psychological, or psycholinguistic, sphere, there are two main types of approach to the question of language development. These have been referred to as the "nativist" and the "environmentalist" position. Everyone agrees, of course, that human beings are biologically endowed with the ability to learn language, and that this is a uniquely human attribute – no other species has it, however much a chimpanzee or a dolphin may be trained to operate with words or symbols. But the nativist view holds that there is a specific language-learning faculty, distinct from other learning faculties, and that this provides the human infant with a ready-made and rather detailed blueprint of the structure of language. Learning one's mother tongue consists in fitting the patterns of whatever language he hears around him into the framework which he already possesses. The environmentalist view considers that language learning is not fundamentally distinct from other kinds of learning; it depends on those same mental faculties that are involved in all aspects of the child's learning processes. Rather than having built in to his genetic make-up a set of concrete universals of language, in this view what the child has is the ability to process certain highly abstract types of cognitive relation which underlie (among other things) the linguistic system; the very specific properties of language are not innate, and therefore the child is more dependent on his environment – on the language he hears around him, together with the contexts in which it is uttered – for the successful learning of his mother tongue. In a sense, therefore, the difference of views is a recurrence of the old controversy of nature and nurture, or heredity and environment, in a new guise.

Each of these views can be criticized, although the criticisms that are actually made often relate to particular models of the learning process that have no necessary connection with a nativist or environmentalist position. For example, it is sometimes assumed that an environmentalist interpretation implies some form of behaviourist theory, an essentially stimulus–response, associationist view of learning; but this is totally untrue. Equally, the nativist view is by no means dependent on the notion that learning proceeds by fitting items into the marked slots which nature provided and running the machine to test whether the match is appropriate. The differences between nativist and environ-mentalist are differences of emphasis, among other things in their ideas concerning the essential character of language, where they stem from two rather different traditions. Broadly speaking, the nativist model reflects the philosophical-logical strand in the history of thinking about language, with its sharp distinction between the ideal and the real (which Chomsky calls "competence" and "performance") and its view of language as "rules" – essentially rules of syntax. The environmentalist represents the ethnographic tradition, which rejects the distinction of ideal and real, defines what is grammatical as, by and large, what is acceptable, and sees language as relations based on meaning, with meaning defined in terms of function. To this extent the two interpretations are complementary rather than contradictory; but they have tended to become associated with conflicting psychological theories and thus to be strongly counterposed one against the other.

One argument often put forward in support of a nativist approach must be dismissed as fallacious; this is the theory of the unstructured input, according to which the child cannot be dependent on what he hears around him because what he hears is no more than bits and pieces – unfinished or ungrammatical sentences, full of hesitations, back-tracking, unrelated fragments and the like. This idea seems to have arisen because the earliest tape recordings of connected discourse that linguists analysed were usually recordings of intellectual conversations, which do tend to be very scrappy, since the speakers are having to plan as they go along and the premises are constantly shifting, and which are also largely insulated from the immediate situation, so that there are no contextual clues. But it is not in fact true of the ordinary everyday speech that typically surrounds the small child, which is fluent, highly structured, and closely related to the non-verbal context of situation. Moreover it tends to have very few deviations in it; I found myself when observing the language spoken to, and in the presence of, a small child that almost all the sequences were well formed and whole, acceptable even to the sternest grammatical lawgiver. Of course the fact that the notion of unstructured input is unsound does not disprove the nativist theory; it merely removes one of the arguments that has been used to support it.

More important than the grammatical shape of what the child hears, however, is the fact that it is functionally related to observable features of the situation around him. This consideration allows us to give another account of language development that is not dependent on any particular psycholinguistic theory, an account that is functional and sociological rather than structural and psychological. The two are not in competition; they are about different things. A functional theory is not a theory about the mental processes involved in the learning of the mother tongue; it is a theory about the social processes involved. As we expressed it in the first section, it is concerned with language between people (interorganism), and therefore learning to speak is interpreted as the individual's mastery of a behaviour potential. In this perspective, language is a form of interaction, and it is learnt through interaction; this, essentially, is what makes it possible for a culture to be transmitted from one generation to the next.

In a functional approach to language development the first question to be asked is, 'what are the functions that language serves in the life of an infant?' This might seem self-contradictory, if an infant is one who does not yet speak; but the paradox is intentional – before he has mastered any recognizable form of his mother tongue the child already has a linguistic system, in the sense that he can express certain meanings through the consistent use of vocal sounds. There are, perhaps, four main reasons for putting the question in this form.

1. We can ask the same question at any stage in the life of the individual, up to and including adulthood; there have in fact been a number of functional theories of adult and adolescent language.
2. It is much easier to answer the question in respect of a very young child; the earlier one starts, the more clear-cut the functions are (whereas with an approach based on structure, the opposite is the case; it is in general **harder** to analyse the structure of children's speech than of adults).
3. We can reasonably assume that the child is functionally motivated; if language is for the child a means of attaining social ends – that is, ends which are important to him as a social being – we need look no further than this for the reasons why he learns it.
4. A functional approach to language, if it includes a developmental perspective, can throw a great deal of light on the nature of language itself. Language is as it is because of what it has to do.

To these we might add a fifth, though this is not so much a reason for asking the question as an incidental bonus for having done so. One of the problems in studying the language of a very young child is that of knowing what is language and what is not. We can answer that, in a functional context, by saying that any vocal sound (and any gesture, if the definition is made to include gesture) which is interpretable by reference to a recognized function of language is language – provided always that the relationship of sound to meaning is regular and consistent. The production of a sound for the purpose of practicing that sound is a means of **learning** language, but is not itself an instance of language. The production of a sound for the purpose of attracting attention **is** language, once we have reason to assert that 'attracting attention' is a meaning that fits in with the functional potential of language at this stage of development.

Looking at the early stages of language development form a functional viewpoint, we can follow the process whereby the child gradually 'learns how to mean' – for this is what first-language learning is. If there is anything which the child can be said to be acquiring, it is a range of potential, which we could refer to as his ***meaning potential***. This consists in the mastery of a small number of elementary functions of language, and of a range of choices in meaning within each one. The choices are very few at first, but they expand rapidly as the functional potential of the system is reinforced by success: the sounds that the child makes do in fact achieve the desired results, at least on a significant number of occasions, and this provides the impetus for taking the process further. As an example, Nigel, whose language I studied in successive six-weekly stages from the age of nine months onwards, started apparently with just two functions and one or two meanings in each. At $10\frac{1}{2}$ months, when he first had a recognizable linguistic system, he could express a total of 12 different meanings; these were derived from four clearly identifiable functions (the first four in the list below) and included, among others, what we might translate as 'do that right now!', 'I want my toy bird down' and 'nice to see you; shall we look at this picture together?' By $16\frac{1}{2}$ months, when he was on the threshold of the second phase of language development, the move into English (or whatever language is going to be the mother tongue), he had six functions and a total of 50 meanings that he could, and regularly did, express.

In studying Nigel's progress I used as the framework a set of functions which I had worked out – before he was born – in the course of discussion with my colleagues in the Programme in Linguistics and English Teaching. Teachers taking part in the trials of the materials which were being produced by the Programme had often felt the need for more information about how children learn language, with the emphasis on use rather than on structure; and the Home Office Children's Department Development Group, on behalf of those of the teachers who were from approved schools (as they were then), had called a conference on "Language, Life and Learning", at which I put forward an outline of what language means to the pre-school child, as understood in terms of what be is able to do with it. This involved a set of seven initial functions, as follows:

1. Instrumental ('I want'): satisfying material needs
2. Regulatory ('do as I tell you'): controlling the behaviour of others
3. Interactional ('me and you'): getting along with other people
4. Personal ('here I come'): identifying and expressing the self
5. Heuristic ('tell me why'): exploring the world around (and inside one)
6. Imaginative ('let's pretend'): creating a world of one's own
7. Informative ('I've got something to tell you'): communicating new information.

These headings served as a useful basis for following the developmental progress of an infant, whose early vocal sounds, although still prelinguistic in the sense that they were not modelled on the English language, were used effectively for just these purposes – to obtain goods or services that he required (instrumental), to influence the behaviour of those closest to him (regulatory), to maintain his emotional ties with them (interactional), and so on. The meanings that he can express at this stage – the number of different things that he can ask for, for example – are naturally very restricted; but he has internalized the fact that language serves these purposes, and it is significant that for each of them he has one generalized expression, meaning simply 'I want that' or 'do that!' etc., where the interpretation is given by the situation (e.g. 'I want that spoon' or 'go on singing'), as well as a number of specific expressions, very few at first but soon growing, and soon becoming independent of the presence of the object or other visible sign of his intent.

So by adopting a functional standpoint we can go back to the beginning of the child's language development, reaching beyond the point where he has started to master structures, beyond even his first words, if by "words" we mean items derived from the adult language; and taking as the foundations of language those early utterances which are not yet English or French or Swahili or Urdu but which every parent recognizes as being meaningful, quite distinct from crying and sneezing and the other non-linguistic noises the child makes. At this stage, the child's utterances cannot readily be 'translated' into the adult language. Just as we cannot adequately represent the sounds he makes by spelling them, either in the orthography of the mother tongue or even in phonetic script, because the system which these symbols impose is too detailed and specific, so also we cannot adequately represent the meanings the child expresses in terms of adult grammar and vocabulary. The child's experience differs so widely from that of the adult that there is only a very partial correspondence between his meanings and those that the adult is predisposed to recognize. But if his utterances are interpreted in the light of particular functions, which are recognizable to the adult as plausible ways of using language, it becomes possible to bridge the gap between them – and in this way to show how the infant's linguistic system ultimately evolves and develops into that of the adult, which is otherwise the most puzzling aspect of the language development process. By the time he reached the age of 18 months, Nigel could use language effectively in the instrumental, regulatory, interactional and personal functions, and was beginning to use it for pretend-play (the 'imaginative' function), and also heuristically, for the purpose of exploring the environment. Now for the first time he launched into English, making rapid strides in vocabulary and grammar; and it was very clear from a study of his speech that his principal motive for doing so was the use of language as a learning device.

In order for language to be a means of learning, it is essential for the child to be able to encode in language, through words and structures, his experience of processes of the external world and of the people and things that participate in them.

4. Language and social structure

In Section 3, we considered the process of learning the mother tongue from a functional point of view, interpreting it as the progressive mastery of a number of basic functions of language and the building up of a 'meaning potential' in respect of each. Here we are adopting a sociolinguistic perspective on language – or rather a perspective which in terms of the earlier discussion would be interorganism. Language is being regarded as the encoding of a 'behaviour potential' into a 'meaning potential'; that is, as a means of expressing what the human organism 'can do', in interaction with other human organisms, by turning it into what he 'can mean'. What he can mean (the semantic system) is, in turn, encoded into what he 'can say' (the lexicogrammatical system, or grammar and vocabulary); to use our own folk-linguistic terminology, meanings are expressed in wordings. Wordings are, finally, recoded into sounds (it would be nice if we could say 'soundings', but this usage, although not impossible, is rare), or spellings (the phonological and orthographic systems).[1]

This perspective is valuable to the linguist because it affords an insight into **why** language is as it is. There is no *a priori* reason why human language should have taken just the evolutionary path that it has taken and no other; our brains could have produced a symbolic system of quite a different kind. But if we consider what language is required to do for us, there are certain functions which it must fulfil in all human cultures, regardless of differences in the physical and material environment. These are functions of a very general kind.

1. Language has to interpret the whole of our experience, reducing the indefinitely varied phenomena of the world around us, and also of the world inside us, the processes of our own consciousness, to a manageable number of classes of phenomena: types of processes, events and actions, classes of objects, people and institutions, and the like.
2. Language has to express certain elementary logical relations, like 'and' and 'or' and 'if', as well as those created by language itself such as 'namely', 'says' and 'means'.
3. Language has to express our participation, as speakers, in the speech situation; the roles we take on ourselves and impose on others; our wishes, feelings, attitudes and judgements.
4. Language has to do all these things simultaneously, in a way which relates what is being said to the context in which it is being said, both to what has been said before and to the 'context of situation'; in other words, it has to be capable of being organized as relevant discourse, not just as words and sentences in a grammar book or dictionary.

It is the demands posed by the service of these functions which have moulded the shape of language and fixed the course of its evolution. These functions are built in to the semantic system of language, and they form the basis of the grammatical organization, since the task of grammar is to encode the meanings deriving from these various functions into articulated structures. Not only are these functions served by all languages, at least in their adult form; they have also determined the way human language has evolved.

So when we study the language development of young children, we are really investigating two questions at once. The first concerns the language they invent for themselves, on the basis of the set of elementary uses or functions of language which reflect the developmental needs, potentialities and achievements of the infant – instrumental, regulatory and so on. The second concerns their transition to the adult language, a language which is still functional in its origins but where the concept of 'function' has undergone a significant change: it is no longer simply synonymous with 'use', but has become much more abstract, a kind of 'metafunction' through which all the innumerable concrete uses of language which the adult engages in are given symbolic expression in a systematic and finite form. To what extent the individual child traces the evolutionary path in moving from one to the other is immaterial; it appears that at a certain point he abandons it, and takes a leap directly into the adult system. Be that as it may, he has to make the transition, and in doing so he carves out for himself a route that reflects the particular circumstances of his own individual history and experience. Geoffrey Thornton expresses this very well when he says that the language which each child learns "is a unique inheritance. It is an inheritance because he is endowed, as a human being, with the capacity to learn language merely by growing up in an environment in which language is being used around him. It is unique, because ... no two people occupy identical places in an environment where language learning is taking place, and this must mean that the language learnt is unique to the individual" (*Exploring Language*, p. 48).

This takes us back to the perspective outlined in Section 2. Biologically, we are all alike, in so far as the language-learning capacity is concerned; we have this ability, as a species, just as we have the ability to stand upright and walk, and it is quite independent of the usual measures of "intelligence" in whatever form. Ecologically, on the other hand, each one of us is unique, since the environmental pattern is never exactly repeated, and one individual's experience is never the same as another's.

However, the uniqueness of the individual, in terms of his personal experience, must be qualified by reference to the culture. Our environment is shaped by the culture, and the conditions under which we learn language are largely culturally determined. This point is significant at two levels, one of which is very obvious, the other less so. It is obviously true in the sense that a child learns the language he hears around him; if he is growing up in an English-speaking society, he learns English. This is a matter of the **linguistic** environment, which is itself part of the culture, but in a special sense. Moreover he learns that dialectal variety of English which belongs to his particular socioregional subculture: working-class London, urban middle-class Northern, rural Dorset, and so on. (He may of course learn more than one dialect, or more than one language, if the culture is a pluralistic one, or under other special conditions.) It is equally true, but much less obvious, in another sense: namely that the culture shapes our behaviour patterns, and a great deal of our behaviour is mediated through language. The child learns his mother tongue in the context of behavioural settings where the norms of the culture are acted out and enunciated for him, settings of parental control, instruction, personal interaction and the like; and, reciprocally, he is 'socialized' into the value systems and behaviour patterns of the culture through the use of language at the same time as he is learning it.

We can now see the relevance of this to linguistic theories of educational failure, which were referred to briefly in the last section. There has been much discussion of educability lately, and various theories have been put forward. One school of thought has concentrated on the effect of the child's **linguistic** environment – namely, the particular form of language he has grown up to speak. In practice, since educational failure is largely a symptom found in the urban lower working class, this means the particular socioregional dialect; and we find two versions of the 'language failure' theory here, sometimes known as the "deficit theory" and the "difference theory". According to the deficit theory, the child's language is simply defective; it lacks some essential elements – it is deficient, perhaps, in sounds, or words, or structures. Now this is not merely nonsense; it is dangerous nonsense. Unfortunately it has rarely been explicitly denied; probably because, as the American educator Joan Baratz put it, "linguists . . . consider such a view of language so absurd as to make them feel that nobody could possibly believe it and therefore to refute it would be a great waste of time". There is no such thing as a deficient social dialect. But, on the other hand, if a teacher believes that there is, and that some or all of his pupils speak one, then, as Frederick Williams has very convincingly shown in his investigations in American schools, he thereby predisposes the children to linguistic failure. This is known as the "stereotype hypothesis". children, no less than adults, will come to behave like the stereotype to which they are consigned.[2]

This then leads us into the "difference" version of the theory, according to which the problem is not that the child's speech is deficient but that it is different – different, in implication, from some received standard or norm. This would obviously be important if it meant that the child did not understand the language in which he was being taught (as happens with many immigrant children). But for the native English-speaking child, this is not the problem. Wherever he comes from, and whatever section of society he comes from, the speech differences are relatively slight and superficial, and in any case he has heard the teacher's language frequently on television and elsewhere, so that he never has more than very temporary difficulty in understanding it, and in fact is usually rather competent at imitating it – an activity, however, which he tends to consider more appropriate to the playground than to the classroom. So the difference theory resolves

84

itself into a question of prejudice: if the child fails as a result of differences between his language and that of the school, it is not because there are difficulties of understanding, but because the child's variety of English carries a social stigma: it is regarded by society as inferior. If 'society' here includes the teacher, the child is, effectively, condemned to failure from the start.

To that extent, then, the difference theory, unlike the deficit theory, is at least partially true: there **are** prejudices against certain varieties of English, and they **are** shared by some teachers. But they are by no means shared by all teachers; and it is difficult to believe that this factor by itself could be sufficient explanation of the full extent of educational failure, especially since children have a great capacity for adaptation – if one form of behaviour does not pay off they will usually switch to another, and they are quite capable of doing so where language is concerned. Moreover the prejudices are getting less, whereas the general view is that educational failure is increasing.

We have then to try another angle, and this is where the functional perspective comes in. Fundamentally, educational failure is a social problem, not a linguistic one; but it has a linguistic aspect, which we can begin to understand if we consider the cultural environment in the second of the two senses mentioned above. It is not the linguistic environment in the sense of which language or dialect the child learns to speak that matters, so much as the cultural or subcultural environment as this is embodied in and transmitted through the language. In other words, the 'language difference' may be significant, but if so it is a difference of function rather than of form.

It is this fundamental insight which lies behind Professor Bernstein's theoretical and empirical work in the field of language and society; together with a further insight, namely that what determines the actual cultural-linguistic configuration is, essentially, the social structure, the system of social relations, in the family and other key social groups, which is characteristic of the particular subculture. Bernstein (*Class, Codes and Control, Vol. 1.*, p. 122) writes: "A number of fashions of speaking, frames of consistency, are possible in any given language and . . . these fashions of speaking, linguistic forms or codes, are themselves a function of the form social relations take. According to this view, the form of the social relation or, more generally, the social structure generates distinct linguistic forms or codes and *these codes essentially transmit the culture and so constrain behaviour*" (his italics). Since, in the words of the American sociologist and linguist William Stewart, "so much of human behaviour is socially conditioned rather than

85

genetically determined", it is not difficult to suppose an intimate connection between language on the one hand and modes of thought and behaviour on the other.[3]

Bernstein has investigated **how** this connection is made, and suggests that it is through linguistic codes, or fashions of speaking, which arise as a consequence of the social structure and the types of social relation associated with it. As Mary Douglas put it, "The control [of thought] is not in the speech forms but in the set human relations which generate thought and speech" (1972, p. 312).

What are these linguistic codes, or fashions of speaking? They relate, essentially, to the functional account of language. It is not the words and the sentence structures – still less the pronunciation or "accent" – which make the difference between one type of code and another; it is the relative emphasis placed on the different functions of language, or, to put it more accurately, the kinds of meaning that are typically associated with them. The "fashions of speaking" are sociosemantic in nature; they are patterns of meaning that emerge, more or less strongly, in particular contexts, especially those relating to the socialization of the child in the family. Hence although each child's language-learning environment is unique, he also shares certain common features with other children of a similar social background; not merely in the superficial sense that the material environments may well be alike – in fact they may not – but in the deeper sense that the forms of social relation and the role systems surrounding him have their effect on the kind of choices in meaning which will be highlighted and given prominence in different types of situation. Peter Doughty comments "the terms *elaborated* and *restricted* refer to characteristic ways of using language to interact with other human beings; they do not suggest that there are two kinds of 'meaning potential' (*Exploring Language*, pp. 104–5).

This dependence on social structure is not merely unavoidable, it is essential to the child's development; he can develop only as **social** man, and therefore his experience must be shaped in ways which make him a member of society and his particular section of it. It becomes restrictive only where the social structure orients the child's thinking **away from** the modes of experience that the school requires. To quote Bernstein again, "the different focusing of experience . . . creates a major problem of educability only where the school produces discontinuity between its symbolic orders and those of the child" (1971, pp. 183–4). In other words, the processes of becoming educated require that the child's meaning potential should have developed along certain lines in certain types of context, especially in relation to the exploration of the environment and of his own part in it. To what extent this requirement is inherent in the very concept of education, and to what extent it is merely a feature of education as it is at present organized in Britain and other highly urbanized societies, we do not know; but as things are, certain ways of organizing experience through language, and of participating and interacting with people and things, are necessary to success in school. The child who is not predisposed to this type of verbal exploration in this type of experiential and interpersonal context "is not at home in the educational world", as Bernstein puts it. Whether a child is so predisposed or not turns out not to be any innate property of the child as an individual, an inherent limitation on his mental powers, as used to be generally thought; it is merely the result of a mismatch between his own symbolic orders of meaning and those of the school, a mismatch that results from the different patterns of socialization that characterize different sections of society, or subcultures, and which are in turn a function of the underlying social relations in the family and elsewhere. Mary Douglas says of Bernstein that he asks "what structuring in society itself calls for its own appropriate structures of speech" (1972, p. 5); and she goes on to add "A common speech form transmits much more than words; it transmits a hidden baggage of shared assumptions", a "collective consciousness that constitutes the social bond".

It is all too easy to be aware of subcultural differences in speech forms, because we are all sensitive to differences of dialect and accent. Unfortunately this is precisely where we go wrong, because differences of dialect and accent are in themselves irrelevant; in Bernstein's words, "There is nothing, but nothing, in the dialect as such, which prevents a child from internalizing and learning to use universalistic meanings", and dialect is a problem only if it is **made** a problem artificially by the prejudice and ignorance of others. It is much harder to become aware of the **significant** differences, which are masked by dialectal variation (and by no means always correspond to dialect distinctions), and which do not appear in any obvious form, as differences in vocabulary or grammatical structure. We are still far from being able to give a comprehensive or systematic account of the linguistic realizations of Bernstein's codes or of the ways in which language operates in the transmission of culture. But the perspective is that of language and social man, and the functional investigation of language and language development provides the basis for understanding.

In essence, what seems to happen is this. The child first constructs a language in the form of a range of meanings that relate directly to certain of his basic needs. As time goes on, the meanings become more complex, and he replaces this by a symbolic system – a semantic system with structural realizations – that is based on the language he hears around him; this is what we call his "mother tongue". Since this is learnt, and has in fact evolved, in the service of the same basic functions, it is, essentially, a functional system; but its functionality is now built in at a very abstract level. This is what was referred to at the beginning of this section, when we said that the adult linguistic system has, in effect, the four generalized functional components, or *metafunctions*, experiential, logical, interpersonal and textual. These form the basis for the organization of meaning when the child moves from his original protolanguage into language proper.

But he does not abandon the original concrete functional elements of the system as he invented it. These still define the purpose for which language is used; and out of them evolve the social contexts and situation types that make up the patterns of use of language in daily life – including those contexts that Bernstein has shown to be critical in the socialization process. Herein lies the basis of the significant subcultural variation that we have been looking at. In **which** particular contexts of use will the child bring to bear **which** portions of the functional resources of the system? Seen from a linguistic point of view, the different "codes", as Bernstein calls them, are different strategies of language use. All human beings put language to certain types of use, and all of them learn a linguistic system which has evolved in that context; but what aspects of the system are typically deployed and emphasized in one type of use or another is to a significant extent determined by the culture – by the systems of social relations in which the child grows up, including the roles he himself learns to recognize and to adopt. All children have access to the meaning potential of the system; but they may differ, because social groups differ, in their interpretation of what the situation demands.

5. Language and situation

Children grow up, and their language grows up with them. By the age of two and a half or even earlier the child has mastered the adult language **system**; the framework is all there. He will spend the rest of his childhood – the rest of his life, even – mastering the adult **language**.

Language, as we have stressed, is a potential: it is what the speaker can do. What a person can do in the linguistic sense, that is, what he can do as speaker/hearer, is equivalent to what he 'can mean'; hence the description of language as a 'meaning potential'.

To describe language as a potential does not mean we are not interested in the actual, in what the speaker does. But in order to make sense of what he does, we have to know what he can do. This is true whatever our particular angle on language, whether we are looking at it as behaviour, or as knowledge (Chomsky's "competence"), or as art: what is, the actual sentences and words that constitute our direct experience of language, derives its significance from what could be. But it is in the social perspective that we are best able to explain what **is**, because we can pay attention to situations of language use, taking account of the non-linguistic factors which serve as the controlling environment. It is at least theoretically possible to look at the 'actual' from a psycholinguistic viewpoint (so-called "theories of performance"), but it has not yet been shown to be very fruitful.

When we come to examine the adult language in its contexts of use, we at once run up against the difficulty that the one thing we cannot specify is what the 'use' of any given utterance is. Nor can we enumerate the total set of possible uses for language as a whole. We cannot draw up a general list setting out the adult's uses of language, in the way that we were able to do for the developmental functions in the language of the very small child. Or rather – what amounts to the same thing – we could draw up a hundred and one such lists, and there would be no means of preferring one list over another. Then when we came to consider actual instances we should have to recognize that in any particular utterance the speaker was in fact using language in a number of different ways, for a variety of different purposes, all at the same time. The use of language is not a simple concept.

Nevertheless it is a very helpful one, without which we cannot explain either the variation we find within a language – the different styles, levels of formality and so on – or the nature of language itself. The latter is outside our scope here, although we referred in the preceding section to the inherently functional organization of the linguistic system.[1]

But the former is fundamental to any consideration of language in an educational context. The ability to control the varieties of one's language that are appropriate to different uses is one of the cornerstones of linguistic success, not least for the school pupil. (For an excellent

1. See further M. A. K. Halliday, *Explorations in the Functions of Language*, London: Edward Arnold, 1973.

discussion of 'differences according to use' see Doughty, Pearce and Thornton 1972, Chapter 11: 'Diversity in written English' by John Pearce.)

The basic concept here is that of 'context of situation', originally suggested by Malinowski and subsequently elaborated by Firth (see J. R. Firth 1950: 'Personality and language in society'). Essentially what this implies is that language comes to life only when functioning in some environment. We do not experience language in isolation – if we did we would not recognize it as language – but always in relation to a scenario, some background of persons and actions and events from which the things which are said derive their meaning. This is referred to as the "situation", so language is said to function in "contexts of situation" and any account of language which fails to build in the situation as an essential ingredient is likely to be artificial and unrewarding.

It is important to qualify the notion of 'situation' by adding the word "relevant". The 'context of situation' does not refer to all the bits and pieces of the material environment such as might appear if we had an audio and video recording of a speech event with all the sights and sounds surrounding the utterances. It refers to those features which are relevant to the speech that is taking place. Such features may be very concrete and immediate, as they tend to be with young children whose remarks often bear a direct pragmatic relation to the environment, e.g. *some more!* 'I want some more of what I've just been eating'. But they may be quite abstract and remote, as in a technical discussion among experts, where the 'situation' would include such things as the particular problem they were trying to solve and their own training and experience, while the immediate surroundings of objects and events would probably contain nothing of relevance at all. Even where the speech does relate to the immediate environment, it is likely that only certain features of it will be the relevant ones; for example, is it the presence of a particular individual that matters, or is it a certain role relationship, no matter who is occupying the roles in question? If John says *I love you*, it presumably does matter that it was said to Mary and not Jane; but if he says *Can you put up a prescription for me?*, what is relevant in that situation is the **role** of dispensing chemist, and not the identity of the individual who happens to be occupying it at that particular time and place.

In general, the ability to use language in abstract and indirect contexts of situation is what distinguishes the speech of adults from that of children. Learning language consists in part in learning to free it from the constraints of the immediate environment. This process **begins** very early in life, when the child first learns to ask for things that are not visible and to recall objects and events which he has observed earlier. But it is a gradual process, which takes place in different ways with different children; this is one of the variables which Bernstein has found to be significant – which **types** of situation serve as the gateway to more abstract and generalized contextual meanings. As he says, "certain groups of children, through the forms of their socialization, are oriented towards receiving and offering universalistic meanings in *certain contexts*". This in itself is not important; but it becomes important if there are certain **types** of situation which play a central part in the child's total development, since these are the ones where he will need to use language in ways that are least dependent on the here and now.

This leads us to the notion of a situation type. Looking at how people actually use language in daily life, we find that the apparently infinite number of different possible situations represents in reality a very much smaller number of general **types** of situation, which we can describe in such terms as 'players instructing novice in a game', 'mother reading bedtime story to child', 'customer ordering goods over the telephone', 'teacher guiding pupils', 'discussion of a poem' and the like. Not all these situation types are equally interesting, and some are obviously very trivial; but in the last resort the importance of any abstract category of this kind depends on what we are going to make of it, and the significance of the notion of 'context of situation' for the present discussion is that some situation types play a crucial role in the child's move into the adult language. For example, if a mother or father is playing with a child with some constructional toy, such as a set of building bricks, this type of situation is likely to contain some remarks of guidance and explanation, with utterances like *I don't think that one will go on there; it's too wide*. The context of situation for this utterance is one in which the child is gaining instruction relating to his handling of objects, and although any one instance is not by itself going to make much difference, an accumulation of experiences of this kind may be highly significant. And if it regularly happens that the remarks relate not just to **this particular** tower that is being built with **these particular** bricks, but to tower-building in general – in other words, if the context of situation is not limited to the actual physical surroundings, but extends to more general and less immediate environments, as would be implied by a remark such as *the smaller ones have to go at the top* – then language is now serving a primary function in this aspect of the child's development. Hence he will have a strong sense of **this** use of language,

91

of language as a means of learning about the physical environment and about his own ability to interact with it and control it.

The types of situation which seem to be most critical to the child's socialization, which have been identified by Bernstein in the most general terms,[4] are already anticipated in the developmental functions through which the child has first started to build up a linguistic system of his own: the instrumental, regulatory and so on, described in Section 3 above. For example, those types of situation which involve explanation and instruction, Bernstein's "instructional context", typically pick up the developmental thread that first appeared in the form of a "heuristic" function, the child's early use of language to explore his environment. They are therefore critical also in the child's learning of **language**, since it is through using language in situations of these types that he builds on and expands his meaning potential.

This is where the notions of context of situation, and situation type, become important for the school. The school requires that the child should be able to use language in certain ways: first of all, most obviously, that he should be able to use language to learn. The teacher operates in contexts of situation where it simply has to be taken for granted that for every child, by the time he arrives in school, language is a means of learning; and this is an assumption that is basic to the educational process. Less obvious, but perhaps no less fundamental, is the assumption that language is a means of personal expression and participation: that the child is at home, linguistically, in interpersonal contexts, where his early use of language to interact with those who were emotionally important to him, and to express and develop his own uniqueness as an individual (the interactional and personal functions), has in the same way been taken up and extended into new realms of meaning. No doubt both these assumptions are true, as they stand: every normal child has mastered the use of language both for entering into personal relationships and for exploring his environment. But the **kinds** of meaning which he associates with the contexts of situation where these uses of language are prominent may vary considerably from one child to another. Here we are back to Bernstein's codes again, which we have now approached from another angle, seeing them as differences in the meaning potential which may be typically associated with given situation types. As we have seen, these differences have their origin in the social structure. In Ruqaiya Hasan's words, "the "code" is defined by reference to its semantic properties" and "the semantic properties of the codes can be predicted from the elements of social structure which, in fact, give rise to them" (1973, p. 258).

Now the very young child, in his first ventures with language, keeps the functions of language fairly clearly apart; when he speaks, he is doing only one thing at a time – asking for some object, responding to a greeting, expressing interest or whatever it is. When he starts learning his mother tongue, however, the contexts of situation in which he uses it are already complex and many-sided, with a number of threads of meaning running simultaneously. To vary the metaphor, we could say that all speech other than the protolanguage of infancy is polyphonic: different melodies are kept going side by side, and each element in the sentence is like a chord which contributes something to all of them. This is perhaps the most striking characteristic of human language, and one which distinguishes it from all other symbolic communication systems.

6. Register

This last point is a reflection of the contexts of situation in which language is used, and the ways in which one type of situation may differ from another. Types of linguistic situation differ from one another, broadly speaking, in three respects: first, as regards what is actually taking place; secondly, as regards what part the language is playing; and thirdly, as regards who is taking part. These three variables, taken together, determine the range within which meanings are selected and the forms which are used for their expression. In other words, they determine the "register".

The notion of register is at once very simple and very powerful.[5] It refers to the fact that the language we speak or write varies according to the type of situation. This in itself is no more than stating the obvious. What the theory of register does is to attempt to uncover the general principles which govern this variation, so that we can begin to understand **what** situational factors determine **what** linguistic features. It is a fundamental property of all languages that they display variation according to use; but surprisingly little is yet known about the nature of the variation involved, largely because of the difficulty of identifying the controlling factors.

An excellent example of register variation (and of how to investigate and describe it) is provided by Jean Ure in a paper entitled 'Lexical density and register differentiation' (1971). Here Jean Ure shows that, at least in English, the lexical density of text, which means the proportion of lexical items (content words) to words as a whole, is a function first of the medium (that is whether it is spoken or written – written language has a higher lexical density than speech) and, within that, of the social function (pragmatic language, or 'language in action', has the lowest lexical density of all). This is probably true of all languages; but whether it is or not, it is a basic fact about English and a very good illustration of the relation between the actual and the potential that we referred to at the beginning of this section. We could say, following Dell Hymes, that it is part of the speaker's "communicative competence" that he knows how to distribute lexical items in a text according to different kinds of language use; but there is really no need to introduce here the artificial concept of 'competence', or 'what the speaker knows', which merely adds an extra level of psychological interpretation to what can be explained more simply in direct sociolinguistic or functional terms.

It is easy to be misled here by posing the question the wrong way, as a number of writers on the subject of register have done. They have asked, in effect, 'what features of language are determined by register?' and then come up with instances of near-synonymy where one word differs from another in level of formality, rhetoric or technicality, like *chips* and *French fried potatoes*, or *deciduous dentition* and *milk teeth*. But these are commonplaces which lie at the fringe of register variation, and which in themselves would hardly need any linguistic or other kind of 'theory' to explain them. Asked in this way, the question can lead only to trivial answers; but it is the wrong question to ask. **All** language functions in contexts of situation, and is relatable to those contexts. The question is not what peculiarities of vocabulary, or grammar or pronunciation, can be directly accounted for by reference to the situation. It is **which** kinds of situational factor determine **which** kinds of selection in the linguistic system. The notion of register is thus a form of prediction: given that we know the situation, the social context of language use, we can predict a great deal about the language that will occur, with reasonable probability of being right. The important theoretical question then is: what do we need to know about the social context in order to make such predictions?

Let us make this more concrete. If I am talking about gardening, I may be more likely to use words that are the names of plants and other words referring to processes of cultivation; and this is one aspect of the relation of language to situation – the subject matter of gardening is part of the social context. But, in fact, the probability of such terms occurring in the discourse is also dependent on what I and my interlocutor are doing at the time. If we are actually engaged in gardening while we are talking, there may be very few words of this kind. Jean Ure quotes an amusing example from some Russian research on register: "The recording was of people frying potatoes, and frying potatoes was what they were talking about; but since, it seems, neither frying nor potatoes were represented lexically in the text, the recording was a mystification to all who had not been in the kitchen at the time." The image of language as merely the direct reflection of subject matter is simplistic and unsound, as Malinowski pointed out exactly 50 years ago; there is much more to it than that, and this is what the notion of register is all about.

What we need to know about a context of situation in order to predict the linguistic features that are likely to be associated with it has been summarized under three headings: we need to know the *field of discourse*, the *mode of discourse* and the *tenor of discourse*.[6] We shall say a little more about these in Section 7; here it will be helpful to quote John Pearce's summary, from Doughty, Pearce and Thornton 1972:

> Field refers to the institutional setting in which a piece of language occurs, and embraces not only the subject-matter in hand but the whole activity of the speaker or participant in a setting [we might add: 'and of the other participants'] ...
>
> Mode refers to the channel of communication adopted: not only the choice between spoken and written medium, but much more detailed choices [we might add: 'and other choices relating to the role of language in the situation'] ...
>
> Tenor or Style refers to the relationship between participants ... not merely variation in formality ... but ... such questions as the permanence or otherwise of the relationship and the degree of emotional charge in it.

These are the general concepts needed for describing what is linguistically significant in the context of situation. They include the subject matter, as an aspect of the 'field of discourse' – of the whole setting of relevant actions and events within which the language is functioning; for this is where subject matter belongs. We do not, in fact, first decide what we want to say, independently of the setting, and then dress it up in a garb that is appropriate to it in the context, as many writers on language and speech events seem to assume. The 'content' is part of the total planning that takes place. There is no clear line between the 'what' and the 'how'; all language is language-in-use, in a context of situation, and all of it relates to the situation, in the abstract sense in which we are using the term here.

We should here make a passing reference to dialects, which are part of the picture of language and social man, although not primarily relevant in the educational context except as the focus of linguistic attitudes. Our language is also determined by who we are; that is the basis of dialect, and in principle a dialect is with us all our lives – it is not subject to choice. In practice, however, this is less and less true, and the phenomenon of "dialect switching" is widespread. Many speakers learn two or more dialects, either in succession, dropping the first when they learn the second, or in coordination, switching between them according to the context of situation. Hence the dialect comes to be an aspect of the register. If for example the standard dialect is used in formal contexts and the neighbourhood one in informal contexts, then one part of the contextual determination of linguistic features is the determination of choice of dialect. When dialects come to have different meanings for us, the choice of dialect becomes a choice of meaning, or a choice between different areas of our meaning potential.

Like the language of the child, the language of the adult is a set of socially contextualized resources of behaviour, a 'meaning potential' that is related to situations of use. Being 'appropriate to the situation' is not some optional extra in language; it is an essential element in the ability to mean. Of course, we are all aware of occasions when we feel about something said or written that it might have been expressed in a way that was more appropriate to the task in hand; we want to 'keep the meaning but change the wording'. But these are the special cases, in which we are reacting to purely conventional features of register variation. In the last resort, it is impossible to draw a line between 'what he said' and 'how he said it', since this is based on a conception of language as existing in isolation from any context. The distinction between one register and another is a distinction of **what** is said as much as of **how** it is said, without any enforced separation between the two. If a seven-year-old insists on using slang when you think he should be using more formal language, this is a dispute about registers; but if he insists on talking about his football hero when you want him to talk about a picture he has been painting, then this is equally a dispute over registers, and one which is probably much more interesting and far-reaching for both teacher and pupil concerned.

Thus our functional picture of the adult linguistic system is of a culturally specific and situationally sensitive range of meaning potential. Language is the ability to 'mean' in the situation types, or social contexts, that are generated by the culture. When we talk about "uses of language", we are concerned with the meaning potential that is associated with particular situation types; and we are likely to be especially interested in those which are of some social and cultural significance, in the light of a sociological theory of language such as Bernstein's. This last point is perhaps worth stressing. The way that we have envisaged the study of language and social man, through the concept of 'meaning potential', might be referred to as a kind of 'socio-semantics', in the sense that it is the study of meaning in a social or sociological framework. But there is a difference between 'social' and 'sociological' here. If we describe the context of situation in terms of *ad hoc* observations about the settings in which language is used, this could be said to be a 'social' account of language but hardly a 'sociological' one, since the concepts we are drawing on are not referred to in any kind of general social theory. Such an account can be very illuminating, as demonstrated in a brilliant paper, published some 20 years ago, by T. F. Mitchell (1957), called 'The language of buying and selling in Cyrenaica' – though since the language studied was Cyrenaican Arabic and the paper was published in a learned journal in Morocco, it is not widely known. But for research of this kind to be relevant to a teacher who is professionally concerned with his pupils' success in language, it has to relate to social contexts that are themselves of significance, in the sort of way that Bernstein's "critical contexts" are significant for the socialization of the child. The criteria would then be sociological rather than simply social – based on some theory of social structure and social change. In this respect, the earlier terms like Firth's "sociological linguistics", or "sociology of language" as used by Bernstein, are perhaps more pointed than the currently fashionable label "sociolinguistics".

7. Some topics to explore

In this final section we shall suggest some topics which offer the possibility of further exploration. These are topics which can be followed up in various ways: they can be explored through further reading, or in study groups; one can enquire into them by means of one's own investigations; and in many instances pupils in the class can be enlisted to help in the enquiry, for example by keeping a language diary, or by noting down things they hear said by a small brother or sister. The issues are ones which teachers have found to be relevant to

97

their own work, and which can be 'researched' in the course of one's daily life, through observation and questioning, without the need for a year's leave of absence and a research foundation grant. The headings are:

1. Language development in young children
2. Language and socialization
3. Neighbourhood language profile
4. Language in the life of the individual
5. Language and situation
6. Language and institutions
7. Language attitudes.

1. Language development in young children

Anyone with a young child in the family can make himself a positive nuisance trying to record its speech, not only by cluttering up the house with concealed microphones and other equipment but also by accumulating vast quantities of unprocessed tape. (It takes ten hours to listen to ten hours of tape, and a great deal longer than that to transcribe it.) The most useful piece of research equipment is actually a notebook and pencil; and the most important research qualification (as in many other areas) is the ability to **listen to language**, which is not difficult to acquire and yet is surprisingly seldom developed. This means the ability to attend to the actual words that are being spoken, as distinct from the usual kind of listening which involves the automatic decoding and processing of what is said. To put it another way, 'listening to language' means listening to the wording, or else the sounding (if the interest is in the phonetics), instead of only to the meaning. Skulking behind the furniture and writing down what a small child says, and also what is said to and around him, with a brief note on what he is doing at the time (this is essential), is a useful source of insight, provided of course it is not carried to extremes. Pupils who have small brothers and sisters can do some valuable research here; the older ones can keep accurate records, while the younger ones, though they cannot be expected to do very much field work, will make up for this by virtue of the intrinsic interest of their own glosses and their interpretative comments.

What are we looking for? There are various kinds of understanding to be gained from listening to a child – not in the romantic sense, as a fount of intuitive wisdom (we shall never know whether he possesses such wisdom or not, because whatever he has disappears in the process of his learning to communicate it to us), but as a young human being struggling to grow up, linguistically as in other ways. We can see what are the functions for which he is building up a linguistic system, and how these functions relate to his survival and his social well-being. There is no need for an exact phonetic record – that is something to be left to the specialist – and no need to wait until we hear complete sentences or even recognizable words of English. The child of nine to 18 months will have a range of vocal signals that are meaningful and understandable to those around him, such as Nigel's 'nanana' meaning 'give me that!'; in other words, he will have a range of **meanings**, which define what he can do in the various spheres of action to which vocal resources are applied (see the set of initial functions given in Section 3).

What the child does with language, at this early stage, is all the time shaping his own image of what language is. At a certain point, round about 18 months old, he will abandon his laborious attempt to work through half a million years of human evolution creating his own language, and short-circuit the process by 'going adult' and taking over the language he hears around him. The impetus for this move is still a functional one; the demands he makes on language are increasing, and his own 'do-it-yourself' system can no longer meet them. His language is now further strengthened and enriched as a resource for living and learning, by the addition of a whole new range of semantic choices; and his image of what language is, and what it can do, is enriched correspondingly. With this image he comes ready equipped to school; and the sad thing is that so few teachers in the past have either shared the image or even sought to understand what, in fact, the child can already do with language when he comes to them, which is a very great deal. To look into the functional origins of language, at the beginning of the developmental process, is to go a long way towards a sympathetic appreciation of what language means to the child when he first sets foot in school. In the absence of such an appreciation, much of what goes on in the classroom may be largely irrelevant to his needs.

Points to look for:

(a) Very young children

What are the functions for which the very young child first
   begins to learn language?

What meanings does he learn to express, within these
   functions?

What sort of meanings can he respond to (e.g. 'Do you want
   ...')?

Who does he (a) talk to (b) listen to? In what types of situation?

What kind of reinforcement does he get for his efforts? Who
   understands him most readily? Has he an interpreter (e.g. an
   older brother or sister)?

(b) Children nearer school age

What are the functions for which the child is now using
   language?

Is it possible, in fact, to recognize from among the mass of
   particular instances any general types of use that might be
   significant: learning about the material environment, learning about social relations and cultural values, controlling
   behaviour, responding emotionally and so on?

What sort of difficulties does he encounter? Are there things
   he cannot make language do for him?

What are the functions for which he is now beginning to need
   the **written** language, and writing as a medium? This is the
   key question for the child first coming into school. Will
   learning to read and write make sense to him, matching his
   experience of what language is and what it is for, so that he
   sees it as a means of enlarging that experience; or will it
   seem to be a meaningless exercise which is unrelated to any
   of his own uses of language?

2. Language and socialization

This topic is closely related to the last; but here the focus of attention is
shifted away from the learning of language as a whole on to the role of
language in relation to the child as 'social man', and the ways in which
language serves to initiate the child into the social order.

Every child is brought up in a culture, and he has to learn the
patterns of that culture in the process of becoming a member of it. The
principal means whereby the culture is made available to him is

through language: language is not the only channel, but it is the most significant one. Even the most intimate of personal relationships, that of the child with its mother, is from an early age mediated through language; and language plays some part in practically all his social learning.

Bernstein's work has provided the key to an understanding not merely of the part played by language in the home life and the school life of the child but, more significantly, of **how** language comes to play this central part; and hence of how it happens that some children fail to meet the demands that are made by the school on their linguistic capacities, not because these capacities are lacking but because they have typically been deployed in certain ways rather than in others.

The types of social context which Bernstein identifies as critical to the process of the child's socialization were mentioned in Section 5: the regulative, the instructional, the imaginative or innovative and the interpersonal. These are, clearly, related to the developmental functions of language as I outlined them: instrumental, regulatory, and so on. But whereas I was asking 'what are the key linguistic functions through which the child first **learns language?**', the underlying question being about language development and the nature of language itself, Bernstein is asking 'what are the key linguistic contexts through which the child **learns the culture?**', with the emphasis on social development and cultural transmission. For example, the ways in which a parent controls the behaviour of a child reveal for the child a great deal about statuses and roles, the structure of authority, and moral and other values in the culture.

There are various possible lines of approach if one is enquiring into the part played by language in significant social contexts. One interesting type of investigation was devised and carried out by Bernstein and Henderson, who took a number of specific tasks involved in bringing up a child, for example 'teaching children everyday tasks such as dressing or using a knife and fork', 'showing them how things work', 'disciplining them' and 'dealing with them when they are unhappy', and asked mothers how much more difficulty they thought parents would have in carrying out these tasks if they had no language with which to do it – imagining, for example, that they were deaf and dumb. The answers do not, of course, tell us what the mothers actually say to their children on these occasions; but they give an idea of their orientation towards different functions of language, and there turn out to be certain significant differences which go with social class.

It is not impossible to examine actual samples of the language used in particular instances of the types of situation that are significant for the child's socialization; and to ask what the child might have learnt about the culture from the things that were said to him. For example, a form of control such as 'you mustn't touch things that don't belong to you' carries a great deal of potential information about private property and ownership. Naturally one or two such remarks by themselves would not tell him very much; but from their constant varied repetition and reinforcement he would learn a lot about the culture of which he had involuntarily taken out membership. And the interesting point is that this learning would have taken place not only without instruction, but without organized knowledge behind it, through the most ordinary everyday uses of language in ordinary everyday kinds of situation.

For a teacher there is the additional question of the role of language in the classroom – or rather roles, since the school is a complex institution and language has many different parts to play in it. The key question, perhaps, is this: to the extent that the school is a new culture into which the child has been socialized (and, as we have seen, this makes greater demands on some children than it does on others), is the actual pattern of language use in the daily life of the school adequate to the socializing task? If it is not – and in many instances at present it almost certainly is not – what can be done to remedy the situation?

A study of the use of language in the classroom may reveal some of the assumptions that are made by the teacher about the school as a social institution – assumptions about the nature of educational processes, about teacher-pupil relationships, about the values accorded to objects, their schemes of classification, and the like – while at the same time showing that the children get no help in becoming aware of these things, or in learning the relevant schemes of social relations and social values. Or, on the other hand, it might turn out that the school provides very adequate means for making such matters explicit: again, not by **teaching** them, but by encouraging and developing a use of language that is culturally rich and socially enlightened. Either way, there is much to be gained from watching language at work in the socializing process.

Points to consider:

(a) What part does language play in the socialization of the child?

What types of situation are likely to be significant at the pre-school stage (e.g. listening to stories, having meals, playing with other children)? Can these be seen as concrete instances of Bernstein's four "critical contexts for socialization"?

What might the child learn from these situations, about social relations, social values, the structure of knowledge and the like?

How would he learn these things – from what kinds of use of language (for example, in games with adults, *my turn . . . your turn*, leading to a concept of a particular kind of role relation, with a privilege that is shared and exercised by turns)?

What demands on his own linguistic abilities, in terms of the developmental functions of language, are made by these situations (e.g. verbal games, teasing, helping mother in the kitchen, going shopping, competing with other children)?

(b) How do the forms of the child's socialization find linguistic expression in his modes of behaving and learning?

What differences appear between children from different cultures, such as British, West Indian, Pakistani? Between children from different subcultures, such as social class groups within the native British population? How are these expressed in language? (For example, different concepts of family relationships, expressed partly by different modes of address.) [The point is not that such groups speak different languages or dialects; the emphasis should be on the way they **use** language, on the meanings that are expressed.]

What is the significance for the school of the child's pre-school experience, seen in terms of patterns of language use? Are certain ways of using language in school likely to be less familiar to him, and if so can they be made explicit in a manner that is likely to help?

3. Neighbourhood language profile

There has never been any lack of interest in the local varieties of English speech, and numerous accounts of the vocabulary and pronunciation of different dialects have appeared since the Elizabethan period.

Systematic linguistic study of rural dialects began about a hundred years ago, in France, Germany and Switzerland; since that time dialect surveys have been undertaken in many countries ranging from China to the United States. These are designed to show the particular characteristics of the speech in each locality, and to trace its derivation from an earlier stage of the language.

Dialect studies are based on the assumption, which is largely borne out in practice, that there are homogeneous speech communities: the people of one locality all speak alike. The notion of a 'dialect' is defined on this assumption. "The dialect of Littleby" means the speech that one learns by virtue of growing up as an inhabitant of Littleby. The researcher typically searches out the oldest inhabitant, among those who have lived in the village all their lives, and takes his speech as representative, rather than that of younger people or of those who have moved in to the area from outside, whose speech will probably not be "pure Littleby".

Recently, and particularly in the United States, attention has turned to urban dialects; and it has been found out that the traditional concepts of dialectology do not hold good for large industrial cities. In one respect, of course, this is obvious: everyone knows that the inhabitants of a city like London do not all speak alike. There is not only geographical variation, distinguishing the speech of one **locality** from that of another – South-East London, North London and so on – but also social variation, distinguishing the speech of one **social class** from that of another. (No doubt this was true of Littleby too, if one took the squire and the parson into account.) But the pattern of urban dialects is much more complex than this. Our understanding of the nature of city speech is largely due to the work of one scholar, William Labov, whose pioneer studies of New York speech gave a radically different picture of the dialect structure of an industrial community.

Labov showed up the extraordinary complexity of the social stratification: not only in the sense that there are some very minute distinctions separating different speech varieties, but also, more importantly, that such distinctions may have great social significance in the community. The interesting finding is that, while the typical New Yorker is very inconsistent in his own speech habits, switching from one pronunciation to another according to the situation, and particularly according to the degree of conscious attention to speech that is involved, he is almost entirely consistent in his judgement of the speech of other people, and can be extremely sensitive to the slightest variation in what he **hears**. He is quite unaware that such variation occurs within his own speech, although he may be subconsciously troubled by the fact (Labov devised an "index of linguistic insecurity" which brings this out); but he responds to subtle differences and changes in the speech of others, and uses the information to identify their social status. Labov found, for instance, that if he played a tape recording of just one sentence to a sample of New Yorkers, not only would those who heard it agree in large measure about what sort of employment the speaker they were listening to would be best fitted for, but also, if he 'doctored' the tape at just one point – altering it in a way which would be equivalent, in London terms, to dropping just one *h* – the subjects rated the same speaker one notch lower on their employment scale. Labov concluded from these investigations that an urban speech community (unlike a rural one) is not so much a group of people who speak in a certain way, but rather a group of people who share the same prejudices about how others speak.

If the townsman, or "megalopolitan" in current jargon, does vary in his speech habits, the variation is normally not random, but relates to the context of situation. He may switch between a neighbourhood dialect and some form of standard speech, perhaps with some intermediate degrees; but the choice, though probably entirely subconscious, is likely to depend on who he is speaking to, what sort of occasion it is and what kind of environment they are in – in other words, on the field, mode and tenor of discourse, as we defined these above. That is to say, his dialect switching is actually an expression of register variation. This phenomenon is by no means confined to urban communities; in fact it was first studied in detail, by the American linguist John Gumperz, in villages and small towns, in countries as different from each other as India and Norway. But it is characteristic of the city-dweller that he does not keep to one constant set of speech habits. His pronunciation, at least, is likely to vary according to circumstances; and even those who, as adults, do not display any noticeable variation in their speech have almost certainly moved away in certain respects from the neighbour-hood dialect they learnt as children.

Neighbourhood speech patterns in the city are always liable to be complicated by movements of population, as is happening in English cities with the arrival of large groups of immigrants, so that even the neighbourhood is not always a homogeneous speech unit. Nevertheless neighbourhood speech has a very powerful influence among children, in their own peer group; it is remarkable that children coming into a neighbourhood from outside, even if they outnumber those from the locality, tend to grow up speaking the local language, so that the concept of a neighbourhood dialect is a valid and important one. It is the language of the children's peer group, in the street, the park and later on in the school playground; and it serves for the child as his badge of membership in the culture. It should be added we still know very little about the linguistic characteristics of children's peer group dialects, which show a number of special peculiarities, some of which are significant for an understanding of how languages change.

Points to look for:

(a) Is it possible to identify a neighbourhood dialect in your area?

Would there be general agreement on what is the characteristic speech of the neighbourhood?

How specifically can it be tied to a particular area? Is it, for example, Home counties? London? South-East London? Catford? Brownhill Road area?

Taking some such locality, perhaps intermediate in size, what is noticeable and distinctive about the speech habits, in terms of grammar, vocabulary or pronunciation? (The best way to find out is to listen to yourself imitating the neighbourhood speech. In doing so you probably produce a caricature rather than a photographic likeness; but a caricature exaggerates precisely the features that we in fact find distinctive. Do you find yourself saying 'a cup of t^{s}ea', 'in the p^{f}ark', with *t* and *p* affricated at the beginning of a stressed syllable? If so this is obviously a noticeable feature of the dialect, though probably less pronounced than you yourself make it appear.)

How widespread is each of the particular features that enter into the picture? (Some will be confined to the immediate locality, others will be characteristic of the whole city or region.)

(b) Are there noticeable differences of speech within the neighbourhood?

If so: Are there social class differences? Other subcultural differences (e.g. between native and immigrant groups)? Generational differences? Institutional differences (e.g. between one school and another)?

Do all children begin by learning the same type of speech? (If so, this is probably the most differentiated type, the variety that is most specific to the locality in question; and it is this to which the term "neighbourhood dialect" is most strictly applicable.)

Do adult and adolescent speakers typically use more than one variety? If so, under what circumstances? When do they switch from one to another, and why?

Can the "language profile" of the neighbourhood be related to the social structure?

(c) What is the relation of the neighbourhood speech to "standard English"?

Is the neighbourhood speech itself a form of standard English, an "accent" rather than a dialect in the strict sense of the term?

What are its limits of tolerance? Is it acceptable in school?

Do adults (a) recognize the desirability of using, and (b) themselves actually use, a form of speech that is closer to standard English? If so, when do they use it? How do they learn it? Are there speakers who do not learn it, and if so what are the consequences for them?

4. Language in the life of the individual

It is surprisingly difficult to get any very clear impression of what we actually do with language in the course of our daily lives. If we were asked to make up out of our heads a linguistic record for the day, most of us would be at a loss to reconstruct what was actually said to us and what we ourselves said – let alone **why** we said some of the things we did say.

Yet the day's language makes up a significant part of the total experience of a typical human being, whether adult or child. It can be a useful as well as entertaining exercise to investigate how a child spends a typical day, as far as using language is concerned: what he says, what is said to and around him, and also what he reads and what he writes, if these are applicable. (It can also be illuminating to look into how one spends one's own linguistic day.)

One technique that has been used is that of the "language diary".

This is exactly what the name implies: an account of the day's linguistic doings, in which are recorded in as much detail as possible the language activities of the day, showing the time span, the type of language event and some observations on the language used. The record might contain no more than entries like: 8:30–8:35 At the newsagent's: buying newspaper, transactional dialogue, self and newsagent; structure of language events: (a) greeting, (b) transaction, (c) comment on weather, (d) valediction. The actual text might have been something like the following:

Morning, Tom!
Good morning to you, sir!
Have you got a *Guardian* left this morning?
You're lucky; it's the last one. Bit brighter today, by the looks of it.
Yes, we could do with a bit of a dry spell. You got change for a pound?
Yes, plenty of change; here you are. Anything else today?
No, that's all just now, Tom. Be seeing you.
Mind how you go.

Children can be asked to keep language diaries, noting down instances of language use at home and in school. The kind of observation they can make will, of course, depend on the age group; but once the concept has been understood it does not much matter what the format is – any form of record keeping is appropriate. From accumulated samples of this kind one builds up a picture of types of interaction among individuals; and this, in turn, brings out something of the complex patterns of daily life as lived in a particular community in a particular culture.

In a community where there is dialect switching, the diary can record the circumstances under which different varieties of speech are employed, using categories such as "neighbourhood" and "standard". Language diaries have in fact mainly been used in multilingual situations, to show how the different languages figure in the lives of individual members of the community: which language do they hear on radio or in the cinema, in which language does one speak to one's wife or husband, consult the doctor, fill up official forms, do the shopping, and so on. But the same principle applies in 'multidialectal' communities, where the language diary helps to make one aware of some of the social complexities of everyday activities. (It is easier to start by noting examples of other people's language behaviour before attempting to be one's own diarist.)

There are various ways of recording language behaviour, which essentially resolve themselves into four: one can record sounds, wordings, meanings or registers. Recording sounds, that is, giving accurate accounts of pronunciation, is a task for the specialist, although we are all amateur phoneticians when it comes to reacting to other people's accents, and a few key features can often be identified as indices of dialect variation. Recording wordings means taking down in full the actual words that are used; this can be done with a notebook and pencil, especially with the aid of shorthand, but also, given sufficient practice, in longhand. Recording meanings means paraphrasing and précising what is said as one notes it down. These three ways of recording language correspond to the three levels of language itself, the levels of sound, of form (grammar and vocabulary) and of meaning; hence each of the three is concerned with a different aspect of linguistic reality. With a tape recorder, of course, one can obtain a 'photographic' image of the whole, and process it at any level one likes; but working with a tape recorder tends to restrict one to the less interesting uses of language, those where the participants remain relatively static, and it is also liable to become somewhat obsessive, so on the whole in linguistic journalism it is probably better to rely on a notebook and pencil, combined with one's own intuition about what is important and what can be left out – an intuition that is notably lacking in tape recorders.

For certain purposes it is very useful to record the actual wordings, particularly in studying the part played by language in the life of a child. Here is an extract – from an account of a linguistic 'day in the life of' a two-and-a-half-year-old boy, Nigel; the dramatis personae here are Nigel, his mother, his father and his aunt:

N. You want **biscuit** <2>
A. Do you want a **biscuit**? <2>
N. Yē
M. Have you washed your **hands**? <2>
A. **Come**, <1> I'll **help** you <1>
N. You want **Mummy** to **help** you <2>
A. Mummy's **busy** <1>
N. You want **Daddy** to **help** you <2>
A. Shall **I** …?
F. **No** <1> it's all **right**, <3> I'll go **with** him <3> [They go]

109

N. [Suiting actions to words] More **water** <2> ... turn the **tap on** <2> ... pull the **plug out** <2> [returning] ... you want to have half of Daddy's biscuit and Daddy have the **other half** <2> ... oh you didn't roll your **sleeves** down <1>

F. Oh you didn't roll your **sleeves** down! <1>

N. You **roll them** <2> [does so] ... where's the **biscuit** <2> [takes it and eats] ... the train picture you tore **up** <1> ... that was very **bad** <1> ... you want **another biscuit** <2> ... want to have half of **Daddy's biscuit** <2> ... want to **break it** <2>

F. All **right**, <3> ... this is the last **one** <1>

The numbers in angle brackets show the intonation patterns, which in English as it happens are an important element in the wording, though they are not shown in our orthography; those occurring here are <1> falling tone, <2> rising tone, <2> falling-rising tone, and <3> half-rising tone. The bold type indicates the word or words on which the tone is made prominent. The conversation is quite trivial in itself, but it reveals a number of things about the child's use of language. Nigel happens at this stage to refer to himself as **you**; also, he uses a tone ending on a rise, <2> or <2>, when the language function is pragmatic (instrumental or regulatory), and a falling tone otherwise. The passage happens to illustrate all the three main types of pragmatic function: instrumental **you want a biscuit**, regulatory **you want Mummy to help you**, and regulatory in the special sense of asking permission **turn the tap on** ('may I?', though in fact permission is assumed and the pattern comes to mean simply 'I'm going to'). Interposed with the dominant motive of obtaining the biscuit are various non-pragmatic elements with their own functions, heuristic (rehearsing a moral judgement) and personal-informative. When one examines the wording closely, there is a great deal to be learnt from a simple exchange of this kind, about the very essential part that is played by ordinary everyday language in the socialization of the child.

However, for many purposes it is enough to record the 'register' that is being used; and here the concepts of 'field', 'mode' and 'tenor' that we referred to in Section 6 provide a valuable framework for giving information about language use in as succinct a way as possible.

(a) *Field*. The kind of language we use varies, as we should expect, according to what we are doing. In different contexts, we tend to select different words and different grammatical patterns – simply because we are expressing different kinds of meaning. All we need add to this, in order to clarify the notion of register, is that the 'meanings' that are involved are a part of what we are doing; or rather, they are part of the expression of what we are doing. In other words, one aspect of the field of discourse is simply the subject matter; we talk **about** different things, and therefore use different words for doing so. If this was all there was to it, and the field of discourse was **only** a question of subject matter, it would hardly need saying; but, in fact, 'what we are talking about' has to be seen as a special case of a more general concept, that of 'what we are doing', or 'what is going on, within which the language is playing a part.' It is this broader concept that is referred to as the "field of discourse". If, for example, the field of discourse is football, then no matter whether we are playing it or discussing it around a table we are likely to use certain linguistic forms which reflect the football context. But the two are essentially different kinds of activity and this is also reflected in the language. This difference, between the language of playing football and the language of discussing football, is also a reflection of the "mode of discourse"; see below.

The "field", therefore, refers to what the participants in the context of situation are actually engaged in doing, like 'buying-selling a newspaper' in our example above. This is a more general concept than that of subject matter, and a more useful one in the present context since we may not actually be **talking about** either buying and selling or newspapers. We may be talking about the weather; but that does not mean that the field of discourse is meteorology – talking about the weather is part of the strategy of buying and selling.

(b) *Mode.* Secondly, the language we use differs according to the channel or wavelength we have selected. Sometimes we find ourselves, especially those of us who teach, in a didactic mode, at other times the mode may be fanciful, or commercial, or imperative: we may choose to behave as teacher, or poet, or advertiser, or commanding officer. Essentially, this is a question of what function language is being made to serve in the context of situation; this is what underlies the selection of the particular rhetorical channel.

This is what we call the "mode of discourse"; and fundamental to it is the distinction between speaking and writing. This distinction partly cuts across the rhetorical modes, but it also significantly determines them: although certain modes can be realized through either medium, they tend to take quite different forms according to whether spoken or written – written advertising, for example, does not say the same things as sales talk. This is because the two media represent, essentially, different **functions** of language, and therefore embody selections of different kinds. The question underlying the concept of the mode of discourse is, what function is language being used for, what is its specific role in the goings-on to which it is contributing? To persuade? to soothe? to sell? to control? to explain? or just to oil the works, as in what Malinowski called "phatic communion", exemplified above by the talk about the weather, which merely helps the situation along? Here the distinction between the language of **playing** a game, such as bridge or football, and the language of **discussing** a game becomes clear. In the former situation, the language is functioning as a part of the game, as a pragmatic expression of play behaviour; whereas in the latter, it is part of a very different kind of activity, and may be informative, didactic, argumentative, or any one of a number of rhetorical modes of discourse.

(c) *Tenor*. Thirdly, the language we use varies according to the level of formality, of technicality, and so on. What is the variable underlying this type of distinction? Essentially, it is role relationships in the situation in question: who the participants in the communication group are, and in what relationship they stand to each other.

This is what, following Spencer and Gregory, we called the "tenor of discourse". Examples of role relationships, that would be reflected in the language used, are teacher/pupil, parent/child, child/child in peer group, doctor/patient, customer/salesman, casual acquaintances on a train, and so on. It is the role relationships, including the indirect relationship between a writer and his audience, that determine such things as the level of technicality and degree of formality. Contexts of situation, or settings, such as public lecture, playground at playtime, church service, cocktail party, and so on can be regarded as institutionalized role relationships and hence as stabilized patterns of "tenor of discourse".

It will be seen from the foregoing that the categories of *field of discourse*, *mode of discourse* and *tenor of discourse* are not themselves kinds or varieties of language. They are the backdrop, the features of the context of situation which determine the kind of language used. In other words, they determine what is often referred to as the register: that is, the types of meaning that are selected, and their expression in grammar and vocabulary. And they determine the register collectively, not piecemeal. There is not a great deal that one can predict about the language that will be used if one knows **only** the field of discourse or **only** the mode or the tenor. But if we know all three, we can predict quite a lot; and, of course, the more detailed the information we have, the more linguistic features of the text we shall be able to predict.

It is possible, nevertheless, to make some broad generalization about each of these three variables separately, in terms of its probable linguistic consequences.

The field of discourse, since it largely determines the "content" of what is being said, is likely to have the major influence on the selection of vocabulary, and also on the selection of those grammatical patterns which express our experience of the world that is around us and inside us: the types of process, the classes of object, qualities and quantities, abstract relations, and so on.

The mode of discourse, since it specifies the "channel" of communication, influences the speaker's selection of mood (what kind of statements he makes, such as forceful, hesitant, gnomic, qualified or reassertive; whether he asks questions and so on) and of modality (the judgement of probabilities); and also, in the distinction between speech and writing, it affects the whole pattern of grammatical and lexical organization, the **density** of the lexical content.

In general, written language is more highly 'lexicalized' than spoken language; it has a more complex vocabulary. This does not necessarily mean that written language uses words that are more unusual, though this may be true too; but it means that it has a greater lexical **density**, packing more content words into each phrase or clause or sentence. To express this in another way, written language contains more lexical information per unit of grammar. By the same token, written language also tends to be simpler than spoken language in its grammatical organization; speech, especially informal speech such as casual conservation, displays complexities of sentence structure that would be intolerable (because they would be unintelligible) in writing. Naturally, there is considerable variety within both the written and the spoken modes: there are forms of writing that are more like speech, and forms of spoken language that are very close to the written ('he talks like a book'). But this kind of variation also largely depends on the rhetorical channel or genre, as it is still a function of the mode of discourse. Jean Ure remarks, for example, that the lexical density is determined by the extent to which the language is what she calls "language-in-action".

Both the choice of vocabulary, which is largely a matter of the field of discourse, and its distribution in grammatical structures, which is mainly dependent on the mode, are also affected by factors of the third type, the tenor of the discourse: the types of social relationship, both temporary and permanent, that obtain between a speaker and his

113

hearers, or between a writer and his readers (and such a relationship is presumed to exist even if a writer is writing for an unknown public – this is often a big factor in his success), tend to influence the level of formality and technicality at which the speaker or writer is operating, and hence lead him to prefer certain words over others and to pitch his discourse at a certain point on the Joosian style scale.[7] Equally, however, it is the tenor of discourse that primarily determines which dialectal or other speech variant the speaker is going to select for the occasion: whether he is going to put on his verbal Sunday best and talk proper, or wear the linguistic garb that is suited to the works, the family or the club.

So there is some tendency for the field of discourse to determine the content of what is said, and for the mode and tenor to determine the manner or style of it, with the mode selecting the particular genre to be used and the tenor determining the social dialect. But this is, at best, only a crude approximation. In the first place the distinction between style (or "form", or "manner") and content is largely illusory; we cannot really separate what is said from how it is said, and this is just as true of everyday language as it is of myth and poetry. In the second place, the factors of field, mode and tenor operate as a whole, not in isolation from each other; the linguistic reflection of any one of them depends on its combination with the other two. There is not a great deal that one can say about the language of football, taken as a rubric just by itself (field of discourse), or the language of public lectures (mode), or the language of teacher and pupil (tenor), although these are certainly meaningful concepts, as is proved by the fact that if we hear a recording or read a passage out of context we can usually identify it in precisely such terms as these. But such identification is often made by means of linguistic clues which are themselves rather trivial, like the lecturer's voice quality or the urgent 'sir!' of the schoolboy; whereas in order to predict the interesting and important features of the language that is used we need to characterize the situation in terms of all three variables in interaction with each other. Suppose, on the other hand, that the setting is described in some such terms as these:

Field: Instruction: the instruction of a novice
- in a board game [e.g. Monopoly] with equipment present
- for the purpose of enabling him to participate
Mode: Spoken: unrehearsed

Didactic and explanatory, with undertone of non-seriousness
- with feedback: question-and-answer, correction of error

Tenor: Equal and intimate: three young adult males, acquainted
- but with hierarchy in the situation [two experts, one novice]
- leading to superior-inferior role relationship

Here we can predict quite a lot about the language that will be used, in respect of the meanings and the significant grammatical and lexical features through which they are expressed. If the entries under field, mode and tenor are filled out carefully and thoughtfully, it is surprising how many features of the language turn out to be relatable to the context of the situation. This is not to claim that we know what the participants are going to say; it merely shows that we can make sensible and informed guesses about certain aspects of what they might say, with a reasonable probability of being right. There is always, in language, the freedom to act untypically; but that in itself confirms rather than denies the reality of the concept of what is typical.

There is an experiment well known to students of linguistics in which the subject listens to a recording that is 'noisy' in the technical sense (badly distorted or jammed), so much so that he cannot understand anything of what is being said. He is then given a simple clue as to the register; and next time he listens he understands practically the whole text. We always listen and read with expectations, and the notion of register is really a theory about these expectations, providing a way of making them explicit.

To gain some impression of 'language in the life of the individual', it is hardly necessary, or possible, to keep detailed records of who says what, who to, when and why. But it is not too difficult to take note of information about register, with entries for field, mode and tenor in the language diary. This can give valuable insights into what language means to the individual. It will also effectively demolish any suspicion that there are individuals whose language is impoverished or deficient, since it goes straight to language as behaviour potential, to the semantic system that lies behind the wordings and the 'soundings' which are so often ridiculed or dismissed from serious attention.

Points to look for:

(a) What does the language profile of an individual's daily life look like?

What roles has he adopted, that have been expressed through language? What forms of interaction have these involved (e.g. the role of 'eldest daughter' implies interaction with parent(s) on the one hand and with younger brother(s) or sister(s) on the other; that of 'teacher' suggests interaction with pupils and also, perhaps, with headmaster)?

In what language events (types of linguistic situation) has he participated?

Has he made use of different variants (dialect switching), and if so, with what kind of linguistic variation and under what circumstances?

(b) What is the pattern of register variation?

Can we specify the relevant background features for particular instances of language use?

field of discourse: the nature of the activity, and subject matter

mode of discourse: the channel, and the part played by language in the total event

tenor of discourse: the role relationships among the participants

Where are the properties of the field, mode and tenor revealed in the language spoken or written? How far could the eavesdropper fill in the situational background; and conversely, what features of the language could have been predicted from the structural information?

(c) How much more difficult would it have been for the individual to survive **without** language?

5. Language and the context of situation

Like all the headings in our list, this is closely related to the others; in particular, it overlaps with the previous one, that of language in the life of the individual. But there is a difference of perspective: here we are focusing attention on the generalized contexts of language use and the function of language within these contexts, rather than on the linguistic profile of an individual speaker. The question that is raised is not so much what language means to an individual in his daily life as what the typical social contexts are in which he participates as an articulate being.

As in the last section, there is no difficulty in understanding the general principle: it is obvious that we use language in contexts of situation, and that these can be described in various ways. The problem here has always been how best to describe the various kinds of setting, and especially how to bring out what is significant and distinguish it from all the irrelevant particularities that are associated with specific instances.

This already arises in the treatment of register, as a problem of what Ellis calls "delicacy of focus". Suppose, to take a trivial example, that the field of discourse is shopping: do we characterize this as simply 'transaction', or as 'buying' (as distinct from, say, borrowing), or as 'buying in a shop' (as distinct from in the market), or as 'buying in a chemist's shop' (as distinct from a grocer's), or as 'buying a toothbrush' (as distinct from a cake of soap)? And since the criterion is bound to be our assessment, in some form or other, of whether it matters or not, we may as well ask whether we are likely to take any interest in a situation of this kind in the first place.

One way of deciding whether a particular type of situation is of interest or not is to consider, in terms of the second of the headings above, whether it is of any significance for the socialization of a child. For example, it is a good working hypothesis to assume that any type of situation in which a parent is controlling the child's behaviour is potentially important for linguistic and social development; and this suggests not only that these situations are of interest to us but also that a certain amount of information needs to be given about them, specifically information about what aspect of the child's behaviour it is that is being regulated: whether, for example, attention is being focused on his personal relationships ('don't talk to Granny like that!') or on his behaviour towards objects ('don't tear it').

Generally speaking the concept of social man provides the grounds for assessing the importance of a given class of context. The fact that a particular type of language use is relevant to the socialization of the child is one guarantee of significance; but it is not the only one – there are other ways in which it may be of importance in the culture. We might for example think of a linguistic setting such as 'teacher-parent consultation', subdivided into individual contact, parents' association meeting, exchange of letters, and so on; this may be assumed to be of some significance in an educational context, and therefore the forms of linguistic interaction between teacher and parent might well be worth looking into. Even more interesting are the forms of linguistic interaction between teacher and pupil in the classroom, and in other school settings. There have now been a number of useful studies of classroom language, and these all depend on some notion of the relevant contexts of situation.

Another quite different reason for thinking about 'language and situation' is the fact that the pupil, in the course of his education, is expected to become sensitive to the use of language in different situation types, and to be able to vary his own linguistic behaviour in response to them. The move, in schools, away from a total preoccupation with formal composition towards an awareness of the many different types of language use involved a fairly drastic redefinition of the educationally relevant contexts of situation – a redefinition which was not without its dangers and difficulties, as subsequent debate revealed, but which was very necessary nevertheless. Both *Breakthrough to Literacy* and *Language in Use* demand an enlightened and imaginative view of language and situation; because of this, they are an excellent source of insight into questions of relevance. As we have stressed all along, there is no difference between knowing language and knowing how to use it; success in the mother tongue is success in developing a linguistic potential for all the types of context that are engendered by the culture. From this point of view, if we think that a pupil when he leaves school should be able to use language adequately in this or that particular range of contexts, then those contexts are important even if they do not seem to provide any great scope for linguistic virtuosity or the exercise of the creative imagination. And there is some value to be gained from an occasional glance at those types of language use which are not normally regarded as the responsibility of the school. An example is the language of technical instructions: if one looks carefully (and sympathetically) at the leaflets issued by the manufacturers of appliances, not to the general public but to those responsible for the installation and maintenance of these appliances, one can get a very clear picture of how language is related to the context of situation in which it is functioning – or rather that in which it is **intended** to function: one should always remember that a leaflet of this kind is as out of context in the classroom as would be the gas boiler itself, or whatever other object it is designed to accompany.

These are very clearly questions of register, and we almost inevitably use concepts relating to field, mode or tenor of discourse when we talk about language in relation to the situation. Formulations like "the language of the classroom", "the language of technical instructions", are all characterizations of this kind, sometimes relating to just one of the three dimensions, often combining features of more than one. It is, in fact, very revealing to analyse some of the formulations that are commonly used, and taken for granted as meaningful descriptions of types of language use, in order to see what information they provide which might enable us to make predictions about the text; and we can do this by relating them to field, mode and tenor. Anthropologists often use terms like "pragmatic speech", "ritual language" or Malinowski's "phatic communion"; the question is what we can gather from these about the field of activity, the part played by language within it, and the participant roles and role relationships involved.

Some of the terms that typically figure in discussions of language in the context of English teaching are worth considering from this point of view, terms such as "creative writing", "imaginative language", "jargon", "ordinary language". These are rarely as objective and precise as they are made to seem. Jargon, for instance, often means no more than technical terms which the speaker personally dislikes, perhaps because he is not sure how to use them. If we try to interpret these labels in terms of field, mode and tenor, we find that it is not easy to see what they really imply about the kind of language used. It is not that they are not meaningful; but there is no consensus as to **what** they mean, so we have very little clue as to what would be generally regarded as a specimen of such language. What is creative in one type of situation (or in one person's opinion) would not be so in another.

The term "situation" is sometimes misleading, since it conjures up the idea of 'props', the specific concrete surroundings of a particular speech event such as might appear in a photograph of the scene. But this image is much too particular; what is significant is the situation **type**, the configuration of environmental factors that typically fashions our ways of speaking and writing.

Points to look for:

(a) What are examples of socially significant situation types, considered from an educational point of view?

How accurately and specifically do we define them? What is the 'delicacy of focus', e.g. school − classroom − English class − "creative writing" session?

In what ways are such situation types significant for the pupils' success in school (as distinct from those that are critical for the child's 'socialization' in general, as in 2 above)? What do

119

we expect to learn from an imaginative enquiry into the use of language in these contexts?

(b) What are the generalized functions of language within these situation types?

What do we mean when we talk of "creative", "transactional", "practical", "expressive" (etc.) language? How far is an interpretation of language in these terms dependent on our awareness of the situation?

Can we relate the use of language to the interaction of social roles within these situation types? (The notion that the type of language used – expressive, creative, etc. – is solely governed by the free choice or whim of the individual is very much oversimplified, and leads to some highly artificial and unrealistic classroom exercises.)

Are there 'pure' types of language use, or do real situations always generate some kind of mixed type? (This is a vast topic in its own right. Probably most use of language is neither rigidly pure nor hopelessly mixed, but involves a dominant register and one or two subsidiary motives. *Language in Use* provides opportunities for exploring this notion further.)

6. Language and institutions

Again, this is related to the previous headings; it suggests a further angle on the general theme of language and social interaction. In 4 the focus of attention was on the individual; it was the individual who supplied the common thread linking one language event with another. In 5 we took the situation as the basic construct and used that as the means of relating language events. Here we focus attention on social institutions, such as a family, a school, or a factory; these provide continuity of yet another kind, such as is implied by expressions like "language in the home" or "language in school".

We can think of any social institution, from the linguistic point of view, as a communication network. Its very existence implies that communication takes place within it; there will be sharing of experience, expression of social solidarity, decision-making and planning, and, if it is a hierarchical institution, forms of verbal control, transmission of orders and the like. The structure of the institution will be enshrined in the language, in the different types of interaction that take place and the linguistic registers associated with them.

An obvious example is a school, which is examined from this point of view by Peter Doughty in Chapter 6 of *Exploring Language*. Doughty writes:

> In the sense that a school functions as a social group within a discernible social context, it is a speech community: there will be patterns of interaction peculiar to the school, and consequently, there will also be patterns of language in use peculiar to it, and those who work together in the school develop common responses to them (pp. 100–1).

The school is a communication network, composed of many smaller networks that criss-cross each other and may be relatively fixed and constant or fluid and shifting. Consider for example the question of how decisions are transmitted. One communication network is formed by the chain of command, which might run from headmaster to head of department to member of staff to pupil. The detailed pattern is modified and varied from one instance to another; but the mechanisms are usually linguistic, and can be described (again, on the theoretical basis of field, mode and tenor) in terms of a few recognized situation types: formal interview, tête-à-tête, assembly, noticeboard, and so on. It is interesting to follow through what happens in the case of a particular policy decision, from its original discussion (if any) and adoption to its eventual putting into effect, seeing how language is used at each stage and how it signals the social relationships involved. As Doughty puts it, there are "ways of operating through which one individual indicates to another his understanding of their mutual status and relationship".

There are also the linguistic aspects of the processes whereby a decision is made, as distinct from those by which it is transmitted. Suppose it is initiated from a level some way **below** the level of authority required for its adoption; for example, a suggestion from the class for a visit to the docks. How is this formulated for the purpose of being referred upward for decision, from the class to the teacher, or from the teacher to the head?

The making and implementing of decisions is only one of the aspects of the life of an institution that can be considered from this point of view, taking the institution as a communication network.

The characteristics of one type of institution, and the features that set it off from others, are likely to be revealed in unexpected ways in the language. For example, certain institutions, of which the school is one, are distinguished by the existence of a clientele, a group for whom the institution is originally designed but who are distinct from the members of it, the professionals who, typically, earn their living from the institution. The school has pupils; similarly, a hotel has guests, a hospital has patients, an airline has passengers. (These contrast with institutions such as a family, a club, or a union branch, which have only members; and with those which have a 'general public' with whom they communicate only indirectly and through special channels, such as an industrial enterprise, or a government department.) Here the status of the clientele is largely revealed by the nature of the communication that takes place between it and the members. There is a recognized class of jokes about institutions which lose sight of the interests of the clientele who constitute the sole reason for their existence, centring round the basic theme of 'this would be a splendid place to work in if it wasn't for the … (pupils, guests, etc.)'. The reality behind this form of humour, the rather natural tendency on the part of the professionals to regard the customers as an unnecessary intrusion in the smooth running of the institution, is again most clearly revealed through the language.

The school itself, therefore, is only one of many institutions that are of interest from this point of view, as a communication network, a nexus of interpersonal contexts for the use of language. But in one respect it differs from the others mentioned above. Most other institutions of this general type – those with a clientele – serve their clientele in non-linguistic ways. The hospital treats their ailments, the airline moves them from place to place, the hotel feeds and entertains them. In a school, the relation between staff and pupils is essentially one of talk. The whole function of the school is to be a communication network joining professional and client. (Perhaps the nearest type of institution to it in this respect is a church.) Hence an understanding of the institutional use of language is even more fundamental in the school than elsewhere.

Recently we have begun to see some penetrating accounts of the use of language in the classroom, and these will no doubt shed a totally new light on the nature of the school as an institution, and therefore on the educational process. This refers not only to the teacher's own use of language, but also to the sort of language he gets, as well as the sort of language he expects, from the pupils. The latter are no longer enjoined to silence, as they were once; the communication channels are now two-way. But at the same time there are restraints, and only certain types of linguistic behaviour on the part of the pupils are normally regarded as acceptable – depending, of course, on the context: forms of speech which are not acceptable in the classroom or corridor would pass unnoticed on the sportsfield. This is another instance of variation in register.

Finally there is also the external aspect of the communication patterns: communication between the school and the outside world. We have already referred to teacher-parent interaction; but there are many other aspects to this, which taken together reflect the place of the school in the community as a whole. This also is best seen through attention to the language, which is likely to show up many of the assumptions that are made, by the school on the one hand and the community on the other, about the role of the school in the life of social man.

Points to look for:

(a) What do we mean by an institution, from a linguistic point of view? In other words, can we define it by reference to the concept of a communication network?

Who talks to whom, and who writes to whom, as an essential part of the fabric of the institution?

Who talks or writes to whom as a means of contact between the institution and the outside world?

(b) What is the special nature of the school as a communication network? How does it differ, in this regard, from other institutions of a comparable nature?

How are decisions made, and how are they transmitted? What are the **linguistic** features of the decision processes?

What types of communication are necessary to, and characteristic of, the life of the school? [These again can be seen in terms of field, mode and tenor: what significant kinds of activity are carried on through language, what is the specific channel of communication in each case, and what are the role relationships involved?]

(c) Where are the **breakdowns** in communication, and why?

7. *Language attitudes*

The subject of attitudes to language has been discussed frequently over the past ten years. One of the early treatments of it in an educational context was in Halliday *et al.* (1964) *The Linguistic Sciences and Language Teaching* [this volume, chapter 1], where it was stressed that the reason for insisting on public discussion of attitudes to language was that these can be, and have been, extremely harmful in their effects on educational practice.

We referred above to the "stereotype hypothesis", and to the fact that teachers often base their initial judgement of a child, and their expectations of his performance, very largely upon his accent. This is already very damaging, since a child – like an adult – tends to behave as he is expected to do: if he is stereotyped as a failure, he will fail. But it is not only in their initial expectations that teachers have discriminated in this way. They have often totally rejected the child's mother tongue, and tried to stamp it out with the full force of their disapproval and scorn. It is unlikely that a child will come out of this sort of ordeal unscathed. When the authors of *The Linguistic Sciences and Language Teaching* wrote that "A speaker who is made ashamed of his own language habits suffers a basic injury as a human being: to make anyone, especially a child, feel so ashamed is as indefensible as to make him feel ashamed of the colour of his skin" (p. 105), they were actually taken to task in the columns of a women's magazine, on the grounds that whereas a child cannot change the colour of his skin, he can learn to change his language. This seems to imply that if Catholics are discriminated against, the best way to help them is by forcible conversion to Protestantism.

To reject this is not to argue that a teacher ought to learn to talk to the children in their neighbourhood dialect, a gesture which by itself serves little purpose. But he should be prepared to recognize both his own and other people's folk-linguistic attitudes; and, ideally, to explore these attitudes, taking the pupils into his confidence. The pupils' own experience will tell them that language is one of the many aspects of human behaviour that is judged by others as 'good' or 'bad', they can be encouraged to try and find out why this is, and guided by the teacher towards an understanding which enables them to see through and behind these judgements. (It is not unknown for the pupils to guide the teacher, in the first instance.) This puts questions of dialect and accent, standard and non-standard, into a perspective. We all need to learn some form of the standard language – it does not matter much with what accent, and there is little chance of the teacher's influencing this anyway – but if the standard differs from our mother tongue, we do not throw the mother tongue away. There are functions of language to which the one is appropriate but not the other. Learning standard English, in fact, is more a matter of learning new registers than of learning a new dialect.

Social man is, inevitably, his own ethnographer; he has his own model of himself, his society and his language. This model contains a great deal of useful insight; but it is cluttered up with attitudes which may originally have been protective to the individual himself but which no longer serve him any purpose and become harmful if he is in a position to influence others. Such attitudes are difficult to recognize because they are disguised and legitimized as statements of fact. This is why one of the most far-reaching trends of the past decade has been the trend, in education, towards a much greater social and linguistic objectivity and understanding; the approach to language is now on the whole constructive and positive, instead of being largely negative as it was before.

In exploring language, we are very naturally led to explore the folk linguistic that goes with it. An important part of this, as Peter Doughty points out, is derived from experience at school; and the school is a good place in which to explore it. The class can collect cuttings about language from letters to the press, columns in popular magazines and so on, to see what sort of ideas people have; they can note the words that are used to pass judgement on language (*good, correct, wrong, lazy, ugly,* etc.), the explanations that are offered for these judgements, if any (why is something said to be "wrong" or "sloppy"?), and the particular aspects of language that are brought up for discussion (accent, grammar, vocabulary). It is easy to assume that there must be a general consensus about all such matters, but this is largely illusory: apart from the prescriptive rules that were codified in the English textbooks of the previous generation, which have a very strong power of survival, the consensus consists in little more than a general agreement that there must be a right and a wrong in language somewhere.

It is perhaps worth adding a note about phonetics, especially at a point in history when educated Britons are once again becoming linguists, in the other sense of the term (speakers of foreign languages), as they used to be not so very long ago. In any class where some or all of the pupils 'speak with an accent' – which means the vast majority of the schools in the country – it will be easy to show that for learning French or German or Italian or Russian some of the sounds in their own speech are much more helpful that those of RP (= "received pronunciation", not "royal pronunciation", although it could be roughly defined as the Queen's English). In learning foreign languages, the child who speaks RP has no advantages; and it is very disheartening, though not uncommon, to hear children struggling hard to pronounce foreign sounds badly, in good English, when if they had not been taught to disvalue their own native speech they could have used this as a model and pronounced the foreign sounds well and with ease.

The ability to make observations on the speech of the pupils in accurate phonetic terms is, naturally, something that requires training.

125

But one part of this is a training in listening objectively to speech sounds, and in seeing through the folk linguistic jargon of "pure", "harsh", "grating", "rich", and other such terminological obstacles to clear thinking; and this one can achieve on one's own, given a reasonable dash of curiosity and openmindedness. A teacher who is interested in this aspect of language can then try out the "stereotype hypothesis" on himself, and see how far his own expectations of an individual pupil's performance do in fact correlate with how that pupil pronounces English. In the long run, we may find that the advantage lies with the child who has mastered a variety of different speech forms, although this would have more to do with register than with dialect. At the very least we can show that questions of accent and dialect can be the subject of rational and tolerant discussion, instead of being used as a means of type-casting human beings into ready-made categories and labelling them with badges of inferiority and shame. We tend to treat language all too solemnly, yet without taking it seriously; if we could learn to be rather more serious about it, and at the same time a lot less solemn, we might help to reverse what the *Guardian* referred to as "the slow slide to illiteracy", and to inarticulacy.

Points to look for:

(a) What are the most familiar attitudes towards linguistic norms and correctness?

What linguistic opinions are held by (i) the children, (ii) their parents, (iii) your colleagues, (iv) you?

How are these attitudes manifested and expressed?

Are the value judgements concerned mainly with grammar? with vocabulary? with dialect and accent? Is a distinction made between "grammar" (= 'what should be') and "usage" (= 'what is')?

(b) What is the effect of these attitudes on the relationship between teacher and pupil?

Do they provide a clue to (i) the teacher's expectations, (ii) the teacher's assessments of the pupil's performance?

What is the effect of these attitudes on the child's own expectations of the school, and on his feelings about his chances of success?

What is the effect on his actual performance?

Diagram 1: Suggested categories of dialectal variety differentiation

	Situational categories	Contextual categories	Example of English varieties (descriptive contextual categories	
user's	individuality	idiolect	Mr X's English, Miss Y's English	dialectal varieties: the linguistic reflection of reasonably permanent characteristics of the user in language situations
	temporal provenance	temporal dialect	Old English, Modern English	
	geographical provenance	geographical dialect	British English American English	
	social provenance	social dialect	upper-class English, middle-class English	
	range of intelligibility	standard/ non-standard	standard English, non-standard English	

Diagram II: Suggested categories of diatypic variety differentiation

	Situational categories	Contextual categories	Example of English varieties (descriptive contextual categories	
user's	purposive role	field of discourse	technical English, non-technical English	diatypic varieties: the linguistic reflection of recurrent characteristics of the user's use of language in situations
	medium relationship	mode of discourse	spoken English, written English	
	addressee relationship	tenor of discourse		
	(a) personal	personal tenor	formal English, informal English	
	(b) functional	functional tenor	didactic English, non-didactic English	

Source: Michael Gregory, 'Aspects of varieties differentiation', *Journal of Linguistics* 3, 1967.

Postscript

The work of the (originally Nuffield, later Schools Council) Programme in Linguistic and English Teaching spanned the period from 1964 to 1971, and provided the background of thinking, experience and practical endeavour that lies behind the perspective adopted here. It is in the light of this experience that 'language and social man' assumes relevance as an approach to language in an educational context.

Language has for a long time been a depressed area in our educational system; and only a serious concern with language on the part of teachers, a concern that is enlightened, imaginative and humane, can restore it to the central place which it ought to occupy if we are tackling the problem of educational failure at its deepest level.

Lately there has been a considerable amount of research effort that is relevant to this theme, often following up earlier ideas that had been neglected; and reference has been made to some of the important books and papers that have appeared. But the basic discussion of how these ideas may be translated into practice will be found in the two sets of materials produced by the Programme: *Breakthrough to Literacy* (Longman, 1970) for primary schools, and *Language in Use* (Edward Arnold, 1971) for secondary schools.

The title *Breakthrough to Literacy* referred to the child's breakthrough from speech into the new medium of writing. But it is a breakthrough also in another sense: a breakthrough in the whole concept of language in the primary school. The ideas behind it are embodied in the Teacher's Manual, which can be read on its own as a thoughtful discussion of the question of literacy. It was very encouraging that, at the end of the project, the ILEA set up their Centre for Language in Primary Education, and that the person appointed to take charge of it was David Mackay, leader of the *Breakthrough* team.

It is not unreasonable to claim for *Language in Use* a breakthrough of another kind, this time at the secondary level. This takes the perspective of 'language and social man' and gives it a concrete expression in the form of study units for the exploration of language by pupils within the secondary school range. The accompanying volume *Exploring Language* (Edward Arnold, 1971) has been referred to at many points, and provides the best discussion of language in an educational context that has yet appeared.

There is another breakthrough still to come, in the training of teachers, who have so far been left to fend almost entirely for themselves as far as language is concerned. Perhaps we may look forward to a time when language study has some place in the professional training of all teachers, and the central place in the relevant specialist courses, especially those relating to English and to literacy ('teaching of reading'). "Language study" is not meant to imply a diluted version of academic linguistics – a subject which has often been defined much too rigidly in the university context; but, rather, a serious exploration of language from different angles, ignoring the artificial boundaries which universities (like schools) tend to interpose between one discipline and another. The exploration of language cannot be neatly classified as natural science, social science, humanity or fine art; it takes something from each of these world views. If we claim that language has a key place in the processes of education, this is not only for the obvious reason that it is the primary channel for the transmission of knowledge, but much more because it reflects, as nothing else does, the multi-level personality of man.

Notes

1. Terms like *meaning, wording* and *spelling* are so familiar in everyday speech that we are hardly aware of them as ways of talking about language. But when we say, to a pupil, or to a committee chairman perhaps, "I think you'll have to alter the wording", we are bringing into play what Peter Doughty calls 'a "folk linguistic", a "common sense" about the language we live by' (*Exploring Language*, p. 6).
2. For both these references see Frederick Williams, (ed.), *Language and Poverty*.
3. This view is associated first and foremost with the work of the great American linguist Benjamin Lee Whorf, who wrote "An accepted pattern of using words is often prior to certain lines of thinking and modes of behaviour". Whorf emphasized that it is not so much in "special uses of language" (technical terms, political discourse etc.) as "in its constant ways of arranging data and its most ordinary everyday analysis of phenomena that we need to recognize the influence [language] has on other activities, cultural and personal" (*Language, Thought and Reality*, pp. 134–5). Bernstein points out that, in Whorf's thinking, "the link between language, culture and habitual thought is *not* mediated through the social structure", whereas his own theory "places the emphasis on changes in the social structure as major factors in shaping or changing a given culture through their effect on the consequences of fashions of speaking. It shares with Whorf the controlling influence on experience ascribed to "frames of consistency" involved in fashions of speaking. It differs from Whorf by asserting that, in the context of a common language in the sense of a general code, there will

arise distinct linguistic forms, fashions of speaking, which induce in their speakers *different* ways of relating to objects and persons."

4. Bernstein refers to them as "critical contexts" for socialization, using "context" in the sense of a generalized situation type. He identifies the "regulative" context, "where the child is made aware of the rules of the moral order, and their various backings"; the "instructional" context, "where the child learns about the objective nature of objects and persons, and acquires skills of various kinds"; the "imaginative or innovating" contexts, "where the child is encouraged to experiment and re-create his world on his own terms"; and the "interpersonal" context, "where the child is made aware of affective states – his own, and others"(*Class, Codes and Control I*, pp. 181, 198.)

5. Useful discussions of the concept of register, in the present context, will be found in Hasan (1973) and in Ure and Ellis (1972).

6. See Halliday, McIntosh and Strevens (1964), where the term "style of discourse" was used instead of "tenor". Here we shall prefer the term "tenor" introduced by Spencer and Gregory, in Enkvist, Spencer and Gregory (1964). A number of other, more or less related, schemata have been proposed; see especially Jeffrey Ellis (1965, 1966).

7. Martin Joos recognizes five points: intimate, casual, consultative, formal and frozen; see his book *The Five Clocks*, and also the discussion in Chapters 10 and 11 of *Exploring Language* ('Accent and dialect' and 'Diversity in written English', by John Pearce). It is worth remarking, perhaps, that the term "formality" (or "level of formality") is the source of some confusion in discussions of language, because it is used in two different senses. On the one hand it refers to the use of forms of the language – words, or grammatical structures – that are conventionally associated with certain modes: with impersonal letters or memoranda, various types of interview and the like. On the other hand it is used to refer to the degree of respect that is shown linguistically to the person who is being addressed. languages differ rather widely as regards how (and also as regards how much) they incorporate the expression of respect, but there are ways of addressing parents and elders, social and occupational superiors, and so on, that are recognized as the marks of the social relationship involved. Although there is some overlap between these two senses of 'formality', they are in principle rather distinct and have very different manifestations in language.

Chapter Four

SOCIOLOGICAL ASPECTS OF SEMANTIC CHANGE (1975)

In the past five years there has been extensive activity in the various fields that are known collectively as "sociolinguistics". I shall not attempt to survey this work here; for one thing, a number of comprehensive surveys have recently appeared, for example by Fishman and others in Fishman (1971) *Advances in the Sociology of Language I*, and by Gumperz and Hymes (1972) *Directions in Sociolinguistics*; and for another, only a part of this work would bear directly on the theme of linguistic change. What I would like to attempt, however sketchily, is some kind of synthesis, an integration of a number of rather separate strands into an analytic framework that will relate them to linguistic change and in particular to the semantic level and semantic change. Some aspects of sociolinguistic research – Labov's is perhaps the clearest example – bear very directly on change in the linguistic system, and Labov himself has enumerated certain historical principles on the basis of investigations conducted, by himself and others, in terms of his own elegant and rigorous quantitative methodology (Labov, 1970a). Other studies in the field have a rather indirect bearing on linguistic change, but are of special interest inasmuch as they relate to changes in the semantic system. I shall try to bring these together in what amount to three steps, although the steps will not be taken separately in a clearly marked sequence. First, a schematization of the major trends, showing their place in the overall interpretation of language and the social system,

'Sociological Aspects of Semantic Chang', from Luigi Heilmann (ed.), *Proceedings of the Eleventh International Congress of Linguists,* 853-879, (1975). Originally published Bologna: Il Mulino, 1974.
[Rights reverted to author so no copyright line]

with language being considered as part of the social system. Second, more detailed discussion of those which relate to linguistic change. Third, a consideration of the question of change in the semantic system, from the point of view of the sociology of language.

Current fields of investigation that are in some sense 'sociolinguistic' might be enumerated as follows:

1. Macrosociology of language; linguistic demography
2. Diglossia; multilingualism and multidialectalism
3. Language planning; development and standardization
4. Pidginization and creolization
5. Social dialectology; description of non-standard varieties
6. Educational sociolinguistics
7. Ethnography of speaking; speech situations
8. Register; verbal repertoire and code-switching
9. Social factors in phonological and grammatical change
10. Language and socialization; language in the transmission of culture
11. Sociolinguistic approach to language development in children
12. Functional theories of the linguistic system
13. Linguistic relativity
14. Microsociology of knowledge (ethnomethodological linguistics)
15. Theory of text.

1. Text, situation and register

1.1

Let me start with the concept of a text, with particular reference to the text-in-situation, which may be regarded as the basic unit of semantic structure (i.e. of the semantic process). (Perhaps if we are using the term "sociolinguistics" in these discussions I ought to refer to it rather as the basic unit of "sociosemantic" structure). The concept 'text' has no connotations of size; it may be instantiated as speech act, speech event, topic unit, exchange, episode, narrative and so on.

Now from one point of view, the main interest of the text is what it leaves out. For example, the participants in an encounter accord each other certain statuses and roles, and they do so partly by means of attention to the text, the meanings that are exchanged. Yet, as Cicourel has pointed out, we know very little about how they do it; we have no real theory of linguistic interaction. Somehow, symbolic behaviour is interpreted, and meanings are assigned. Cicourel suggests (1969: 186–9) that the member operates with four interpretative principles or

132

assumptions, which he calls "reciprocity of perspectives", "normal forms", "the etcetera principle" and "descriptive vocabulary as indexical expressions". In any exchange of meanings, the individual assumes (i) that interpretations of experience are shared (others see things in the same way); (ii) that there are principles of selection and organization of meaning, and therefore also (iii) of reconstituting and supplementing omissions (we agree on what to leave out, and the other fills it in – these are I think encodings rather than omissions, with shared 'key' or unscrambling procedures), and (iv) that words, or rather words-in-structures, linguistic forms, are referred identically to past experience. These principles act as "instructions for the speaker-hearer for assigning infinitely possible meanings to unfolding social scenes" (*ibid.* 189). The speaker-hearer relies heavily on the social system for the decoding of text.

Cicourel argues for a "generative semantics" "that begins with the member's everyday world as the basic source for assigning meaning to objects and events" (1969: 197); and this kind of approach to the nature and function of text is a characteristic of ethnomethodological linguistic studies such as those of Sacks and Schegloff. An example is Schegloff's (1971) account of how people refer to location, which reveals some of the general principles on which the speaker-hearer relies in the production and understanding of discourse relating to the identification of places and of persons. It is clear from his account that when participants select, from among a number of 'correct' designations (such as those involving geographical and those involving personal reference points), the adequate or (as he puts it) "right" semantic options they are making use of the relevant particulars of the context of situation: in Schegloff's own formulation, "interactants are context-sensitive". This is another instance of the general principle of presupposition that is embodied in the text-forming potential of the linguistic system. Just as the speaker selects the appropriate information focus, distributing the meanings of the text into information that he decides to treat as recoverable to the hearer (given) and information that he decides to treat as non-recoverable (new), so in Schegloff's example the speaker selects the appropriate co-ordinates, and their degree of accuracy, in specifying where things are. Schegloff appears, however, to leave out the important component of 'rightness' that consists in the participant's option of being 'wrong': that is, of selecting a semantic configuration that violates the situational-contextual restraints, with a specific communicative effect – an option which, at least in the case of information focus, participants very readily take up (see the discussion of information structure, and information focus, in Halliday 1967–1968).

1.2

The selection of semantic options by the speaker in the production of text (in other words, what the speaker decides to mean) is regulated by what Hymes (1967) calls the "native theory and system of speaking". The member of the community possesses a "communicative competence" that "enables [him] to know when to speak and when to remain silent, which code to use, when, where and to whom, etc."; in other words, to know the "rules of speaking", defined by Grimshaw (1971: 136) as "generalizations about relationships among components" of the speech situation. Hymes has given a list, now very familiar, of the eight components of speech, which may be summarized, and to a certain extent paraphrased, as follows: form and content, setting, participants, ends (intent and effect), key, medium, genre and interactional norms. We may compare this with various earlier lists, such as that of Firth (1950) which comprised the participants (statuses and roles), relevant features of the setting, verbal and non-verbal action and effective result.

One of the difficulties with such lists is to know what theoretical status to assign to them in relation to the text. Hymes includes "form and content of message", i.e. the text itself, as one of the components; compare Firth's "verbal action of the participants". An alternative approach is to consider the situational factors as **determinants** of the text. This is exemplified in the triadic formula used by Halliday, McIntosh and Strevens (1964), with its categories of *field*, *mode* and *tenor*. These are categories at a more abstract level which are regarded as determining rather than as including the text; they represent the situation in its generative aspect. Field refers to the ongoing activity and the particular purposes that the use of language is serving within the context of that activity; mode covers roughly Hymes' channel, key and genre; and tenor refers to the interrelations among the participants (status and role relationships). There are some theoretical advantages to be gained from working with a triadic construct, advantages which relate to the nature of the linguistic system (see below).

The categories of field, mode and tenor are thus determinants and not components of speaking; collectively they serve to predict text, via the intermediary of the code, or (since "code" has been used in a number of different senses) to predict what I shall call the *register* (Ure and Ellis 1972). These concepts are intended to make explicit the means whereby the observer can derive, from the speech situation, not the text itself, of course, but certain systematic norms governing the particulars of the text. These norms, taken together, constitute the register. In other words, the various sub-categories of field, mode and tenor have associated with them typical semantic patterns – on the assumption, that is, of what Fishman calls "congruence" (1971: 244–5); so that if for a given instance of language use the situational features are specified, in appropriate terms, typical linguistic features can be specified by derivation from them (Halliday 1970a). (Note that we are concerned with the semantic properties of the text and not with the ritual lexicogrammatical variants that are associated with levels of formality and the like, although these form one part of the total picture). If the observer can derive the text from the situation, then by the same token the participant, or 'interactant', who has the same information available to him, can derive the situation from the text: he can supply the relevant information that is lacking. Thus the 'register' concept provides a means of investigating the linguistic foundations of everyday social interaction, from an angle that is complementary to the ethnomethodological one; it takes account of the processes which link the features of the text, considered as the realization of semantic patterns, to the abstract categories of the speech situation. It is these processes which embody the "native theory and system of speaking".

How far are such concepts relatable to the linguistic system? The literature of sociolinguistics abounds with references to the linguist's practice of treating the linguistic system as an invariant, by contrast with the sociolinguist's interest in variation; but all linguists are interested in variation, and the distinction is a largely artificial one. The underlying question is that of the nature of linguistic choice; specifically, of the various types of choice, and their accommodation and interaction in the linguistic system. The distinction is unfortunate since it implies that "code choice" – in the sense of ritual variation, the choice of appropriate levels of formality etc. – is to be isolated from other aspects of choice. Sociolinguistic discussions have often rested on the tacit assumption that there was nothing at all to be said about the choice between *cat* and *dog* – that is a matter of the system – whereas a distinct theory was needed to account for the choice between *cat* and *mog* [*mog* being a slang term for 'cat' in certain British dialects]. But both these choices are choices that are made within the linguistic system; what is needed is a theory which accounts for both.

This points in the direction of a functional semantics, towards a further elaboration of the theories of the Prague school, who always have explicitly concerned themselves with variation. Hymes (1969: 113) recognizes two types of meaning, "social meaning" and "referential meaning": "Languages have conventional units, structures and relations ... that are what I shall call 'stylistic' (serving social meaning) as well as referential". Elsewhere he uses the term "socio-expressive" for the former. In my own work I have used a triadic system, with components *ideational*, *interpersonal* and *textual* (the first two probably equivalent to Hymes' referential and social), the ideational being then further resoluble into experiential and logical (Halliday 1967–1968, 1972). If we assume for the moment that the linguistic system is in fact essentially trimodal at the semantic level (and there is strong internal evidence for this), then on the basis of the three-way categorization of the situational determinants of text into field, mode and tenor, we can make a tentative correlation between the *situation*, the *text* and the *semantic system*: by and large, it is the ideational component of the system that is activated by the choice of field, the interpersonal by the tenor, and the textual by mode. There is, in other words, a general tendency whereby the speaker, in encoding the role relationships in the situation (the tenor; Hymes' "participants" and "key"), draws on the interpersonal component in the semantic system, realized for example by mood; in encoding the activity, including subject matter (the field; Hymes' "setting" and "ends"), draws on the ideational component, realized for example by transitivity; and in encoding the features of the channel, the rhetorical mode and so on (the mode; Hymes' "instrumentalities" and "genre") draws on the textual component, realized for example by the information focus. These are approximations only: but they are suggestive given that the two sets of categories, the components of the speech situation on the one hand and those of the semantic system on the other, are established quite independently of each other.

1.3

Thus one main strand in the sociolinguistic fabric consists in interrelations among the three levels of 1) social interaction (represented linguistically by the text), 2) the speech situation and 3) the linguistic system. This interrelationship constitutes the systematic aspect of everyday speech. From the sociological point of view, the focus of attention here is on the 'micro' level. By contrast, the 'macro' level involves a further classifying of speech situations, a situational typology such as is embodied in Fishman's notion of "domain", defined (1971:

248) as "The large-scale aggregative regularities that obtain between variables and societally recognized functions". A macro-level sociology of language pays attention to a "more generalized description of sociolinguistic variation", in which there is association between a domain, on the one hand, and a specific variety or language on the other. A domain may be defined in terms of any of the components of speech situations: for example, in Paraguay it is found that Guarani is used in settings which are rural, and, among the non-rural, in those which are (the intersection of) non-formal, intimate and non-serious. Spanish is used in settings which are (the intersection of) urban and either formal or, if non-formal, non-intimate. If the setting is non-rural, non-formal, intimate and serious, the choice of language depends on other variables: language order (i.e. which was the mother tongue), language proficiency and sex (Joan Rubin (1968), quoted in Fishman (1971: 289)). Here the situational criteria are extremely mixed. Generalizations of this kind involve the relating of situation types 'upward' to the general "context of culture", in the sense in which that term was used by Malinowski (1924).

Typically in such 'macro-level' descriptions the concern is with communities where there is bi- or multi-lingualism, or at least some form of diglossia. The shift that takes place is between languages, or between "high" and "low" (classical and colloquial) varieties of the same language; and this is seen to reflect certain broad and generalizable categories of situational variable. The situational features that determine "code shift" may themselves be highly specific in nature; for example Gorman, studying the use of English, Swahili and the vernacular by speakers of eight of Kenya's major languages, found that "Swahili is characteristically used more frequently than English in conversations with fathers and less frequently in conversations with siblings, although there are exceptions ..." (1971: 213) – exceptions which were in turn partly relatable to the topic of the conversation.

It is the relative impermanence of these situational factors which leads to the phenomenon of "code-switching", which is code shift actualized as a process within the individual: the speaker moves from one code to another, and back, more or less rapidly, in the course of daily life, and often in the course of a single sentence. Gumperz describes code shift and code-switching as the expression of social hierarchy in its various forms, notably caste and social class. The verbal repertoire of the speaker, his code potential, is a function of the social hierarchy and of his own place in it; while the particular context of interaction, the social-hierarchical properties of the situation, determine, within limits set by other variables (and always allowing for the individual's role discretion; there is personal as well as transactional switching, in Gumperz' terms), the selection that he makes from within that repertoire.

Hence this particular concept of a 'code', in the sense of a language or language variety coexisting with other languages or language varieties in a (multilingual and multidialectal) society, such that the individual typically controls more than one code, extends naturally and without discontinuity to that of code **as social dialect**, dialectal variety in language that is related to social structure, and specifically to social hierarchy. The situation may determine which code one selects, but the social structure determines which codes one controls. The limiting case would be an ideal diglossia in which every member has access to both the superposed or 'high' variety and one regional or 'low' variety. In general, however, the speaker's social dialect repertoire is a function of his personal caste or class history.

Theoretically a social dialect is like a regional dialect, in that it can be **treated as** invariant in the life history of the speaker. This in fact used to be regarded as the norm. In practice, however, it is misleading; as Labov remarks in this connection (1970a; in 1971: 170): "As far as we can see, there are no single-style speakers". Labov refers to "style shift" rather than "code shift", understanding by this a shift in respect of certain specified variables that is governed by one particular situational restraint, namely the level of formality. The variables he finds are grammatical and phonological ones, such as the presence or absence of *be* in copular constructions, e.g. *he (is) wild*; negative concord, as displayed in the music-hall Cockney sentence *I don't suppose you don't know nobody what don't want to buy no dog*, or its absence; θ vs. $t\theta$ vs. t in initial position, e.g. in *think*; plus or minus post-vocalic *r*, etc. Labov's work has shown that one cannot define a social dialect, at least in an urban context, except by having recourse to variable rules as well as categorical rules: in other words, variation must be seen as inherent in the system. Labov's own earlier definition of an urban speech community, as a group of speakers sharing the same linguistic attitudes, which he arrived at after finding that speech attitudes were more consistent than speech habits, could therefore, in the light of his own studies of variation, be revised to read "a group of speakers showing the same patterns of variation" – which means, in turn, reinstating its original definition as a group of speakers who share the same social dialect, since social dialect is now defined so as to include such variation (see Wolfram 1971).

However, as Labov remarks, although "there are a great many styles and stylistic dimensions, ... *all such styles can be ranged along a single dimension, measured by the amount of attention paid to speech*" (1970a; in 1971: 170, Labov's italics). Hence, for example, the five stylistic levels that are postulated in order to show up variation in post-vocalic *r*: casual speech, careful speech, reading, word lists and minimal pairs. In other words the **type** of linguistic variation that is associated with these contexts, through the "amount of attention paid to speech", is itself largely homogeneous; it can be represented in the form of points along a scale of deviation from an implied norm, the norm in this case being a prestige or "standard" form. The speaker is not switching between alternative forms that are equally deviant and thus neutral with regard to prestige norms (contrasting in this respect with rural speakers in dialect boundary areas). He is switching between variants that are value-charged: they have differential values in the social system. This by no means necessarily implies that the so-called "prestige" forms are most highly valued for all groups in all contexts (Labov, 1970a; in 1971: 204), but simply that the effect of such variation on linguistic change cannot be studied in isolation from the social system which determines the sets of values underlying the variation.

1.4

Discussion of language and social structure usually centres around the influence of social structure on language; but in Labov's perspective any such effect is marginal, in terms of the linguistic system as a whole. "The great majority of linguistic rules are quite remote from any social value" (*ibid*. 204); ". . . social values are attributed to linguistic rules only when there is variation" (205). In other words, there is interaction between social hierarchy and certain features of the dialectal varieties that it gives rise to, such that these features are the object of variation; but no general principles relating language and language variety to the social order.

Such principles are to be found, in a very different perspective, in the work of Bernstein. Here the social structure, and social hierarchy, is shown to be related to variety in language; not to social dialect, however, but to register. This distinction is a fundamental one. Whereas social dialects are different **grammatical and phonological representations** of a semantic system, registers are different **semantic configurations** (leaving open the question whether they are derived from identical semantic systems or not). Hence Bernstein's focus of attention is the relation of social structure to meaning – that is, to the meanings that are typically expressed by the members.

Bernstein has drawn attention to principles of semiotic organization governing the choice of meanings by the speaker and their interpretation by the hearer. These he refers to as "codes"; and there is a considerable source of confusion here, as the same term *code* is being used in radically different senses. The codes control the meanings the speaker-hearer attends to (see Cicourel's "socially distributed meanings"). In terms of our general picture, the codes act as determinants of register, operating on the selection of meanings within situation types: when the systemics of language – the ordered sets of options that constitute the linguistic system – are activated by the situational determinants of text (the field, mode and tenor, or whatever conceptual framework we are using), this process is regulated by the codes. (Bernstein, 1971: *passim*).

A unique feature of Bernstein's work is that it suggests **how** the social structure is represented in linguistic interaction. According to Bernstein, the essential element governing access to the codes is the family role system, the system of role relationships within the family; and he finds two main types, the positional role system, and the personal role system. In the former, the part played by the member (for example in decision-making) is largely a function of his position in the family: role corresponds to ascribed status. In the latter, it is more a function of his psychological qualities as an individual; here status is achieved, and typically there are ambiguities of role. The two types are found in all social classes, but sections of the middle class favour the person-oriented types, and **strongly** positional families are found mainly in the lower working class; thus there is a mechanism for the effect of social class on language, via the interrelation of class and family type.

Bernstein postulates two variables within the code: elaborated versus restricted, and person-oriented versus object-oriented. The idealized sociolinguistic speaker-hearer would control equally all varieties of code; there is of course no such individual, but the processes of socialization of the child do demand – and normally lead to – some degree of **access** to all. It appears, however, that some extreme family types tend to limit access to certain parts of the code system **in certain critical socializing contexts**: a strongly positional family, for example, may orient its members away from the personal, elaborated quartile in precisely those contexts in which this type of code is demanded by the processes of formal education, as education is at

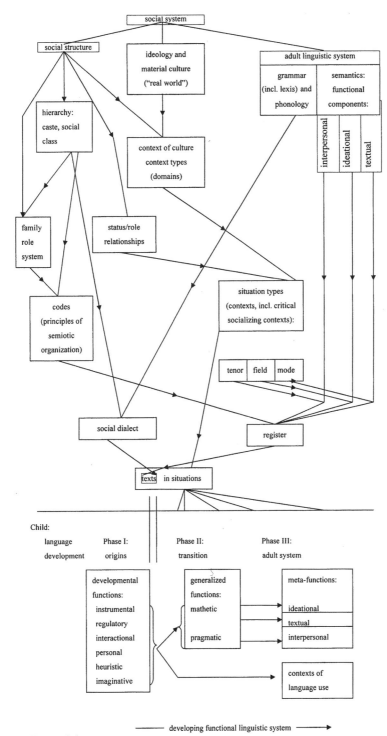

Figure 4.1

present constituted – which may be a contributory factor in the strongly social class-linked pattern of educational failure that is found in Britain, the USA and elsewhere.

It is important to avoid reifying the codes, which are not varieties of language in the sense that registers and social dialects are varieties of language. The relation of code to these other concepts has been discussed by Ruqaiya Hasan, who points out that the codes are located 'above' the linguistic system, at the semiotic level (1973: 258):

> While social dialect is defined by reference to its distinctive formal properties, the code is defined by reference to its semantic properties ... the semantic properties of the codes can be predicted from the elements of social structure which, in fact, give rise to them. This raises the concept "code" to a more general level than that of language variety; indeed there are advantages in regarding the restricted and the elaborated codes as codes of behaviour, where the word "behaviour" covers both verbal and non-verbal behaviour.

The code is actualized in language through register, the clustering of semantic features according to situation type. (Bernstein in fact uses the term "variant", e.g. "elaborated variant", to refer to those character-istics of a register which derive from the choice of code.) But the codes themselves are types of social semiotic, symbolic orders of meaning generated by the social system. Hence they transmit, or rather control the transmission of, the underlying patterns of a culture and sub-culture, acting through the primary socializing agencies of family, peer group and school.

At this point we can perhaps set up some sort of a model in which the linguistic system, and the social system in its restricted sense of social structure, are represented as integral parts of the wider reality of the social system in the more all-embracing sense of the term. For analytical purposes we will add a third component, that of "culture" in the sense of the ideological and material culture, to serve as the source of speech situations and situation types. Malinowski's context of culture (and context of situation) is the product of the social structure together with the culture in this limited sense; so are Fishman's domains. Figure 4.1 (above the line) attempts to present in schematic form the analytic relations that we have set up.

1.5

Naturally there are other components of a sociolinguistic theory which are not included in this summary. Among other things, a sociolinguistic theory implies a theory of text: not merely a methodology of text description, but a means of relating the text to its various levels of meaning. In van Dijk's (1972) account of a "text grammar", text is regarded as "continuous discourse" having a deep or macro structure "as a whole" and a surface or micro structure as a sequence of sentences; a set of transformation rules relates macro to micro structures. In other words, text is the basic linguistic unit, manifested at the surface as discourse. It cannot be described by means of sentence grammars.

Now the last point is worth underlining. The notion of the text as a super-sentence is essentially comparable to that of the sentence as a super-phoneme; it ignores the essential fact, that the two are related by realization, not by size. We have adopted here the view of the text as a **semantic** unit, irrespective of size, with sentences (and other grammatical units) as the realization of it. The essential problem, then, is that of relating, not 'macro' to 'micro' structures (which differ in size), but one **level** (stratum) to another: of relating the text not only 'downwards' to the sentences which realize it but also 'upwards' to a higher level of meaning, of which it is itself the realization or projection. Typically, in a sociolinguistic context, this refers to the sociological meanings that are realized by texts of everyday conversation, perhaps especially those involving the text in its role in cultural transmission; but these are not essentially different in kind from others such as narratives (van Dijk 1972: 273 ff.; see Labov and Waletzky 1967; Greimas, 1971), including children's narratives, and even literary texts.

To say that sociolinguistics implies a theory of text is to say no more than that it implies a **linguistic** theory, one which meets the usual requirement of specifying both system and process (in Hjelmslev's sense of the terms) at all levels (see Dixon 1965). The sentences, clauses and so on which form the material of everyday linguistic interaction (material that is already, of course, highly processed, once it can be referred to in these terms) are to be interpreted both as realizations and as instances: as the *realization* of meanings which are the *instantiation* of the meaning potential. The meaning potential is a functional potential; the analysis of text is in the last resort also functional, being such as to relate the text to the functional components of the semantic system, ideational, interpersonal and textual (or other such frame of reference). These functional components provide the channel whereby the underlying meanings are projected on to the text, via the semantic configurations that we are calling registers.[1] I shall not complicate the exposition further by trying to include in it specific reference to the various other orders of meaning, literary, psychological and so forth, that are projected on to the semantic system and thereby on to the text. But I should like to add one more dimension to the picture. This concerns the learning of language by the child, as this process appears in the light of a sociolinguistic interpretation of language development (Halliday 1975d).

1.6

A child learning his mother tongue is constructing a meaning potential: that is, he is constructing a semantic system, together with its realizations. This process seems to take place in three phases, of which the middle one is functionally transitional. The child begins (Phase I) by developing a semiotic of his own, which is not derived from the adult linguistic system that surrounds him; it is a language whose elements are simple content/expression pairs, having meaning in certain culturally defined and possibly universal functions. These functions can be enumerated tentatively as follows: instrumental, regulatory, interactional, personal, heuristic, imaginative. Typical examples from Nigel, the subject under study:

yī	instrumental: response, positive 'yes I want that'	
ʔ... walk'	regulatory: initiating, specific 'let's go for a	
adādādà	interactional: initiating, greeting + shared pleasure	'nice to see you, & shall we look at this together?'
ʔà it's	interactional: initiating, shared regret	'let's be sad; broken'

Such expressions owe nothing to the mother tongue; this is the stage at which, in many folklores, the child can talk to animals and to spirits, but adults cannot join in.

Then comes a discontinuity, round about 18 months: a point where the child ceases to recapitulate phylogeny and begins to adopt the adult model. From now on the speech around him, the text-in-situation which is a more or less constant feature of his waking environment, comes to determine his language development. He is embarked on a mastery of the adult system, which has an additional level of coding in it: a grammar (including a vocabulary), intermediate between its meanings and its sounds.

Functionally, however, there is no discontinuity; language continues to function for the child in the same contexts as before. But the interpolation of a grammatical system, besides vastly increasing the **number** of possible meanings which the system is capable of storing, also at the same time opens up a new possibility, that of functional combination: it becomes possible to mean more than one thing at once. How does the child help himself over this stage? He appears to generalize from his function set an opposition between language as doing and language as learning: the pragmatic function versus the mathetic function, let us call it. In situational terms, the pragmatic is that which demands some (verbal or non-verbal) response; the mathetic is self-sufficient and does not require a response. Nigel happened to make this distinction totally explicit by means of intonation, producing all pragmatic utterances on a rising tone and all mathetic ones on a falling tone; but that was merely his own individual strategy. The image of language as having a pragmatic and a mathetic potential appears to represent the child's operational model of the adult system at this stage.

Hence the child enters Phase II of the language-learning process with a two-way functional orientation, or grid; and this functional grid, we may assume, acts selectively on the input of text-in-situation, as a semantic filter, rejecting those particulars that are not interpretable in terms of itself, and accepting those which as it were resonate at its own functional frequencies. It is perhaps worth stressing here, in view of the prevailing notion of unstructured or degenerate input, that the utterances the child hears around him are typically both richly structured and highly grammatical, as well as being situationally relevant (see Labov 1970a); the child does not lack for evidence on which to build up his meaning potential.

In Phase II the child is in transition to the adult system. He has mastered the principle of an intermediate, lexicogrammatical level of coding; and he has also mastered the principle of dialogue, namely the adoption, assignment and acceptance (or non-acceptance) of communicative roles, which are social roles of a special kind, those that come into being only through language. The semiotic substance of the pragmatic/mathetic distinction, between language as doing and language as learning, has now been incorporated into the grammar, in the form of the functional distinction between interpersonal and ideational in the adult system. These latter are the ***metafunctions*** of the adult language: the abstract components of the semantic system which correspond to the two basic extrinsic functions of language (those which Hymes calls "social" and "referential"; see above). At the same time the child begins to build in the third component, the "textual" one; this is what makes it possible to create **text**, language that is structured in relation to the context of its use (the "context of situation"). These three components are clearly distinct in the system, as sets of options having strong internal but weak external constraints.

Here is the source of the complex nature of linguistic 'function', which causes some difficulty in the interpretation of functional theories of language, yet which is a major characteristic of the adult semiotic. On the one hand, "function" refers to the social meaning of speech acts, in contexts of language use; on the other hand, it refers to components of meaning in the language system, determining the internal organization of the system itself. But the two are related simply as actual to potential; the system is a potential for use. The linguistic system is a sociolinguistic system.

At this stage, then, the generalized functions which provide the strategy for the child to learn the meaning of the adult language, and which stand to each other in alternation, (an utterance is **either** one thing **or** the other), gradually evolve, via a mode of domination (an utterance is **mainly** one **but also** the other), into a more abstract system with the functions related in combination, by means of their realization in the grammatical system (an utterance is **both** one thing **and** the other). Apparently this enables the child to structure the input which he receives so that any one text comes to be interpreted as a combination of the same kind. To put this another way, being himself at first on any one occasion (predominantly) **either** observer **or** intruder, he can grasp the fact that the adult language allows the speaker – indeed obliges him – to be **both** observer **and** intruder at the same time. When these processes of functional development are completed, the child has effectively entered the adult language **system**; the final phase, Phase III, consists in mastering the adult **language**. Phase III, of course, continues throughout life.

I have attempted to incorporate the developmental components of the sociolinguistic universe of discourse into Figure 1; this is the part below the horizontal line. The double vertical bar cross-cutting this line, towards the left, represents the point of discontinuity in the expression, where the child begins to take over the grammar and phonology of the adult language. In the content, there is a rapid **expansion** from this point on – but no essential discontinuity.

2. Variation and change

2.1

Much of the work referred to above embodies a concept of variation. Typically, this refers to variation between different forms of language within a speech community: between languages or major sub-languages, between dialects, and between speech styles (i.e. minor dialectal variants; Labov's sense of the term). If we distinguish terminologically between *variety*, meaning the existence of (dialectal, etc.) varieties, and *variation*, meaning the movement between varieties (i.e. variety as the state, variation as the process), then the individual speaker displays variation (that is, switches) under certain sociolinguistic conditions; in the typical instance, these conditions relate to the level of formality (degree of attention paid to speech, in Labov's formulation), role relationships, topic of discourse and so on. But there may be variety without variation: this would be the idealized form of the situation studied in rural dialectology, where dialects exist but members do not switch between them.

Just as there may be variety without variation, so also there may be variation without change. Labov has demonstrated the existence of this kind of stable variation, where the variants either are not charged with social value or else are the object of conflicting values which, as it were, cancel each other out – a low prestige form may also have solidarity function, perhaps. But while variation does not always imply change, it is usually presumed to be a feature of sociolinguistic change – change that is related to social phenomena – that it is preceded by, and arises out of, variation, such variation being a product of the interaction of language with the social system, Labov's formulation is as follows (1970; in 1971: 205):

> In the course of change, there are inevitably variable rules, and these areas of variability tend to travel through the system in a wave-like motion. The leading edge of a particular linguistic change is usually within a single group, and with successive generations the newer form moves out in wider circles to other groups. Linguistic *indicators* which show social distribution but no style shift [i.e. variety without variation] represent early stages of this process. *Markers* which show both stylistic and social stratification represent the development of social reaction to the change and the attribution of social value to the

variants concerned. *Stereotypes*, which have risen to full social consciousness, may represent older cases of variation which may in fact have gone to completion; or they may actually represent stable oppositions of linguistic forms supported by two opposing sets of underlying social values.

Taken as a whole, linguistic change involves, in Labov's words, "oscillation between internal pressures and interaction with the social system"; it includes, but is not limited to, change of a "sociolinguistic" kind. The internal pressures Labov sees, as other linguists have done, as a "process of structural generalization", to be explained as a kind of grammatico-semantic equilibrium in which "there is inevitably some other structural change to compensate for the loss of information involved" (1970a; in 1971: 183). An example given is that in Trinidad English the past tense form *gave* was replaced by the present form *give*, and **therefore** the form *do give* was introduced to distinguish present from past: instead of *I give/I gave*, the same system is realized as *I do give/ I give*.

The assumption appears to be that, while sociolinguistic change takes place in the expression, at the grammatical and phonological levels, it cannot affect the content: the semantic system remains unchanged. (Sociolinguistic changes in the expression are usually presented not as changes in the system but as microscopic changes affecting certain **elements** of the system, the implication being that it is the purely internal mechanisms that bring about change in the system – including the change that is required to regulate the balance which has been impaired by socially conditioned changes affecting its elements. But, as Labov himself has pointed out elsewhere (1971), it is difficult to make a very clear-cut distinction between the system and its elements.) If this is to be understood in the limited sense that semantic changes are not brought about by accidental instances of morphological or phonological syncretism, it presumably applies whether such instances are interpreted as the outcome of social processes or not; this question is clearly beyond our present scope. But if it is taken more generally to mean that there are no other forms of linguistic change involving relations between the social system and the linguistic system, this would seem to exclude the possibility of changes of a socio-semantic kind.

Semantic change is an area in which no very clear boundary can be maintained between change that is internal and change that is socially conditioned, although the two are in principle distinguishable; it bears out Hoenigswald's observation (1971: 473) that "The internal and the

...ers is simply the encoding of the one in the other, the one point of ...trariness in the linguistic system.

...n seems possible that the key to some of the problems of areal ...ity may be found in a deeper understanding of creolization, in the ...t of recent studies. The development of areas of affinity is itself ...umably an effect of the creolization process, and hence it is not ...ntially different from historical contact processes in general, but ...er is a natural consequence of them. In the same way the large-scale ...antic innovation referred to above can also be seen as an instance of ...olization, one leading to the development of new lines of semantic ...ity which no longer follow areal (regional) patterns. Neustupny ...71), in an interesting discussion of linguistic distance in which he ...mpts to isolate the notion of "sociolinguistic distance", proposed to ...ne the condition of "contiguity" in social rather than in ...graphical terms. It is not easy to see exactly what this means; it ...not be maintained that a requirement for the development of an area ...affinity is a common social structure, since, quite apart from the ...nomenon of large-scale technical borrowing (which is typically ...ciated with the opposite situation, but might be excluded from ...sideration here), in fact the most diverse social structures are to be ...nd within regions of established linguistic affinity. Yet some concept ...a common social system, at some very abstract level, is presumably ...at is implied by the more usual but vague assertion of a 'common ...ture' as a concomitant of areal resemblances.

...At any rate, areal affinity is a fact, which demonstrates, even though it ...s not explain, that the semantic systems of different languages may be ...e – and therefore that they may be less alike. There is often difficulty ...ough of mutual comprehension within one language, for example ...ween rural and urban speakers, simply because one is rural and the ...er urban. The diachronic analogue to this areal affinity is presumably ...erational affinity; the generation gap is certainly a semiotic one, and ...robably reflected in the semantic system. We do not have the same ...em as our grandfathers, or as ourselves when young. Linguists are ...ustomed to leaving such questions in the hands of specialists in ...nmunication, mass media, pop culture and the like; but they have ...plications for the linguistic system, and for linguistic change. New ...ms of music, and new contexts of musical performance, demand new ...truments, though these are never of course totally new.

external factors in linguistic change are densely interwined, but not... inextricably so". The existence of semantic variety is traditionally taken for granted in language and culture studies; but the instances that can be cited of culturally conditioned semantic change are quite limited in their scope. These changes are typically fairly microscopic, affecting specific sub-systems, especially those concerned with the linguistic expression of social status and role; a well-known example is Friedrich's (1966) study of Russian kin terms, relating the changes in the number and kind of kinship terms in general use to changes in the structure of social relationships in Russian society. Semantic field theory, which takes the *champ de signification* as the constant and examines the changes in the meaning of the elements of the sub-system within it, also lends itself to sociocultural explanations (Trier's classic example of the field of 'knowing' in medieval German). But it seems unlikely that we should expect to find, at the semantic level, 'sociolinguistic' changes of a more general or macroscopic kind.

However, it is not so much major shifts in the linguistic system that are in question, as linguistic changes which relate to general features of the social system, or to sociological constructs that have their own validity apart from being merely a form of the explanation of linguistic phenomena. There are two types of fairly pervasive semantic change, the one well recognized, the other more problematical, that come to mind here. The first is the large-scale introduction of new vocabulary, as in periods of rapid technical innovation; the other is change in what Whorf called "fashions of speaking", or semantic styles.

The first of these processes is characterized by the appearance in the language of a large number of previously non-existent thing-meanings: objects, processes, relations and so forth, realized by a variety of means in the lexicogrammatical structure including – but not limited to – the creation of vocabulary. (To call this process "introduction of new vocabulary" is a misleading formulation; rather it is the introduction of new thing-meanings, which may or may not be expressed by new lexical elements.) One major source of insight into this process is **planned** sociolinguistic change, in the general context of language planning. The key concept in language planning is that of 'developing a language'. It is not entirely clear in which sense "develop" is being used here: does it imply that there are underdeveloped languages (in which case no doubt they should be referred to as "developing" languages – but the linguistic distinction between developed languages and others is a very dubious one), or should the term be interpreted rather in the sense of developing a film, bringing out what is already latently there?

However that may be, "developing a language" typically refers to vocabulary extension, the creation of new terms by some agency such as a commission on terminology, or at least in the course of some officially sponsored activity such as the production of reference works and textbooks.

What is the essential nature of such change, when viewed from a linguistic standpoint? Haugen (1966) refers to it as "elaboration of function", and the relevant concept is, presumably, a functional one: the language is to function in new settings, types of situation to which it has previously been unadapted. This is certainly a true perspective. But it is remarkable how little is yet known about the processes involved, especially about the natural processes of functional adaptation in non-Western languages. There is a fairly extensive literature on technical **innovation** in European languages, tracing the development of industrial and other terminologies (e.g. Wexler 1955, on the evolution of French railway terminology); and on technical vocabularies as they are found in existence in languages everywhere (folk taxonomies; e.g. Frake 1961; Conklin 1962; Basso 1967). But studies of innovation in non-European languages are rare. A notable example is Bh. Krishnamurthi's work on Telugu, investigating how the members of farming, fishing and weaving communities incorporate new thing-meanings – new techniques, new apparatus and equipment – into their own linguistic resources.

2.2

This leads us into the second heading, that of fashions of speaking. It is often held, at least implicitly, that the semantic styles associated with technical English or Russian, or political French, are inseparable from the terminologies, and have to be introduced along with them wherever they travel. Certainly it is a common reproach against speakers and writers using a newly created terminology that they tend to develop a kind of 'translationese', a way of meaning that is derived from English or whatever second language is the main source of innovation, rather than from the language they are using. No doubt it is easier to imitate than to create in the developing language semantic configurations which incorporate the new terminological matter into existing semantic styles. But this is not exactly the point at issue. There is no reason to expect all ideologies to be modelled on the semiotic structure of Standard Average European; there are other modes of meaning in literature than the poetry and the drama of Renaissance

Europe, and it will not be surprising to find oth elsewhere in the social system, including the intellectual activity. This is not to say, however, never change. The alternative in the development of that of either becoming European or staying as i becoming European or becoming something else, di it is but more closely following its own existing patt

It is very unlikely that one part of the semantic syst totally isolated from another; when new meanings are a large scale, we should expect some changes in speaking. It is far from clear how these take place; quite inadequate to interpret the innovations simp subject matter. The changes that are brought about in media, genres, participants and participant relations, al of the situation. New registers are created, whi alignments and configurations in the functional co semantic system. It is through the intermediary of th that the semantic change is brought about. Semantic of the social relationships and situation types genera structure. If it changes, this is not so much because o now speaking **about** as because of who they are spea circumstances, through what media and so on. A shift speaking will be better understood by reference to cha social interaction and social relationships than by the s link between the language and the material culture.

2.3

One phenomenon that shows up the existence of 'sociolinguistic' factor in semantic change is that Abdulaziz (1971) has drawn attention to the areal whereby speakers of East African languages, whether th Swahili or not, find Swahili easier to handle than Engli very high degree of intertranslatability between Swahi language. Gumperz and Wilson's account (1971) identity of Marathi, Kannada and Urdu as spoken in a India along the Marathi-Kannada border is especially respect. Since such instances are typically also characte degree of phonological affinity, the idealized case of a be characterized in Hjelmslevian terms as one in wh systems are identical and the expression systems are

3.1

As with other levels of the linguistic system, the normal condition of the semantic system is one of change. The specific nature of the changes that take place, and their relation to external factors, may be more readily understood if we regard the semantic system as being itself the projection (encoding, realization) of some higher level of extra-linguistic meaning.

From a sociolinguistic viewpoint, the semantic system can be defined as a functional or function-oriented meaning potential; a network of options for the encoding of some extra-linguistic semiotic system or systems in terms of the two basic components of meaning that we have called the ideational and the interpersonal. In principle this higher-level semiotic system may be viewed in the tradition of humanist thought as a conceptual or cognitive system, one of information about the real world. But it may equally be viewed as a semiotic of some other type, logical, ideological, aesthetic – or social. Here it is the social perspective that is relevant, the semantic system as realization of a social semiotic; in the words of Mary Douglas (1971: 389),

> If we ask of any form of communication the simple question what is being communicated? the answer is: information from the social system. The exchanges which are being communicated constitute the social system.

Information from the social system has this property, that it is, typically, presented in highly context-specific doses. Whereas a logical semantics may be a monosystem, a social semantics is and must be a polysystem, a set of sets of options in meaning, each of which is referable to a given social context, situation type or domain.

The semantic system is an interface, between the (rest of the) linguistic system, and some higher order symbolic system. It is a projection, or realization, of the social system; at the same time it is projected on to, or realized by, the lexico-grammatical system. It is in this perspective that the sociolinguistic conditions of semantic change may become accessible.

Let us illustrate the notion of a context-specific semantics from two recent studies. In both cases for the sake of simplicity I will choose very small sets of options, sets which, moreover, form a simple taxonomy. The first is from Turner, somewhat modified. Turner, on the basis of a number of investigations by Bernstein and his colleagues in London, constructs a semantic network for a certain type of regulative context within the family, involving general categories of parental control strategy: "imperative", "positional" and "personal". Each of these is then further sub-categorized, "imperative" into "threat of loss of privilege" and "threat of punishment", "positional" into "disapprobation", "rule-giving", "reparation-seeking" and "positional explanation", "personal" into "recognition of intent" and "personal explanation". Figure 4. 2 shows the system under "threat of loss of privilege"; these are the options that have been shown to be available to the mother who selects this form of control behaviour.

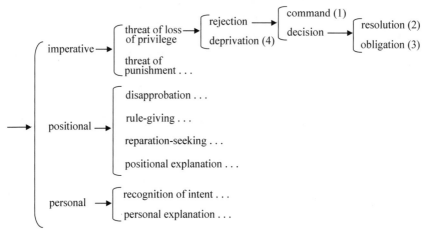

Figure 4.2

In order to show how these options are typically realized in the lexico-grammatical system, we indicate the contribution that each makes to the final structure of the sentence (references are to paragraphs in Roget's *Thesaurus*):

rejection: material process, Roget § 293 Departure or
              § 287 Recession: Hearer *you* = Affected; positive
command: "middle" type; imperative, jussive, exclusive
decision: either "middle" type, or (rarer) "non-middle"
              (active, Speaker *I* = Agent); indicative,
              declarative
resolution: future tense
obligation: modulation, necessity
deprivation: material process, benefactive, Roget § 784
              Giving; "non-middle" type; (optional) Speaker
              I = Agent; Hearer *you* = Beneficiary; indicative,
              declarative; future tense; negative

Examples:

(1) you go on outside
(2) you're going upstairs in a minute
(3) I'll have to take you up to bed
(4) you're not going to be given a sweet/I shan't buy you anything

Taken as a whole the system reveals correlation at a number of points with social class, as well as with other social factors; for example, in the investigation from which this is taken, significantly more middle-class mothers than working-class mothers selected the 'rule-giving' type of positional control.

The second example is taken from Coulthard *et al.* (1972). For a fuller representation of this semantic network, see figure 4.3 from Halliday 1975e; see Sinclair *et al.* 1972 for a fuller report. This is a study of semantics in the classroom. The socializing agent is the school, where presumably regulative and instructional contexts are inseparably associated. The authors investigated the options open to the teacher for the initiation of discourse: he may select "direct", which is predominantly regulative in intent, or he may select "inform" or "elicit", which are predominantly instructional. Figure 4.4 shows some of the options under the "directive" heading; the form of presentation is adapted to match that of Turner.

The unmarked modal realization of the "directive" category is the imperative; but there are marked options in which the other moods occur. "Proscribed action" (1) is a behavioural directive which may be realized through imperative, declarative or interrogative clause types. Directives relating to non-proscribed actions may be (2) isolated exchanges (behavioural) or (3) parts of interactions (procedural); they may be (4) requests, encoded in the various modal forms, or (5) references to an action which ought to have been performed but has not been, typically in past tense interrogative. (see Ervin-Tripp 1969; in 1971: 56 ff.)

Examples:

(1) don't rattle/what are you laughing at/someone is still whistling
(2,4) will you open the door?/I want you to stop talking now
(2,5) did you open that door?
(3,4) you must all stop writing now
(3,5) have you finished?

These illustrations are, of course, very specific in their scope; but they bring out the general point that, in order to relate the linguistic realization

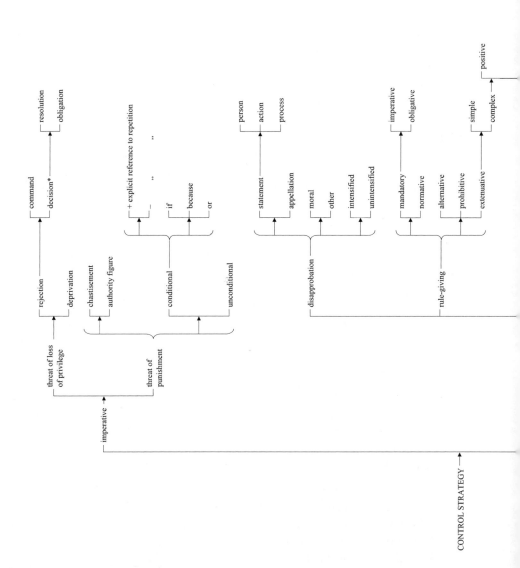

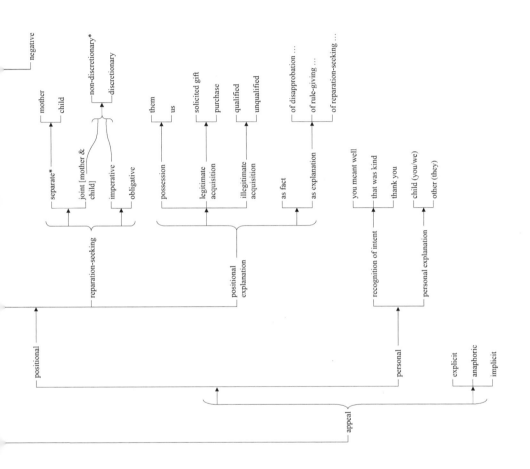

Test situations:

What would you do if — brought you a bunch of flowers and you found out that he/she had got them from a neighbour's garden?

Imagine — had been out shopping with you and when you got home you found he/she'd picked some little thing from one of the counters without you noticing. What should you say or do?

Figure 4.3 Semantic system for a class of regulative [social control] situations

of social meanings to the linguistic system, it is necessary to depart from the traditional monolithic conception of that system, at least at the semantic level, and to consider instead the particular networks of meanings that are operative in particular social contexts. How these various semantic systems combine and reinforce each other to produce a coherent, or reasonably coherent, world view is a problem in what Berger and Kellner call the "microsociology of knowledge". In their analysis of the sociology of marriage, they interpret the marriage relation as a continuing conversation, and observe (1970: 61) "In the marital conversation, a world is not only built, but it is also kept in a state of repair and ongoingly refurnished". This is achieved through the cumulative effect of innumerable microsemiotic encounters, in the course of which all the various semantic sub-systems are brought into play.

3.2

Hymes made the point several years ago that " the role of language may differ from community to community" (1966: 116). Hymes was making a distinction between what he called two types of linguistic relativity: cross-cultural variation in the system (the fashions of speaking, or "cognitive styles" as he called them) and cross-cultural variation in its uses.

But we should not press this distinction too hard. The system is merely the user's potential, or the potential for use; it is what the speaker-hearer 'can mean'. This semantic potential we are regarding as one form of the projection of his symbolic behaviour potential: the "sociosemiotic" system, to use Greimas' term. In any given context of use – a given situation type, in a given social structure – the member disposes of networks of options, sets of semiotic alternatives, and these are realized through the semantic system. From this point of view, as suggested in the last section, the semantic system appears as a set of sub-systems each associated with a particular domain, or context of use. What we refer to as "the system" is an abstract conceptualization of the totality of the user's potential in actually occurring situation types.

In other words, different groups of people tend to mean different things. Hymes is undoubtedly right in recognizing cross-cultural variation in the system, and it would not be surprising if we also find intracultural (i.e. cross-subcultural) variation. One may choose to separate this observation from the observation that different groups of people tend to use language in different ways, using the one observation to explain the other; but in any case, the fact has be accounted for, and

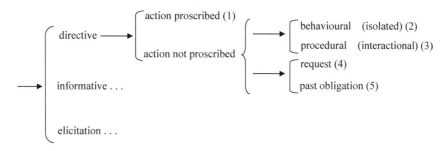

Figure 4.4

cannot readily be accommodated in a conceptual framework which imposes a rigid boundary between competence and performance and reduces the system to an idealized competence which is invariable and insulated from the environment.

Labov has shown how, under conditions of social hierarchy, social pressures act selectively on phonological and grammatical variables, leading to variation and change. How far do such pressures also operate in the case of semantic change? Although Labov himself does not consider the semantic level, his work on non-standard varieties of English has important implications for this question.

In a recent paper (1970b), Labov gives a lively discussion of Negro Non-Standard English for the purpose of demonstrating that it is just as grammatical and just as "logical" as any of the "standard" forms of the language. This is not news to linguists, for whom it has always been a cardinal axiom of their subject; this is why, as Joan Baratz pointed out once, linguists have rarely taken the trouble to deny the various myths and folk-beliefs about the illogicality of non-standard forms. There is no doubting the logicalness of all linguistic systems. But although all linguistic systems are equally 'logical', they may differ in their semantic organization; and there have been serious discussions about the possibility of "deep structure" differences – which we may interpret as semantic differences – among the different varieties of English (Loflin 1969).

It may be tempting to take it for granted that all varieties of a language must be semantically identical, since as we know there are many people who misinterpret variety in evaluative terms: if two systems differ, they hold, then one must be better than the other. It has been difficult enough to persuade the layman to accept forms of English which differ phonologically form the received norm, and still more so those which differ grammatically; there would probably be even greater resistance to the notion of semantic differences. But one should not be browbeaten by these attitudes into rejecting the possibility of sub-cultural variety in the semantic system. In the words of Louis Dumont (1970; 1972: 289),

> The oneness of the human species ... does not demand the arbitrary reduction of diversity to unity; it only demands that it should be possible to pass from one particularity to another, and that no effort should be spared in order to elaborate a common language in which each particularity can be adequately described.

It is not too difficult to interpret this possibility of sub-cultural differences at the semantic level on the basis of a combination of Labov's theories with those of Bernstein. Labov, presumably, is using the term "logic" in his title in imitation of those who assert that non-standard English 'has no logic'; the meaning is 'logicalness', the property of being logical, rather than the **kind** of logic that it displays. There is no reason to believe that one language or language variety has a different logic from another. But this does not mean their semantic systems must be identical. Labov's findings could, with enough contrivance, be reduced to differences of grammar – thereby robbing them of any significance. What they in fact display are differences of semantic style, code-regulated habits of meaning, presumably trans-mitted through social and family structure, that distinguish one sub-culture from another. Bernstein's work provides a theoretical basis for the understanding of this kind of semantic variety, making it possible to envisage a social semiotic of a sufficiently general kind. Some such theory of language and social structure is a prerequisite for the interpretation of sociolinguistic phenomena, including Labov's own findings and the principles he derives from them. It is all the more to be regretted, therefore, that Labov included in his valuable polemic some ill-founded and undocumented criticisms of Bernstein's work; e.g. "The notion is first drawn from Bernstein's writings that ...", followed by a quotation from somebody else which is diametrically opposed to Bernstein's ideas. (Because of his misunderstanding of Bernstein, Labov assumes – one must assume that he assumes it, since otherwise his criticism would lose its point – that the speech which he quotes from Larry is a example of restricted code; in other words, Labov appears to confuse Bernstein's "code" with social dialect, despite Bernstein's explicit distinction between the two (1971: 199, but clear already in 1971: 128, first published in 1965); (see again Hasan 1973). It is my impression that in Larry's speech as Labov represents it the controlling code is predominantly an elaborated one, although it is impossible to categorize such small speech samples with any real significance; but in any case, as Bernstein has been at pains to establish, differences of code are relative – they are tendencies, or orientations, within which each individual displays considerable variation: a fact which helps to explain some of Labov's own findings.)[2] Bernstein would, I have no doubt, agree with the points that Labov purports to make against him; but more important than that, Bernstein's work provides the necessary theoretical support for Labov's own ideas, Since this work has been misunderstood in some quarters it may be helpful to attempt a brief recapitulation of it here.

3.3

We can, I think, identify three stages in the development of Bernstein's theoretical ideas. In the first stage, roughly prior to 1960, Bernstein examined the pattern of educational failure in Britain, and attempted an explanation of it in terms of certain non-linguistic projections of the social system, particularly modes of perception. In the second stage, roughly 1960–65, he came to grips not only with language but also with linguistics, and came up with certain linguistic findings, of considerable interest but still of a rather unsystematic kind. In the third stage he combined his two previous insights and sought explanations in terms of a social semiotic, with the linguistic semiotic, i.e. semantics, as its focal point. This has meant a major step towards a genuinely 'sociolinguistic' theory – one that is at once both a theory of language and a theory of society.

Berstein had begun with the observation that educational failure was distributed non-randomly in the population, tending to correlate with social class; the lower the family in the social scale, the greater the child's chances of failure. Clearly there was some incompatibility between lower working-class social norms and the middle-class ethos and the educational system based on it. The pattern emerged most starkly as a discrepancy between measures of verbal and non-verbal intelligence: the discrepancy was significantly greater in the lower working class – and it tended to increase with age. There was, obviously, therefore, a linguistic element in the process, and Bernstein developed his first version of the "code" theory to try to account for it: "elaborated code" represented the more verbally explicit, context-independent type of language, one which maintained social distance, demanded individuated responses, and made no assumptions about the hearer's intent; while the "restricted code" was the more verbally implicit, context-dependent, socially intimate form in which the hearer's intent could be taken for granted and hence responses could be based on communalized norms. Education as at present organized demanded elaborated code; therefore, if any social group had, by virtue of its patterns of socialization, only partial or conditional control over this code, that group would be at a disadvantage.

Harried by the linguists, Bernstein attempted to define the codes in linguistic terms, beginning with inventories of features and progressing towards a concept of 'syntactic prediction' according to which elaborated code was characterized by a wider range of syntactic choices, restricted code by a more limited range. Those like myself who categorically rejected this interpretation were partly confounded by some interesting early studies which showed that, in the performance of certain tasks, the amount of grammatical variation that was found in respect of (i) modification in the nominal group and (ii) the use of modalities, by children of various ages, was in fact linked to social class. It was clear, however, that any significant linguistic generalizations that could be made would be at the semantic level, since it was through meanings that the codes were manifested in language. Bernstein then went on to identify a small number of "critical socializing contexts", generalized situation types from which the child, in the milieu of the primary socializing agencies of family, peer group and school, derives his essential information about the social system. The hypothesis was that, in a given context, say that of parental control of the child's behaviour, various different sub-systems within the semantic system might typically be deployed; hence the "codes" could be thought of as differential orientation to areas of meaning in given social situations.

It seemed that if in some sense access to the codes is controlled by social class, this control was achieved through the existence of different family types, defined in terms of role relationships within the family: the "positional" and "personal" family types (see 1.3. above). With important qualifications and sub-categorizations, it appeared that strongly positional families would tend towards restricted-code forms of interaction – at least in their modes of parental control, in the regulative context. Family types do not coincide with classes; but it is likely that, in the British context, the more purely positional family is found most frequently among the lower working class – just that section of the population where the proportion of educational failure is the highest. The model then looks something like this:

(different) social classes

(different) family role systems

(different) semiotic codes

(different) "orders of meaning and relevance"

The later development of Bernstein's thought is set out in the final papers of *Class, Codes and Control*, Vol. I, which are too rich to be summarized in a short space. Bernstein's theory is a theory of social learning and cultural transmission, and hence of social persistence and social change. As Mary Douglas puts it (1972: 312),

> Whatever [Bernstein] does, ... he looks at four elements in the social process. First the system of control, second the boundaries it sets up, third the justification or ideology which sanctifies the boundaries, and fourth he looks at the power which is hidden by the rest ...
> I think Professor Bernstein's work is the first to argue that the distribution of speech forms in equally a realization of the distribution of power.

It is a theory of society in which language plays a central part, both as determiner and as determined: language is controlled by the social structure, and the social structure is maintained and transmitted through language. Hence it offers the foundation for interpreting processes of semantic change.

3.4

In terms of the framework we set up in the first section, there are two possible mechanisms of socio-semantic change: feedback and transmission – that is, feedback from the text to the system, and transmission of the system to the child. As far as feedback is concerned, there is the possibility of changes in the meanings that are typically associated with particular contexts or situation types, taking place in the course of time. These changes come about, for example, through changes in the family role systems, under conditions which Bernstein has suggested; or through other social factors – changes in educational ideologies, for example. Such changes could relate to rather specific situation types, such as those in the two illustrations given above.

We are familiar with instances of small sub-systems realizing specific areas of symbolic behaviour. A good example is the "pronouns of power and solidarity" (Brown and Gilman 1960). The semantic system of Modern English is quite different at this point from that of Elizabethan English, so much so that we can no longer even follow for example the detailed subtleties and the shifts which take place in the personal relationship of Celia and Rosalind in *As You Like It*, which is revealed by their sensitive switching between *thou* and *you* (McIntosh 1963). This is simply not in our semantic system. But such instances are limited, not only in that they represent somewhat specific semantic options but also in that they reflect **only those social relationships that are created by language** (and that do not exist independently of language: the form *you* has meaning only as the encoding of a purely linguistic relationship) – or else, as in the case of changes in the use of kin terms, they affect only the direct expression of the social relationships themselves. Bernstein's work allows us to extend beyond these limited instances in two significant ways. First, it provides an insight into how the relations within the social system may come to shape and modify **other** meanings that language expresses, which may be meanings of any kind; socio-semantic variation and change is not confined to the semantics of interpersonal communication. Second, in the light of a functional account of the semantic system, Bernstein's work suggests how the changes in speech patterns that are brought about in this way become incorporated into the system, as a result of the innumerable small momenta of social interaction, and so have an effect on other options, not disturbing the whole system (whatever that would mean), but reacting specifically on those options that are functionally related to them.

Then there is transmission, and here we have considered the child's learning of the mother tongue from a sociolinguistic point of view: suggesting that the developmental origins of the semantic system are to be sought in the systems of meaning potential deriving from certain primary functions of language – instrumental, regulatory and so on. Let us postulate that a particular socializing agency, such as the family, tends to favour one set of functions over another: that is, to respond more positively to the child's meanings in that area, at least in certain significant socializing contexts. Then the semantic system associated with such contexts will show a relative orientation towards those areas of meaning potential. An indication of how this may come about at an early age is given in an interesting study by Katherine Nelson (1971), which suggests that the combination of educational level of parent with position of child in family may lead to differential semantic orientations and thus influence the child's functional strategy for language learning.

There is nothing surprising in this; it would be surprising if it was otherwise. The question that is of interest is to what extent such functional orientations become incorporated into the system. We noted earlier that the child, having begun by inventing his own language, in which the **expression** is unrelated to adult speech, at a certain point abandons the phylogenetic trail and takes over the adult system; there is a discontinuity in the realization. But there is (we suggested) no **functional** discontinuity; the child continues to build on the functional origins of the system, generalizing out of his original functional set a basic distinction of pragmatic versus mathetic – a pragmatic, or 'doing' function, which demands a response from the hearer, and a mathetic or 'learning' function, which is realized through observation, recall and prediction and which is self-sufficient: it demands no response from anyone. This, in turn, is a transitional pattern, which serves to transform the functional matrix so that it becomes the core of the adult language, taking the form of the ideational/interpersonal components in the semantic network; hence there is functional continuity in the **system**. At the same time the primary functions evolve into social contexts, the situation types encountered in the course of daily life. For example, the original interactional function of calls and responses to those on whom the child was emotionally dependent develops into the general interpersonal context within the family and peer group; the imaginative function of sound-play develops into that of songs and rhymes and stories; and so on. Thus there is functional continuity of **use**, that is, in the **contexts in which selections are made from within the system**. The meanings engendered by the social system, in other words, are such that the child is predisposed by his own glossogenic experience to adapt the linguistic mode of meaning to them.

Naturally, he 'makes semantic mistakes' in the process, mistakes which are often revealing. For example, my own subject Nigel at one stage learnt the grammatical distinction between declarative and interrogative. He located it, correctly, in the interpersonal component in the system, and related it to contexts of the exchange of information. But having at the time no concept of asking yes/no questions (i.e. isolating the polarity element in the demand for information), he used the system to realize a semantic distinction which he did make but which the adult language does not, namely that between imparting information to someone who knows it already, who has shared the relevant experience with him (declarative), and imparting information to someone who has not shared the experience and so does not know it (interrogative). Thus for example on one occasion while playing with his father he fell down; he got up and said to his father *you fell down* (*you* referred to himself at this stage). Then his mother, who had not been present, came into the room; he ran up to her and said *did you fall down?* The use of *you* and the use of the interrogative are of course connected; they are both (at the intraorganism level) aspects of the non-internalization of role-playing speech. But the modal pattern reveals a small semantic sub-system, not present in the adult language, which is both stable in terms of the child's meaning potential at the time, and transitional in the wider developmental context.

The functional continuity that we have postulated, according to which both the linguistic system itself and its environment evolve out of the initial set of functions which define the child's earliest acts of meaning, accounts for the fact that the child's meaning potential may develop different orientations under different environmental conditions – including, therefore, under the control of different symbolic codes. "The social structure becomes the developing child's psychological reality by the shaping of his act of speech" (Bernstein 1971: 124). If there are changes in the social structure, especially changes affecting the family role systems, these may lead to changes in the child's orientation towards or away from certain ways of meaning in certain types of situation; and this, particularly in the environment of what Bernstein calls the "critical socializing contexts", may lead to changes in learning strategies, and hence to changes in the meaning potential that is typically associated with various environments – i.e. in the semantic system. These changes in meaning potential would take place gradually and without essential discontinuity. A socio-semantic change of this kind does not necessarily imply, and probably usually does not imply, the complete disappearance of a semantic choice, or the appearance of a totally new one. It is likely to mean rather that certain choices become more, or less, differentiated; or that certain choices are more, or less, frequently taken up. These things too are features of the system. It seems possible, therefore, that semantic changes may be brought about by changes in the social structure, through the operation of the sort of processes described by Labov, in the course of the transmission of language to the child.[3]

The transmission of language is at the same time the linguistic transmission of the culture; the two cannot be separated. Along with many others, including Hymes, Fishman and Labov, I find the concept of 'sociolinguistics' unnecessary; if the goal is the pursuit of system-in-language (Fishman 1971: 8), this is simply linguistics, and linguistics always has, throughout all its shifts of emphasis, accepted what Hymes (1967) calls the "sociocultural dimensions of its subject-matter", the link between language and the social factors that must be adduced to explain observed linguistic phenomena. By the same token, however, we do not need "communicative competence", which has to be adduced only if the system has first been isolated from its social context. If we insist on adopting the 'intraorganism' perspective implied by the notion of competence, looking at 'what the speaker-hearer knows' as distinct from what he can do, then competence **is** communicative competence; there is no other kind (see Hymes 1971). But this is itself a needless complication. The system can be represented directly in 'interorganism' terms, as social interaction; it is 'what the speaker-hearer can do', and more specifically what he can mean. We only know what he knows in the light of what he is able to mean.

The sociology of language is a different question, as Fishman says; here the aims are wider than the characterization of the linguistic system. Sociology of language implies the theoretical relation of the linguistic system to prior, independently established sociological concepts, as in Bernstein's work, where each theory is contingent on the other: the linguistic system is as essential to the explanation of social phenomena as is the social system to the explanation of linguistic phenomena.

In considering the social conditions of linguistic change, we are asking not only the 'sociolinguistic' question, to what extent are changes in the linguistic system relatable to social factors, but also, and perhaps more, the sociology of language question, to what extent are changes in the linguistic system essential concomitants of features of (including changes in) the social system. Labov's work on phonetic change has not yet so far as I know been taken up by sociologists; but it reveals patterns and principles of intra- and inter-group communication which seem to me to have considerable significance for theories of social interaction and social hierarchy. And from another angle, Bernstein's research into language in the transmission of culture is equally central both to an understanding of language, including language development in children and linguistic change, and to an understanding of society, of persistence and change in the social structure. Here we are in a genuine inter-discipline of sociology and

167

linguistics, an area of convergence of two different sets of theories, and ways of thinking about people.

Bernstein once reproached sociologists for not taking into account the fact that humans speak. If linguists seek to understand the phenomena of persistence and change in the linguistic system – how the innermost patterns both of language and of culture are transmitted through the countless microsemiotic processes of social interaction – we for our part must learn to take account of the fact that humans speak, not in solitude, but to each other.

Notes

1. See in this connection Zumthor's characterization of medieval poetry (1972: 171): 'Nombreuses sont les textes où l'une des deux fonctions, idéationnelle ou interpersonnelle, domine absolument, au point d'estomper, parfois d'effacer presque, les effets de l'autre. C'est là, me semble-t-il, un trait fondamental de la poésie médiévale'.
2. It is astonishing that Labov finds in Bernstein a "bias against all forms of working-class behavior"; if anything, Bernstein's sympathies would seem to be the other way. As Mary Douglas puts it, "As far as the family is concerned, Basil Bernstein betrays a preference for "positional" control rather than for "personal" appeals ... [His] analysis cuts us, the middle class parents, down to size. Our verbosity and insincerity and fundamental uncertainty are revealed ... The elaborated code is far from glorious when the hidden implications of the central system that generates it are laid bare". In a generous letter to *The Atlantic* (Vol. 230 no. 5 November 1972), Labov has expressed regret for any way in which his own writings have led to a misinterpretation of Bernstein's work.
3. This in no way conflicts with the point made by Weinreich, Labov and Herzog (p. 145) that "the child normally acquires his particular dialect pattern, including recent changes, from children only slightly older than himself". In fact the whole of the present discussion depends on some general interpretation of linguistic change along the lines of the article just quoted, which is of major importance in the field.

Chapter Five

Language as Social Semiotic: Towards a General Sociolinguistic Theory (1975)[1]

Introductory

Probably the most significant feature of linguistics in the 1970s is that man has come back into the centre of the picture. As a species, of course, he was always there: his brain, so the argument ran, has evolved in a certain way – *ergo*, he can talk. But truly speaking man does not talk; **men** talk. People talk to each other; and it is this aspect of man's humanity, largely neglected in the dominant linguistics of the 1960s, that has emerged to claim attention once more.

Linguistics is a necessary part of the study of people in their environment; and their environment consists, first and foremost, of other people. Man's ecology is primarily a social ecology, one which defines him as 'social man'; and we cannot understand about social man if we do not understand about language. In order to suggest this perspective, linguists came to talk of "sociolinguistics"; and this term has been repeatedly discussed and evaluated in relation to various quasi-synonyms such as "sociological linguistics", proposed by Firth (1935), "institutional linguistics" (Hill 1958) and "sociology of language" (Fishman 1967). There is some consensus to the effect that the study of language in its social context is simply an aspect or facet of linguistics, while anything that is interpreted as significant covariation between

'Language as Social Semiotics: Towards a General Sociolinguistic Theory', from Adam Makkai and Valerie Becker Makkai (eds.), *The First LACUS Forum*, 17–46, (1975). Copyright © Hornbeam Press, California. **[Acknowledgement for chapter: 'The paper was first published in LACUS Forum I, 1975, published by the Linguistics Association of Canada and the United States].**

linguistic and sociological phenomena lies beyond the boundaries of linguistics properly so-called. In practice, however, "sociolinguistics" continues to be used as a cover name for a variety of different topics ranging from linguistic demography at one end to the sociology of knowledge at the other; and the question arises to what extent these very disparate areas of enquiry have anything in common. Is there any sort of integrated picture of the relation of language to other social phenomena, a general framework expressing the social meaning of language, to which these studies relate and through which they relate to each other? It is the intention of the present paper to explore this question. It may be said in advance that, while nothing so definite as a conclusion will be reached, the terminal direction will be towards integration – towards eliminating boundaries rather than imposing them, and towards a unifying conception of language as a form of social semiotic.

Sociolinguistics sometimes appears to be a search for answers which have no questions. Let us therefore enumerate at this point some of the questions that do seem to need answering.

1. How do people decode the highly condensed utterances of everyday speech, and how do they use the social system for doing so?
2. How do people reveal the ideational and interpersonal environment within which what they are saying is to be interpreted? In other words, how do they construct the social contexts in which meaning takes place?
3. How do people relate the social context to the linguistic system? In other words how do they deploy their meaning potential in actual semantic exchanges?
4. How and why do people of different social class or other sub-cultural groups develop different dialectal varieties and different orientations towards meaning?
5. How far are children of different social groups exposed to different verbal patterns of primary socialization, and how does this determine their reactions to secondary socialization especially in school?
6. How and why do children learn the functional-semantic system of the adult language?
7. How do children, through the ordinary everyday linguistic inter-action of family and peer group, come to learn the basic patterns of the culture: the social structure, the systems of knowledge and values, and the diverse elements of the social semiotic?

1. Some areas of sociolinguistic research

A list of topics that come under the heading of sociolinguistics might include the following (from Chapter 4, above):

1. Macrosociology of language; linguistic demography
2. Diglossia; multilingualism and multidialectalism
3. Language planning; development and standardization
4. Pidginization and creolization
5. Social dialectology; description of non-standard varieties
6. Educational sociolinguistics
7. Ethnography of speaking; speech situations
8. Register; verbal repertoire and code switching
9. Social factors in phonological and grammatical change
10. Language and socialization; language in the transmission of culture
11. Sociolinguistic approach to language development in children
12. Functional theories of the linguistic system
13. Linguistic relativity
14. Microsociology of knowledge (ethnomethodological linguistics)
15. Theory of text.

We shall try to take up some of the questions that have been being investigated under these headings, in order to suggest where they link up with each other and to see how far they already form part of a general pattern.

1.1 Linguistic interaction

Somehow the participants in speech encounters interpret one another's symbolic behaviour; they assign each other roles and statuses, accept and act on instructions and explanations, and in general exchange meanings which derive from every kind of social context. They do this first and foremost by attending to text, which is language in a context of situation – language in the environment of other semiotic structures and processes. But we have very little conception of **how** they do it. Cicourel (1969) suggests that participants operate with four interpretative principles, "reciprocity of perspective", "normal forms", "the "etcetera" principle" and "descriptive vocabulary as indexical expressions". In other words, each individual assumes that others (i) see things in the same way as he does, (ii) agree on what to leave out, (iii) fill in what has been left out and (iv) use language in the same way to refer to past experience. These principles act as "instructions for the speaker-hearer for assigning infinitely possible meanings to unfolding social scenes".

Similar ideas are embodied in ethnomethodological linguistic studies such as those of Sacks and Schegloff, for example Schegloff's account of how people refer to location. Schegloff (1971) shows that the speaker derives from the context of situation the relevant criteria for deciding which of a number of possible strategies for identifying places and persons is the 'right' one in the particular circumstances; and he concludes that "interactants are context-sensitive". This is similar to the way in which a speaker selects the appropriate information focus, distributing the text into meanings that he is treating as recoverable to the hearer ("given") and meanings he is treating as non–recoverable ("new") (Halliday 1967b). It is important to stress that a speaker also has the option of being 'wrong' – of deliberately organizing the meaning in a way that runs counter to the context of situation, with marked rhetorical effect.

The difficulty of integrating linguistic interaction studies with other areas of sociolinguistic research lies mainly in the lack of an explicit formulation of the relationship between the text, which is the ***process*** of interaction, and the linguistic ***system***. How are the participants exploiting their semantic potential? And how does this potential relate systematically to features of the context of situation? We need answers to these questions if we are to make generalizations about how semiotic acts are encoded in language and linguistic meanings interpreted as semiotic acts.

1.2 The ecology of speech

From a sociolinguistic standpoint a text is meaningful not so much because the hearer does not know what the speaker is going to say, as in a mathematical model of communication, as because he does know. He has abundant evidence, both from his knowledge of the general (including statistical) properties of the linguistic system and from his sensibility to the particular cultural, situational and verbal context; and this enables him to make informed guesses about the meanings that are coming his way.

The speaker's selection of options in the production of text is regulated by the 'theory and system of speaking' in the culture (Hymes 1967). Hymes postulates that the member has access to a set of sociolinguistic principles or "rules of speaking", so that he knows "when to speak and when to remain silent, which code to use, when, where and to whom, etc."; in Grimshaw's (1971) interpretation, he makes "generalizations about relationships among components" of the speech situation. What are the components of the speech situation? Hymes' own formulation may be summarized as: the form and content of the message, the setting, the participants, the intent and the effect of the communication, the key, the medium, the genre and the norms of interaction. An example of an earlier formulation is provided by Firth (1950): the participants – their statuses and roles, the relevant features of the setting, the verbal and non-verbal action, and the effective result.

The difficulty of relating these notions to other sociolinguistic concepts lies in the fact that we do not know what kind of theoretical validity to ascribe to lists such as these. What are we to understand by "situation", and what is its relation to the text? Both Firth and Hymes include the text itself among the "features" or "components" of the situation: Firth's "verbal action of the participants", Hymes' "form and content of the message". But we shall need to conceive of the 'situation' in more abstract terms, and of situational features as **determinants** of the text, enabling us to predict what the speaker is going to say in the same way that the hearer does (see Hymes 1971). Otherwise it is impossible to relate the text systematically to its environment (or Hymes' ethnography of speaking to Sacks' theory of linguistic interaction).

1.3 Functional theories of language

These have been mainly of four kinds: anthropological, e.g. Malinowski (1923, 1935); psychological, e.g. Bühler (1934); ethological, e.g. Morris (1967); or educational, e.g. Britton (1970). All these have in common the property of being extrinsic in orientation: they are not concerned with language as object but with language in the explanation of other phenomena. Hence they are meant to be interpreted as generalizations about language use rather than as explanations of the nature of the linguistic system (see Greenberg 1963, Chapter 7).

All these theories incorporate in one form or another the basic distinction between two primary semiotic roles that language serves: an ideational role, that of **being about** something, and an interpersonal role, that of **doing** something. Essentially the same distinction is expressed in the pairs of terms "narrative/active"; "representational (or "informative")/expressive and conative"; "cognitive/social"; "semantic/stylistic". Hymes uses the terms "referential/social" (also "socio-expressive" and "stylistic"); he interprets the distinction as one between types of meaning expressed by different linguistic resources: "Languages have conventional units, structures and relations ... that are what I shall call "stylistic" (serving social meaning) as well as referential" (1969). Linguists of the Prague School recognized a third component, which they called "functional sentence perspective"; this is the text-forming or textual role that language serves, and it is a role that is purely intrinsic to language (Daneš (ed.) 1974). So there is a general conception of language as serving two major functions; to which a third has to be added, of a somewhat different kind because intrinsic to language itself, if the functions are to be related systematically to linguistic structure.

The difficulty with the concept of functions of language, and its relation to a general sociolinguistics, is that the functions as usually conceived are neither concrete enough nor abstract enough. On the one hand it is difficult to relate them to the text, to what people actually say, since people nearly always seem to be using language in more than one 'function' at once; and on the other hand it is difficult to relate them to the linguistic system, because there are not, in fact, any recognizable linguistic entities – words, or grammatical constituents – that can be identified as serving just this or just that function, as expressing one type of meaning and not others. The problem arises through a false equation of 'function' with 'use'. It is necessary to separate these two concepts in the sociolinguistic context, and also to suggest how they may come to be separated developmentally in the course of the learning of the mother tongue (Halliday 1975c).

1.4 Variety, variation and variability

It has always been recognized that dialectal variety in language reflected the social as well as the geographical provenance of the speaker, but it was Labov's highly original studies of urban speech patterns which effectively extended the scope of dialectology from the regional to the social dimension (1966).

Unlike rural dialects, which could be and traditionally have been treated as systems of invariant forms, urban dialects display patterns of inherent variation. A city-dweller, at least in our society, typically switches among a range of different forms of a given variable, in general without being aware that he is doing so. A number of factors are involved in this switching, such as monitoring (adjustment to meet

174

the social conditions of the speech situation) and marking (adjustment for the purpose of signalling special social roles) (Labov 1970); but all of them in one way or another derive from the nature of social dialect as a manifestation of the social structure and particularly of its hierarchical nature.

A closely related phenomenon is that of code-switching, studied in detail by Gumperz (1971, Part II), in which speakers in multilingual contexts regularly switch between different languages, often within a sentence or even smaller unit. This likewise reflects the relative status, and also the functional specialization, of each language in the society in question.

Labov has demonstrated very convincingly that variation is inherent in the linguistic system. His work shows that, over and above the kind of variation that consists in socially motivated departure from an essentially stable norm, we have to recognize variability: that is, the system itself embodies variables, to some of which social values then tend to accrue.

The difficulty with variation and variability as **socio**linguistic concepts (see Bickerton 1971) is to know what is the nature of the social meanings that are being realized through these patterns. How do the variants differ in meaning, and what is the **meaning** of choosing one rather than another? In other words, what is the semantics of the social structure that they are being made to express? It is not too difficult to relate variation in language to a general concept of subjective social stratification which has been derived from the study of this variation in the first place. The problem is to go further than this, by relating the linguistic phenomena to, and integrating them into, an independently established social theory with its own interpretation of social structure and social change.

1.5 Language, social structure and education

It is not difficult to demonstrate that, where there is a high rate of educational failure in urban areas, this failure tends to be associated with social class; roughly, the lower the family on the social scale (whether this is assessed intuitively or by means of some standardized measures) the greater the child's chances of failure.

Investigators concluded from this that there was a linguistic element in the situation; in some sense, language was to blame. If lower working-class children show significantly greater discrepancy between measures of verbal and non-verbal intelligence, a discrepancy which tends to increase with age, then their language is holding them back; and this must mean their dialect, since it is the dialect that is distinctive. So educational failure is explained as language failure, with language interpreted as social dialect (Baratz and Shuy 1969; Shuy 1971; Williams 1970).

The language failure theory has taken two alternative forms, usually known as "deficit" and "difference". The deficit version lays the blame on language as a **system.** According to this version, the language of the children concerned is deficient in some respect – it has not enough words, or not enough structures. The difference version lays the blame on language as an **institution**. It holds that the language of the children who fail is not deficient, but that the fact that it is different (from the standard language) acts just as much to their disadvantage because the standard language is required by the educational process, or else simply by social prejudice on the part of teachers and others. Either way, the child suffers.

Neither version of the theory is satisfactory, though for different reasons: the deficit version because it is not true, the difference version because, although it is true, it does not explain. There is no convincing evidence that children who fail in school have fewer words and structures at their command than those who succeed; and the notion of a defective dialect is in any case self-contradictory. But if children are failing because they speak a dialect that is different, they can certainly learn a second one, as children do in many cultures the world over. (This is not to deny, of course, that the attitudes towards their own speech forms are harmful and unjust. In fact, non-standard-speaking children often do learn standard speech forms, though not always for scholastic purposes.) This argument does not in any way destroy the sociolinguistic concept of a social dialect, as a language variety that is related to the social structure, one which expresses and symbolizes social hierarchy. But it removes it from the centre of the picture of the educational crisis.

1.6 Language and cultural transmission

What then are the significant social class differences in language, if any, and what are the social processes that give rise to them? Bernstein was the first to suggest an interpretation in terms of the transmission of the culture from one generation to the next.

It is a commonplace that a child's primary socialization in family and peer group takes place largely through language. What Bernstein's work has shown is how the social structure comes to be represented and transmitted in the process. This takes place also through language. Bernstein postulated that linguistic interaction is regulated by socio-linguistic "codes", or coding orientations, embodying two major variables: elaborated versus restricted, and person-oriented versus object-oriented. These determine the speech variants or types of discourse typically associated with particular situations. The meaning of 'orientation towards persons or objects' is clear. 'Elaboration or restriction' is more opaque; but an 'elaborated' variant is one which is more verbally explicit, which maintains social distance, demands individuated responses and makes minimal assumptions about the hearer's intent; it thus tends towards less ambiguity in the situational reference and more ambiguity in the role relationships. The codes are general tendencies governing the range of meanings that speakers typically deploy.

The individual child's exposure to the codes is, Bernstein suggests, a function of the system of role relationships within the family; and in particular of the balance between the "positional" system, in which role corresponds to ascribed status (the part played by the member is a function of position in the family), and the "personal" system, in which role corresponds to achieved status (the part played by the member is a function of his qualities as an individual). All combinations are found in all social classes, but, in Britain at least, strongly positional role systems tend to be found mainly in lower working-class families (where educational failure is high). It seems that a positional family structure tends to orient the members away from the elaborated, personal mode, in just those socializing contexts in which learning is associated with an adult authority figure, for example the context of parental control. But it is predominantly this mode that is demanded by the principles and processes of education as at present constituted. Hence the styles of meaning through which the culture is transmitted produce an incompatibility between lower working-class social norms and the middle-class ethos and the educational system that is based on it (Bernstein 1971). The difficulty here for a sociolinguistic theory is to understand how the codes are translated into linguistic interaction. By what mechanism do the differences in elaboration and orientation manifest themselves in the way people talk, to each other and to their children? Bernstein has made it clear from the start that these are not matters of social dialect, of varieties of lexicogrammatical and phonological realization. Either the codes are to be interpreted as different semantic systems, which as a general interpretation is implausible (and has also been rejected by Bernstein, at one point), or there must be some channel through which they intercede between the semantic system and the text.

1.7 Sociolinguistics and language development

The learning of the mother tongue can be interpreted from one point of view as a sociolinguistic process, and such an interpretation is one component of the general sociolinguistic universe. Aside from Bernstein's work, and that which is derivative from him, there are currently three main avenues of research which lead in the direction of a developmental sociolinguistics. One is through semantics, one is along the lines of 'sociolinguistic competence' and the third is via a functional approach to the linguistic system.

Recent interest in the semantics of language development arose as an extension of psycholinguistic studies in the learning of vocabulary and structure; hence it has tended to focus on word meanings, conceptual structures and logical relations (see Eve V. Clark 1973). The study of the acquisition of sociolinguistic competence is concerned with how the child learns the social uses of language, the "rules of speaking" whereby his language meets the demands of the situation and the social structure (Susan M. Ervin-Tripp 1972, 1973). In the functional approach, learning the mother tongue has been interpreted as learning the set of functions that language serves and developing a meaning potential in respect of each (Halliday 1975c).

Each of these three approaches presents certain difficulties, including that of isolation from the other two. Work in the field of child semantics has focused on the acquisition of concepts as an aspect of cognitive development; but it has not sought to relate meaning to social context, or to interpret language as the realization of social meanings and the semantic system as the linguistic encoding of the social system. The concept of sociolinguistic or communicative competence derives from the acceptance of a sharp distinction between a highly idealized "competence" and a correspondingly belittled "performance", a distinction which is at best irrelevant, and at worst obstructive, in a sociolinguistic perspective; this tends to isolate the system from its use, and hence to obscure the fact that the system develops through interaction, as a meaning potential that is always related to social contexts. The problem for the functional approach is that of showing how meanings evolve in a functional context, and how a postulated initial set of developmental functions of language come to be incorporated into the linguistic system (see 1.3 above). Finally the problem for all three approaches is to give some indication of how, and why, a child develops a linguistic system that has just the properties that human language has, and of how, and why, the human species developed such a system in the first place.

2. Elements of a sociosemiotic theory of language

In this section we shall refer to certain general concepts, inherent in these and related sociolinguistic studies, which form essential ingredients in any social-interactional theory of language. These are the text, the situation, the text variety or register, the code (in Bernstein's sense), the linguistic system (including the semantic system) and the social structure.

2.1 Text

Let us begin with the concept of text, the instances of linguistic interaction in which people actually engage: whatever is said, or written, in an operational context, as distinct from a citational context like that of words listed in a dictionary.

For some purposes it suffices to conceive of a text as a kind of 'supersentence', a linguistic unit that is in principle greater in size than a sentence but of the same kind. It has long been clear, however, that discourse has its own structure that is not constituted out of sentences in combination (sometimes referred to as a "macro" structure; see van Dijk 1972); and in a sociolinguistic perspective it is more useful to think of text as **encoded** in sentences, not as composed of them. (Hence what Cicourel refers to as omissions by the speaker are not so much omissions as encodings, which the hearer can decode because he shares the principles of realization that provide the key to the code.) In other words, a text is a semantic unit; it is the basic unit of the semantic process. It may be instantiated in various ways, as speech act, speech event, topic unit, exchange, episode, narrative and so on.

At the same time, text represents choice. A text is 'what is meant', selected from the total set of options that constitute what can be meant. In other words, text can be defined as actualized meaning potential.

The meaning potential, which is the paradigmatic range of semantic choice that is present in the system, and which the members of a culture have access to in their language, can be characterized in two ways, corresponding to Malinowski's distinction between the "context of situation" and the "context of culture" (1923, 1935). Interpreted in the context of culture, it is the entire semantic system of the language. This is a fiction, something we cannot hope to describe. Interpreted in the context of situation, it is the particular semantic system, or set of sub-systems, which is associated with a particular type of situation or social context. This too is a fiction; but it is something that may be more easily describable (see 2.5 below). In sociolinguistic terms the meaning potential can be represented as the range of options that is characteristic of a specific situation type.

2.2 Situation

The situation is the environment in which the text comes to life. This is a well-established concept in linguistics, going back at least to Wegener (1885). It played a key part in Malinowski's ethnography of language, under the name of "context of situation"; Malinowski's notions were further developed and made explicit by Firth, who maintained that the context of situation was not to be interpreted in concrete terms as a sort of audio–visual record of the surrounding 'props' but was, rather, an abstract representation of the environment in terms of certain general categories having relevance to the text. The context of situation may be totally remote from what is going on round about during the act of speaking or of writing. Firth's characterization was referred to in 1.2 above.

It will be necessary to represent the situation in still more abstract terms if it is to have a place in a general sociolinguistic theory; and to conceive of it not as situation but as situation **type**, in the sense of what Bernstein refers to as a "social context". This is, essentially, a semiotic structure. It is a constellation of meanings deriving from the semiotic system that constitutes the culture.

If it is true that a hearer, given the right information, can make sensible guesses about what the speaker is going to mean – and this seems a necessary assumption, seeing that communication does take place – then this 'right information' is what we mean by the social context. It consists of those general properties of the situation which collectively function as the determinants of text, in that they specify the semantic configurations that the speaker will typically fashion in contexts of the given type.

However, such information relates not only 'downward' to the text but also 'upward', to the linguistic system and to the social system. The 'situation' is a theoretical sociolinguistic construct; it is for this reason that we interpret a particular situation type, or social context, as a semiotic structure. The semiotic structure of a situation type can be represented as a complex of three dimensions: the ongoing social activity, the role relationships involved, and the symbolic or rhetorical channel. We shall refer to these respectively as *field, tenor* and *mode* (following Halliday, McIntosh and Strevens 1964, as modified by Spencer and Gregory 1964; and see Gregory 1967). The field, corresponding roughly to Hymes' "setting" and "ends", is the field of social action in which the text is embedded; it includes the subject matter, as one special manifestation. The tenor, which corresponds in general to Hymes' "participants" and "key", is the set of role relationships among the relevant participants; it includes levels of formality as one particular instance. The mode, roughly Hymes' "instrumentalities" and "genre", is the channel or wavelength selected, which is essentially the function that is assigned to language in the total structure of the situation; it includes the medium (spoken or written), which is explained as a functional variable.

Field, tenor and mode are not kinds of language use, nor are they simply components of the speech setting. They are a conceptual framework for representing the social context as the semiotic environ-ment in which people exchange meanings. Given an adequate specification of the semiotic properties of the context in terms of field, tenor and mode we should be able to make sensible predictions about the semantic properties of texts associated with it. To do this, however, requires an intermediary level – some concept of text variety, or register.

2.3 *Register*

The term *register* was first used in this sense, that of text variety, by Reid (1956); the concept was taken up and developed by Jean Ure (Ure and Ellis 1972), and interpreted within Hill's (1958) "institu-tional linguistic" framework by Halliday, McIntosh and Strevens (1964). The register is the semantic variety of which a text may be regarded as an instance.

Like other related concepts, such as "speech variant" and "(socio-linguistic) code" (Ferguson 1971, Chapters 1 and 2; Gumperz 1971, Part I), register was originally conceived of in lexicogrammatical terms. Halliday *et al.* drew a primary distinction between two types of language variety: dialect, which they defined as variety according to the user, and register, which they defined as variety according to the use. The dialect is what a person speaks, determined by who he is; the register is what a person is speaking, determined by what he is doing at the time. This general distinction can be accepted, but, instead of characterizing a register largely by its lexicogrammatical properties, we shall suggest, as with text, a more abstract definition in semantic terms.

A register can be defined as the configuration of semantic resources that the member of a culture typically associates with a situation type. It is the meaning potential that is accessible in a given social context. Both the situation and the register associated with it can be described to varying degrees of specificity; but the existence of registers is a fact of everyday experience – speakers have no difficulty in recognizing the semantic options and combinations of options that are 'at risk' under particular environmental conditions. Since these options are realized in the form of grammar and vocabulary, the register is recognizable as a particular selection of words and structures. But it is defined in terms of meanings; it is not an aggregate of conventional forms of expression superposed on some underlying content by 'social factors' of one kind or another. It is the selection of meanings that constitutes the variety to which a text belongs.

2.4 Code

Code is used here in Bernstein's sense; it is the principle of semiotic organization governing the choice of meanings by a speaker and their interpretation by a hearer. The code controls the semantic styles of the culture.

Codes are not varieties of language, as dialects and registers are. The codes are so to speak 'above' the linguistic system; they are types of social semiotic, or symbolic orders of meaning generated by the social system (see Hasan 1973). The code is actualized in language through the register, since it determines the semantic orientation of speakers in particular social contexts; Bernstein's own use of "variant" (as in "elaborated variant") refers to those characteristics of a register which derive from the form of the code. When the semantic systems of the language are activated by the situational determinants of text – the field, tenor and mode – this process is regulated by the codes.

Hence the codes transmit, or control the transmission of, the underlying patterns of a culture or sub-culture, acting through the socializing agencies of family, peer group and school. As a child comes to attend to and interpret meanings, in the context of situation and in the context of culture, at the same time he takes over the code. The culture is transmitted to him with the code acting as a filter, defining and making accessible the semiotic principles of his own sub-culture, so that as he learns the culture he also learns the grid, or sub-cultural angle on the social system. The child's linguistic experience reveals the culture to him through the code, and so transmits the code as part of the culture.

2.5 The linguistic system

Within the linguistic system, it is the **semantic system** that is of primary concern in a sociolinguistic context. Let us assume a tristratal model of language, with a semantic, a lexicogrammatical and a phonological stratum; this is the basic pattern underlying the (often superficially more complex) interpretations of language in the work of Troubetzkoy, Hjelmslev, Firth, Jakobson, Martinet, Pottier, Pike, Lamb, Lakoff and McCawley (among many others). We can then adopt the general conception of the organization of each stratum, and of the realization between strata, that is embodied in Lamb's stratification theory (Lamb 1971, 1974).

The semantic system is Lamb's "semological stratum"; it is conceived of here, however, in functional rather than in cognitive terms. The conceptual framework was already referred to in 1.3 above, with the terms *ideational*, *interpersonal* and *textual*. These are to be interpreted not as functions in the sense of uses of language, but as functional components of the semantic system – *metafunctions* as we have called them elsewhere (Halliday 1974). (Since in respect both of the stratal and of the functional organization of the linguistic system we are adopting a ternary interpretation rather than a binary one, we should perhaps explicitly disavow any particular adherence to the magic number three. In fact the functional interpretation could just as readily be stated in terms of four components, since the ideational comprises two distinct subparts, the experiential and the logical; but the distinction happens not to be very relevant here.)

What are these functional components of the semantic system? They are the modes of meaning that are present in every use of language in every social context. A text is a product of all three; it is a polyphonic composition in which different semantic melodies are interwoven, to be realized as integrated lexicogrammatical structures. Each functional component contributes a band of structure to the whole.

The ideational function represents the speaker's meaning potential as an observer. It is the content function of language, language as about something. This is the component through which the language encodes the cultural experience, and the speaker encodes his own individual experience as a member of the culture. It expresses the phenomena of the environment: the things – creatures, objects, actions, events, qualities, states and relations – of the world and of our own consciousness, including the phenomenon of language itself; and also the 'metaphenomena', the things that are already encoded as facts and as reports. All these are part of the ideational meaning of language.

The interpersonal component represents the speaker's meaning potential as an intruder. It is the participatory function of language, language as doing something. This is the component through which the speaker intrudes himself into the context of situation, both expressing his own attitudes and judgements and seeking to influence the attitudes and behaviour of others. It expresses the role relationships associated with the situation, including those that are defined by language itself, relationships of questioner–respondent, informer–doubter and the like. These constitute the interpersonal meaning of language.

The textual component represents the speaker's text-forming potential; it is that which makes language relevant. This is the component which provides the texture; that which makes the difference between language that is suspended *in vacuo* and language that is operational in a context of situation. It expresses the relation of the language to its environment, including both the verbal environment – what has been said or written before – and the non-verbal, situational environment. Hence the textual component has an enabling function with respect to the other two; it is only in combination with textual meanings that ideational and interpersonal meanings are actualized.

These components are reflected in the lexicogrammatical system in the form of discrete networks of options. In the clause (simple sentence), for example, the ideational function is represented by transitivity, the interpersonal by mood, and the textual by a set of systems that have been referred to collectively as "theme". Each of these three sets of options is characterized by strong internal but weak external constraints: for example, any choice made in transitivity has a significant effect on other choices within the transitivity systems, but has very little effect on choices within the mood or theme systems. Hence the functional organization of meaning in language is built in to the core of the linguistic system, as the most general organizing principle of the lexicogrammatical stratum.

2.6 Social structure

Of the numerous ways in which the social structure is implicated in a sociolinguistic theory, there are three which stand out. In the first place, it defines and gives significance to the various types of social context in which meanings are exchanged. The different social groups and communication networks that determine what we have called the "tenor" – the status and role relationships in the situation – are obviously products of the social structure; but so also in a more general sense are the types of social activity that constitute the "field". Even the "mode", the rhetorical channel with its associated strategies, though more immediately reflected in linguistic patterns, has its origin in the social structure; it is the social structure that generates the semiotic tensions and the rhetorical styles and genres that express them (Barthes 1970).

Secondly, through its embodiment in the types of role relationship within the family, the social structure determines the various familial patterns of communication; it regulates the meanings and meaning styles that are associated with given social contexts, including those contexts that are critical in the processes of cultural transmission. In this way the social structure determines, through the intermediary of language, the forms taken by the socialization of the child. (See 1.6 above, and Bernstein 1971, 1974)

Thirdly, and most problematically, the social structure enters in through the effects of social hierarchy, in the form of caste or class. This is obviously the background to social dialects, which are both a direct manifestation of social hierarchy and also a symbolic expression of it, maintaining and reinforcing it in a variety of ways: for example, the association of dialect with register – the fact that certain registers conventionally call for certain dialectal modes – expresses the relation between social classes and the division of labour. In a more pervasive fashion, the social structure is present in the forms of semiotic interaction, and becomes apparent through incongruities and disturbances in the semantic system. Linguistics seems now to have largely abandoned its fear of impurity and come to grips with what is called "fuzziness" in language; but this has been a logical rather than a sociological concept, a departure from an ideal regularity rather than an organic property of sociosemiotic systems. The 'fuzziness' of language is in part an expression of the dynamics and the tensions of the social system. It is not only the text (what people mean) but also the semantic system (what they can mean) that embodies the ambiguity, antagonism, imperfection, inequality and change that characterize the social system and social structure. This is not often systematically explored in linguistics, though it is familiar enough to students of communication and of general semantics, and to the public at large. It could probably be fruitfully approached through an extension of Bernstein's theory of codes (see Mary Douglas 1972). The social structure is not just an ornamental background to linguistic interaction, as it has tended to become in sociolinguistic discussions. It is an essential element in the evolution of semantic systems and semantic processes.

3. A sociolinguistic view of semantics

In this section we shall consider three aspects of a sociological semantics: the semantics of situation types, the relation of the situation to the semantic system, and the socio-semantics of language development. The discussion will be illustrated from a sociolinguistic study of early language development.

3.1 The semantics of situation types

A sociological semantics implies not so much a general description of the semantic system of a language but rather a set of context-specific semantic descriptions, each one characterizing the meaning potential that is typically associated with a given situation type (see 2.2 above; also Halliday 1972). In other words, a semantic description is the description of a register.

This approach has been used to great effect by Turner in a number of studies carried out under Bernstein's direction in London (Turner 1973). Turner's contexts in themselves are highly specific; he constructs semantic networks representing, for example, the options taken up by mothers in response to particular questions about their child control strategies. At the same time they are highly general in their application, both because of the size of the sample investigated and, more especially, because of the sociological interpretation that is put upon the data, in terms of Bernstein's theories of cultural transmission and social change.

The sociolinguistic notion of a situation type, or social context, is variable in generality, and may be conceived of as covering a greater or smaller number of possible instances. So the sets of semantic options that constitute the meaning potential associated with a situation type may also be more or less general. What characterizes this potential is its truly 'sociolinguistic' nature. A semantics of this kind forms the interface between the social system and the linguistic system; its elements realize social meanings and are realized in linguistic forms. Each option in the semantic network, in other words, is interpreted in the semiotics of the situation and is also represented in the lexicogrammar of the text. (Note that this is not equivalent to saying that the entire semiotic structure of the situation is represented in the semantic options, and hence also in the text, which is certainly not true.)

Figure 5.1 shows an outline semantic network for a particular situation type, one that falls within the general context of child play; more specifically, it is that of a small child manipulating vehicular toys in interaction with an adult. The network specifies some of the principal options, together with their possible realizations. The options derive from the general functional components of the semantic system (2.5 above) and are readily interpretable in terms of the grammar of English; we have not attempted to represent the meaning potential of the adult in the situation, but only that of the child. The networks relate, in turn, to a general description of English, modified to take account of the child's stage of development.

3.2 Structure of the situation, and its relation to the semantic system

The semiotic structure of a situation type can be represented in terms of the three general concepts of field, tenor and mode (see 2.2 above). The 'child play' situation type that was specified by the semantic networks in Figure 5.1 might be characterized, by reference to these concepts, in something like the following manner:

Field   Child at play: manipulating movable objects (wheeled vehicles) with related fixtures, assisted by adult; concurrently associating (i) similar past events, (ii) similar absent objects; also evaluating objects in terms of each other and of processes.

Tenor   Small child and parent interacting: child determining course of action, (i) announcing own intentions, (ii) controlling actions of parent; concurrently sharing and seeking corroboration of own experience with parent.

Mode   Spoken, alternately monologue and dialogue, task-oriented; pragmatic, (i) referring to processes and objects of situation, (ii) relating to and furthering child's own actions, (iii) demanding other objects; interposed with narrative and exploratory elements.

187

Realizations in text (Figure 5.1a):

be located/2 participants	put
be located/1 participant	be (in, on)
be located: in	in
be located: on	on
move/2 participants: person	send
move/2 participants: object	carry
move/1 participant	go
move: straight	down
move: in circle	round and round
possess/2 participants	[give]
possess/1 participant	have
exist/2 participants	find
exist/1 participant	be (there's)
benefactive ('for me')	for you
movable: type of vehicle	train, engine, lorry
movable: identifying property	blue, black
immovable	chair, floor, railway line
capable	will
suitable	(be) for
efficient	(go) well
past	(past tense)
present	(present tense)

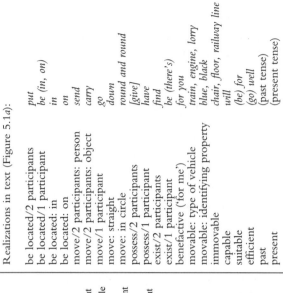

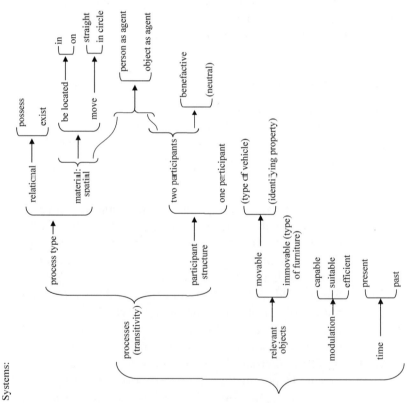

Systems:

Figure 5.1(a): Ideational

188

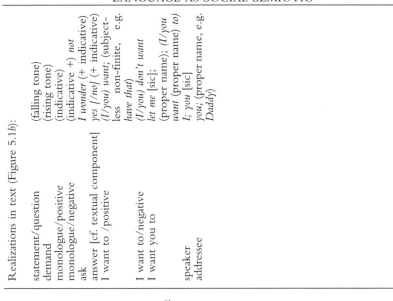

Realizations in text (Figure 5.1*b*):

statement/question (falling tone)
demand (rising tone)
monologue/positive (indicative)
monologue/negative (indicative +) *not*
ask *I wonder* (+ indicative)
answer [cf. textual component] *yes* [*/no*] (+ indicative)
I want to /positive (*I/you) want*; (subjectless non-finite, e.g.
have that)
I want to/negative (*I/you) don't want*
I want you to *let me* [sic];
(*proper name*); (*I/you
want* (proper name) *to*)
speaker *I; you* [sic]
addressee *you*; (proper name, e.g.
Daddy)

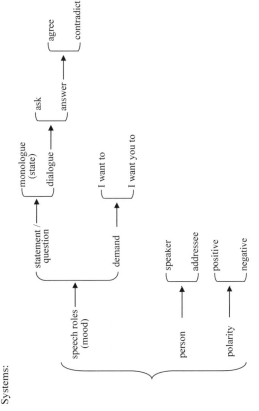

Figure 5.1(b): Interpersonal

189

Realizations in text (Figure 5.1c):

person theme: child — *I/you* (initial); subjectless (non-finite)
person theme: parent — (proper name initial)
object theme — (object name initial)
exophoric: demonstrative — *this, that, the, here*
exophoric: possessive — *your* ('my')
anaphoric — *it, that, the*
adversative — *but;* (fall-rise tone)
ellipsis: 'yes/no' — *yes [no]*
ellipsis: modal — (modal element, e.g. *it is, it will*)
lexical: repetition of items — (e.g. *train ... train*)
lexical: collocations — (e.g. *chair ... floor, train ... railway line*)
information structure: text units — (organization in tone groups)
information structure: given-new — (location of tonic nucleus)

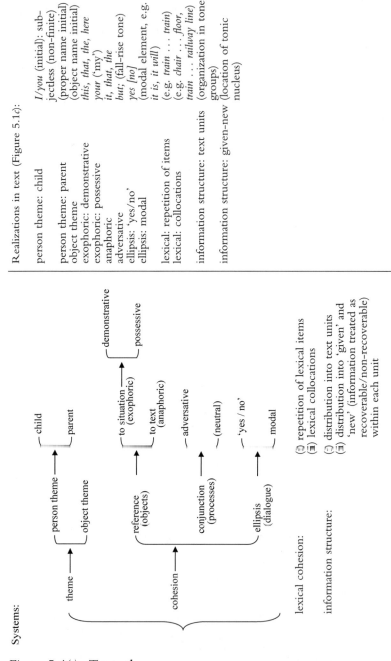

Systems:

theme → person theme → child / parent
object theme

cohesion → reference (objects) → to situation (exophoric) → demonstrative / possessive
to text (anaphoric)
conjunction (processes) → adversative
ellipsis (dialogue) → (neutral) / 'yes / no' / modal

lexical cohesion: (i) repetition of lexical items (ii) lexical collocations

information structure: (i) distribution into text units (ii) distribution into 'given' and 'new' (information treated as recoverable/non-recoverable) within each unit

Figure 5.1(c): Textual
Figure 5.1: Semantic systems and their realizations, as represented in Nigel's speech (text in 3.2)

Below is a specimen of a text having these semiotic properties. It is taken from a study of the language development of one subject, Nigel, from nine months to three and a half years; the passage selected is from age 1; 11. [Note: ` = falling tone; ´ = rising tone; ˇ = fall-rise tone; tonic nucleus falls on syllables having tone marks; tone group boundaries within an utterance shown by ... . For analysis of intonation, see Halliday 1967a.]

> Nigel [small wooden train in hand, approaching track laid along a plank sloping from chair to floor]: *Here the ràilway line ... but it not for the trǎin to go on that.* Father: *Isn't it?* Nigel: *Yès tís. ... I wonder the train will carry the lòrry* [puts train on lorry (sic)]. Father: *I wonder.* Nigel: *Oh yes it wíll. ... I don't wànt to send the train on this flóor ... you want to send the train on the ràilway line* [runs it up plank on to chair] *... but it doesn't go very well on the chǎir. ...* [makes train go round in circles] *The train all round and ròund ... it going all round and ròund ...* [tries to reach other train] *have that tráin ... have the blue tráin* ('give it to me') [Father does so] *... send the blue train down the ráilway line ...* [plank falls off chair] *lèt me put the railway line on cháir* ('you put the railway line on the chair!') [Father does so] *...* [looking at blue train] *Daddy put sèllotape on it* ('previously') *... there a very fierce lìon in the train ... Daddy go and see if the lion still thére ... Have your éngine* ('give me my engine'). Father: *which engine? The little black engine?* Nigel: *Yès ... Daddy go and fìnd it fór you ... Daddy go and find the black éngine for you.*

Nigel's linguistic system at this stage is in a state of transition, as he approximates more and more closely to the adult language, and it is unstable at various points. He is well on the way to the adult system of mood, but has not quite got there – he has not quite grasped the principle that language can be used **as a substitute for** shared experience, to impart information not previously known to the hearer; and therefore he has not yet learnt the general meaning of 'yes/no question'. He has a system of person, but alternates between *I/me* and *you* as the expression of the first person 'I'. He has a transitivity system, but confuses the roles of Agent (Actor) and Medium (Goal) in a non-middle (two participant) process. It is worth pointing out perhaps that adult linguistic systems are themselves unstable at many points – a good example being transitivity in English, which is in a state of considerable flux; what the child is approximating to, therefore, is not something

	Situational	Semantic
Field	manipulation of objects assistance of adult movable objects and fixtures movability of objects and their relation to fixtures recall of similar events evaluation	process type and participant structure benefactive type of relevant object type of location and movement past time modulation
Tenor	interaction with parent determination of course of action enunciation of intention control of action sharing of experience seeking corroboration of experience	person mood and polarity demand, 'I want to' demand, 'I want you to' statement/question, monologue statement/question, dialogue

Mode	dialogue
	reference to situation
	textual cohesion: objects
	textual cohesion: processes
	furthering child's actions
	
	orientation to task
	spoken mode
		ellipsis (question-answer)
		exophoric reference
		anaphoric reference
		conjunction
		theme (in conjunction with transitivity
		    and mood; typically, parent or
		    child in demands, child in two–
		    participant statements, object in
		    one-participant statements)
		lexical collocation and repetition
		information structure

Figure 5.2: Determination of semantic features by elements of semiotic structure of situation (text in 3.2)

fixed and harmonious but something shifting, fluid and full of indeterminacies.

What does emerge from a consideration of Nigel's discourse is how, through the internal organization of the linguistic system, situational features determine text. If we describe the semiotic structure of the situation in terms of features of field, tenor and mode, and consider how these various features relate to the systems making up the semantic networks shown in Figure 5.1, we arrive at something like the picture presented in Figure 5.2.

192

There is thus a systematic correspondence between the semiotic structure of the situation type and the functional organization of the semantic system. Each of the main areas of meaning potential tends to be determined or activated by one particular aspect of the situation:

Semantic components		Situational elements
Ideational	systems activated by features of	Field
Interpersonal	systems activated by features of	Tenor
Textual	systems activated by features of	Mode

In other words, the type of symbolic activity (field) tends to determine the range of meaning as content, language in the ideational function; the role relationships (tenor) tend to determine the range of meaning as participation, language in the interpersonal function; and the rhetorical channel (mode) tends to determine the range of meaning as texture, language in its relevance to the environment. There are of course many indeterminate areas – though there is often some system even in the indeterminacy: for example, the child's evaluation of objects lies on the borderline of "field" and "tenor", and the system of "modulation" likewise lies on the borderline of the ideational and interpersonal components of language (Halliday 1969a). But there is an overall pattern. This is not just a coincidence: presumably the semantic system evolved as symbolic interaction among people in social contexts, so we should expect the semiotic structure of these contexts to be embodied in its internal organization. By taking account of this we get an insight into the form of relationship among the three concepts of situation, text and semantic system. The semiotic features of the situation activate corresponding portions of the semantic system, in this way determining the register, the configuration of potential meanings that is typically associated with this situation type, and becomes actualized in the text that is engendered by it.

3.3 Socio-semantics of language development

A child learning his mother tongue is learning how to mean; he is building up a meaning potential in respect of a limited number of social functions (see 1.7 above). These functions constitute the semiotic environment of a very small child, and may be thought of as universals of human culture.

The meanings the child can express at this stage derive very directly from the social functions. For example, one of the functions served by the child's "proto-language" is the regulatory function, that of controlling the behaviour of other people; and in this function he is likely to develop meanings such as 'do that some more' (continue or repeat what you've just been doing), and 'don't do that'. How does he get from these to the complex and functionally remote meanings of the adult semantic system?

These language-engendering functions, or 'proto-contexts', are the origin at one and the same time both of the social context and of the semantic system. The child develops his ability to mean by a gradual process of generalization and abstraction, which in the case of Nigel appeared to go somewhat along the following lines. Out of the six functions of his proto-language (instrumental, regulatory, interactional, personal, heuristic and imaginative), he derived a simple but highly general distinction between language as a means of doing and language as a means of knowing – with the latter, at this stage, interpretable functionally as 'learning'. As he moved into the phase of transition into the adult system, at around 18 months, he assigned every utterance to one or another of these generalized functional categories, encoding the distinction by means of intonation: all 'learning' utterances were on a falling tone, and all 'doing' utterances on a rising tone. As forms of interaction, the latter required a response (increasingly, as time went on, a **verbal** response) while the former did not.

From the moment when this semantic principle was adopted, however, it ceased to satisfy, since Nigel already needed a semiotic system which would enable him to do both these things at once – to use language in both the learning mode and the doing mode within a single utterance. Without this ability he could not engage in true dialogue; the system could not develop a dynamic for the adoption and assignment of semiotic roles in verbal interaction. At this point, two steps were required, or really one complex step, for effectively completing the transition to the adult system. One was a further abstraction of the basic functional opposition, such that it came to be incorporated into his semantic system, as the two components of "ideational" and "inter-personal"; in the most general terms, the former developed from 'learning' function, the latter from the 'doing' function. The other step was the introduction of a lexicogrammar, or syntax, making it possible for these two modes of meaning to be expressed simultaneously in the form of integrated lexicogrammatical structures.

The term "socio-semantics of language development" refers to this process, whereby the original social functions of the infant's proto-language are reinterpreted first as *macro-functions*, and then as *meta-*

194

functions, functional components in the organization of the semantic system. These components, as remarked earlier (2.5), are clearly seen in the adult language; the options show a high degree of mutual constraint within one component but a very low degree of constraint between components. At the same time, looked at from another point of view, what the child has done is finally to dissociate the concept of 'function' from that of 'use'; the functions evolve into components of the semantic system, and the uses into what we are calling social contexts or situation types. For a detailed treatment of this topic see Halliday (1975c).

4. Towards a general sociolinguistic theory

In this final section we shall try to suggest how the main components of the sociolinguistic universe relate to one another, the assumption being that this network of relations is the cornerstone of a general sociolinguistic theory.

4.1 Meaning and text

The *text* is the linguistic form of social interaction. It is a continuous progression of meanings, combining both simultaneously and in succession. The meanings are the selections made by the speaker from the options that constitute the *meaning potential*; text is the actualization of this meaning potential, the process of semantic choice.

The selections in meaning derive from different functional origins, and are mapped on to one another in the course of their realization as lexicogrammatical structure. In our folk linguistic terminology, the "meaning" is represented as "wording" – which in turn is expressed as "sound" ("pronouncing") or as "spelling". The folk linguistic, incidentally, shows our awareness of the tristratal nature of language.

4.2 Text and situation

A text is embedded in a context of *situation.* The context of situation of any text is an instance of a generalized social context or situation type. The situation type is not an inventory of ongoing sights and sounds but a semiotic structure; it is the ecological matrix that is constitutive of the text.

Certain types of situation have in their semiotic structure some element which makes them central to the processes of cultural transmission; these are Bernstein's "critical socializing contexts". Examples are those having a regulative component (where a parent is regulating the child's behaviour), or an instructional component (where the child is being explicitly taught).

4.3 Situation as semiotic structure

The semiotic structure of the situation is formed out of the three socio-semiotic variables of *field, tenor* and **mode.** These represent in systematic form the type of activity in which the text has significant function (field), the status and role relationships involved (tenor) and the symbolic mode and rhetorical channels that are adopted (mode). The field, tenor and mode act collectively as determinants of the text through their specification of the register (4.5 below); at the same time they are systematically associated with the linguistic system through the functional components of the semantics (4.4).

4.4 Situation and semantic system

The semiotic components of the situation (field, tenor and mode) are systematically related to the functional components of the semantics (ideational, interpersonal and textual): *field* to the *ideational* component, representing the 'content' function of language, the speaker as observer; *tenor* to the *interpersonal* component, representing the 'participation' function of language, the speaker as intruder; and *mode* to the *textual* component, representing the 'relevance' function of language, without which the other two do not become actualized. There is a tendency, in other words, for the field of social action to be encoded linguistically in the form of ideational meanings, the role relationships in the form of interpersonal meanings, and the symbolic mode in the form of textual meanings.

4.5 Situation, semantic system and register

The semiotic structure of a given situation type, its particular pattern of field, tenor and mode, can be thought of as resonating in the semantic system and so activating particular networks of semantic options; typically options form within the corresponding semantic components (4.4). This process specifies a range of meaning potential, or *register*: the semantic configuration that is typically associated with the situation type in question.

196

4.6 Register and code

The specification of the register by the social context is in turn controlled and modified by the *code*: the semiotic style, or "socio-linguistic coding orientation" in Bernstein's term, that represents the particular sub-cultural angle on the social system. This angle of vision is a function of the social structure. It reflects, in our society, the pattern of social hierarchy, and the resulting tensions between an egalitarian ideology and a hierarchical reality. The code is transmitted initially through the agency of family types and family role systems, and subsequently reinforced in the various peer groups of children, adolescents and adults.

4.7 Language and the social system

The foregoing synthesis presupposes an interpretation of the social system as a *social semiotic*: a system of meanings that constitutes the 'reality' of the culture. This is the higher-level system to which language is related: the semantic system of language is a realization of the social semiotic. There are many other forms of its symbolic realization besides language; but language is unique in having its own semantic stratum.

This takes us back to the 'meaning potential' of 4.1. The meaning potential of language, which is realized in the lexicogrammatical system, itself realizes meanings of a higher order; not only the semiotic of the particular social context, its organization as field, tenor and mode, but also that of the total set of social contexts that constitutes the social system. In this respect language is unique among the modes of expression of social meanings: it operates on both levels, having meaning both in general and in particular at the same time. This property arises out of the functional organization of the semantic system, whereby the meaning potential associated with a particular social context is derived from corresponding sets of generalized options in the semantic system.

4.8 Language and the child

A child begins by creating a proto-language of his own, a meaning potential in respect of each of the social functions that constitute his developmental semiotic. In the course of maturation and socialization he comes to take over the adult language. The text-in-situation by

197

which he is surrounded is filtered through his own functional-semantic grid, so that he processes just what is interpreted in terms of his own social semiotic at any particular stage.

As a strategy for entering the adult system he generalizes from his initial set of functions an opposition between language as doing and language as learning. This is the developmental origin of the interpersonal and ideational components in the semantic system of the adult language. The concept of function is now abstracted from that of use, and has become the basic principle of the linguistic organization of meaning.

4.9 The child and the culture

As a child learns language, he also learns **through** language. He interprets text not only as being specifically relevant to the context of situation but also as being generally relevant to the context of culture. It is the linguistic system that enables him to do this; since the sets of semantic options which are characteristic of the situation (the register) derive from generalized functional components of the semantic system, they also at the same time realize the higher order meanings that constitute the culture, and so the child's focus moves easily between the microsemiotic and the macrosemiotic environment.

So when Nigel's mother said to him, 'Leave that stick outside; stop teasing the cat; and go and wash your hands. It's time for tea,' he could not only understand the instructions but could also derive from them information about the social system: about the boundaries dividing social space, and 'what goes where'; about the continuity between the human and the animal world; about the regularity of cultural events; and more besides. He does not, of course, learn all this from single instances, but from the countless socio semiotic events of this kind that make up the life of social man. And as a corollary to this, he comes to rely heavily on the social system for the decoding of the meanings that are embodied in such day-to-day encounters.

In one sense a child's learning of his mother tongue is a process of progressively freeing himself from the constraints of the immediate context – or, better, of progressively redefining the context and the place of language within it – so that he is able to learn through language, and interpret an exchange of meanings in relation to the culture as a whole. Language is not the only form of the realization of social meanings, but it is the only form of it that has this complex property: to

198

mean, linguistically, is at once both to reflect and to act – and to do these things both in particular and in general at the same time. So it is first and foremost through language that the culture is transmitted to the child, in the course of everyday interaction in the key socializing agencies of family, peer group and school. This process, like other semiotic processes, is controlled and regulated by the code; and so, in the course of it, the child himself also takes over the coding orientation, the sub-cultural semiotic bias that is a feature of all social structures except those of a (possibly non-existent) homogeneous type, and certainly of all complex societies of a pluralistic and hierarchical kind.

4.10 Summary

Figure 4.1 (p. 141) is an attempt to summarize the discussion in diagrammatic form; the arrow is to be read as 'determines'. What follows is a rendering of it in prose.

Social interaction typically takes a linguistic form, which we call *text*. A text is the product of indefinitely many simultaneous and successive choices in meaning, and is realized as lexicogrammatical structure, or *wording*. The environment of the text is the context of situation, which is an instance of a social context, or *situation type*. The situation type is a semiotic construct which is structured in terms of *field, tenor* and *mode*: the text-generating activity, the role relationships of the participants, and the rhetorical modes they are adopting. These situational variables are related respectively to the *ideational, interpersonal* and *textual* components of the *semantic system*: meaning as context (the observer function of language), meaning as participation (the intruder function) and meaning as texture (the relevance function). They are related in the sense that each of the situational features typically calls forth a network of options from the corresponding semantic component; in this way the semiotic properties of a particular situation type, its structure in terms of field, tenor and mode, determine the semantic configuration or *register* – the meaning potential that is characteristic of the situation type in question, and is realized as what is known as a "speech variant". This process is regulated by the *code*, the semiotic grid or principles of the organization of social meaning that represent the particular sub-cultural angle on the social system. The sub-cultural variation is in its turn a product of the *social structure*, typically the social hierarchy acting through the distribution of family types having different familial role systems. A child, coming into the picture, interprets text-in-situation in terms of his generalized functional categories of *learning (mathetic)* and *doing (pragmatic)*: from here by a further process of abstraction he constructs the functionally organized semantic system of the adult language. He has now gained access to the social semiotic; this is the context in which he himself will learn to mean, and in which all his subsequent meaning will take place.

The aim of this paper has been to interrelate the various components of the sociolinguistic universe, with special reference to the place of language within it. It is for this reason that we have adopted the mode of interpretation of the social system as a semiotic, and stressed the systematic aspects of it: the concept of system itself, and the concept of function within a system. It is all the more important, in this context, to avoid any suggestion of an idealized social functionalism, and to insist that the social system is not something static, regular and harmonious, nor are its elements held poised in some perfect pattern of functional relationships.

A 'socio-semiotic' perspective implies an interpretation of the shifts, the irregularities, the disharmonies and the tensions that characterize human interaction and social processes. It attempts to explain the semiotic of the social structure, in its aspects both of persistence and of change, including the semantics of social class, of the power system, of hierarchy and of social conflict. It attempts also to explain the linguistic processes whereby the members construct the social semiotic, whereby social reality is shaped, constrained and modified – processes which, far from tending towards an ideal construction, admit and even institutionalize myopia, prejudice and misunderstanding (Berger and Luckmann 1967, Chapter 3).

The components of the sociolinguistic universe themselves provide the sources and conditions of disorder and of change. These may be seen in the text, in the situation, and in the semantic system, as well as in the dynamics of cultural transmission and social learning. All the lines of determination are *ipso facto* also lines of tension, not only through indeterminacy in the transmission but also through feedback. The meaning of the text, for example, is fed back into the situation, and becomes part of it, changing it in the process; it is also fed back, through the register, into the semantic system, which it likewise affects and modifies. The code, the form in which we conceptualize the injection of the social structure into the semantic process, is itself a two-way relation, embodying feedback from the semantic configurations of social interaction into the role relationships of the family and other social groups. The social learning processes of a child, whether those of learning the language or of learning the culture, are among the most permeable surfaces of the whole system, as one soon becomes aware in listening to the language of young children's peer groups – a type of semiotic context which has hardly begun to be seriously studied. In the light of the role of language in social processes, a sociolinguistic perspective does not readily accommodate strong boundaries. The 'sociolinguistic order' is neither an ideal order nor a reality that has no order at all; it is a human artefact having some of the properties of both.

★This article was first written during my tenure of a fellowship at the Center for Advanced Study in the Behavioral Sciences, Stanford, California. I should like to express my gratitude to the Center for the opportunities which this afforded.

Notes

1. The present paper is reprinted by permission from *The First LACUS Forum 1974*, pp. 17–46, edited by Adam Makkai and Valerie Becker Makkai, published by Hornbeam Press, Columbia, SC.

Chapter Six

ASPECTS OF SOCIOLINGUISTIC RESEARCH (1975)

1. Language and social context

1.1. The social context of speech events

One of the earliest attempts to describe language in its social context was made by Malinowski in the course of his ethnographic studies in the South Pacific (1935). Malinowski called this the "context of situation"; and since his interest lay in the organization of culturally significant activities such as gardening and fishing expeditions, he interpreted the context of situation in concrete terms as a kind of scenario, a background of what was going on around at the time of the speech events. He also recognized, however, that to understand the meaning of what was said it was necessary to know the "context of culture", the systems of knowledge and belief, the social values and social structure of the community in question; and that this was equally true of all types of social organization at whatever level of technology.

In order to relate the specific context of a particular speech event to the broader environment of the culture as a whole, Firth proposed certain general headings for describing the context of situation: the participants (their status and roles), the relevant features of the setting, the verbal and non-verbal action, and the effective result (1950). A more recent set of categories proposed by Hymes reads (slightly paraphrased) as: "form and content, setting, participants, ends (intent and effect), key, medium, genre, and interactional norms" (1967). When people exchange meanings, interacting with each other through

'Some Aspects of Sociolinguistics', from *Interactions between Linguistics and Mathematical Education*, Report on a Symposium Sponsored by UNESCO – CEDO – ICMI, Nairobi, September 1974, ED-74/CONF. 808 (64–73). Reproduced by permission of UNESCO.

talk or writing, they have such background information available to them; and they make use of it all the time in order to understand each other. It may be concluded that anyone who is either studying verbal interaction or trying to influence it through some form of language planning is likely to need information of the same kind.

In a later section (1.4.) we shall summarize these findings in slightly different terms.

1.2. The speech community

A speech community might be thought of as homogeneous: as a group of people linked by a common social organization, who talk to each other and who all speak alike. This is an idealized construct, to which no human group would be expected to conform exactly, but which could serve as a model by reference to which actual communities could be described.

Actual communities, however, depart from this pattern in very radical ways. (1) A community speaking one language may still have a wide range of different styles; the range of any one individual will typically depend on his place in the social structure, and probably no member commands all styles. Geertz has described this situation in Java (1960). (2) A community may have a colloquial and a classical version of 'the same' language (often so different as to be mutually unintelligible), the two being recognized by consensus as appropriate in distinct social contexts. Ferguson has described this under the name of "diglossia" (1959). (3) A community may have two or more languages, related or unrelated. Furthermore, any combination of (1), (2) and (3) may occur.

Gumperz' definition of a speech community takes account of these possibilities. He defines it as "any human aggregate characterized by regular and frequent interaction by means of a shared body of verbal signs and set off from similar aggregates by significant differences in language usage" (1968). Gumperz himself has studied a number of communities displaying different kinds of linguistic plurality, dialectal, diglossic and multilingual, with particular reference to the conditions which determine the patterns of switching among the various languages or dialects (1971).

A major advance in our understanding of the nature of a speech community came about as a result of the work of Labov in New York City. Labov found an immense diversity in speech habits, both between individuals and also within each individual: not only does one New

Yorker not speak like another – he does not even speak like himself. By contrast, he found a remarkable homogeneity in speech attitudes: all New Yorkers tend to share the same linguistic prejudices, and to use the speech of their fellow citizens as a social index with striking accuracy and consistency. Furthermore, this combination of diversity of performance with uniformity of judgement is greater among the young (ages 18–40; before 18, Labov found, the attitudes were still being formed) than among the old, suggesting that it was increasing over time. Labov concluded: "it seems plausible to define a speech community as a group of speakers who share a set of social attitudes towards language" (1970a).

In the light of Labov's work, the conception of a sociolinguistically homogeneous speech community no longer appears very useful even as an idealization. For the sort of social and cultural pluralism that is increasingly typical of all parts of the world, it is too remote from the actual facts.

1.3. Variation theory

Labov's findings have been corroborated in other cities in North America and Europe; these features seem to be typical of urban communities which are marked by a strongly hierarchical social structure.

Arising out of these studies there has developed what is known as "variation theory", or sometimes "variability theory". According to this theory, which is now widely though not universally accepted, variation is inherent in the system of language.

In philosophical linguistics, language is isolated from its social context and studied in an idealized form, with a sharp boundary drawn between the system and the use of the system (what Chomsky called "competence" and "performance").

By contrast, in social and anthropological linguistics language is studied in context, and no sharp line is drawn between the system and its use: language is regarded as equivalent to 'speech potential'.

Labov argued that the patterns he uncovered could arise only if dialect-like variation was built into the system, such that it was the norm for any individual to produce variable speech forms, and to react to them when he heard them. Then, since every member of the community takes part in this systematic variation, some of the variants come to be charged with social value.

Variation theory implies that, for any one meaning, there may be a range of possible 'wordings' to express it; and for any one wording, there may be a range of possible 'soundings' to express it. In technical linguistic terms, in place of an invariant norm we postulate a norm of diversification in both the lexicogrammatical realization of semantic elements and the phonological realization of lexicogrammatical elements. For any one variable, the range of variants may be greater or less, and they may be continuous (like the different qualities of a vowel) or discontinuous (like different words or structures); but there is no single norm to which the speaker is always approximating. In terms of the linguistic 'schools' of a generation ago, variation theory has its precursors in the Prague school and the 'London' school rather than in American structuralism (or its Chomskyan derivative).

There are two versions of variation theory, differing however only in emphasis. Labov's "quantitative paradigm" stresses the statistical regularity of variation over a whole population. He uses two vectors, each with roughly five values: one representing the social class of the speaker, the other the "speech style", which he defines as "the amount of attention paid [by the speaker] to speech", and which ranges through casual – careful – reading – word lists – minimal pairs. (We shall suggest below that these two vectors are special instances of more general criteria, and that for explanatory purposes a third needs to be added.) The idea is that for each cell in the resulting matrix – say, lower middle-class speaker in careful speech – it is possible to predict which variant will occur, with a significantly high probability of being right; and furthermore, that the variants turn out to be systematically ordered along the rows and columns.

Bailey and Bickerton offer an alternative model, the "implicational series", in which the variants are ordered according to their tendencies of co-occurrence one with another (1971, 1974). This stresses the role of the linguistic environment, rather than the social environment, and hence interprets variation more as individual choice than as social index. The difference may be largely attributed to the fact that Labov works in large urban communities and Bickerton in isolated rural ones. It is worth mentioning here that Bickerton's work in Guyana is part of another important development through which we are coming to understand a great deal more about the processes of creolization and decreolization, and their very central place in the history of language in general (1973).

The significance of variation theory is that it provides a basis for understanding how language variants come to function as symbols of different social groups and sub-cultures, and of the different models of reality that they present. In this way particular sounds or words or structures become the focus of social attitudes, and serve both to express and to maintain the existing social structure.

This work has considerable implications for multilingual communities. It suggests that 'many-languaged-ness', or "polylectalism" as Bailey calls it, is the norm for human societies, and that it represents in a significant fashion the plurality of different facets of, or 'angles' on, each given culture. This in turn goes some way towards explaining how it comes about that different languages that have coexisted over a long period in a more or less common cultural context come to resemble each other in systematic ways. We return to both these topics in Section 2 below.

1.4. Language varieties: dialect and register

Let us now relate this back to the theme of language and social context. The general notion that links the two is that of 'language variety', of which we can recognize two kinds: dialects (dialectal varieties) and registers (sometimes called diatypic or functional varieties).

1. A dialect is a variety 'according to the user': it is what a person speaks (habitually), determined by who he is. Who he is means, in turn, where he comes from: geographically and socially – the relative weight of these two criteria is highly variable. In principle, dialects are different ways of saying the same things.

In terms of variation theory, a dialect is a regular configuration of variants. In practice, speakers do not mix variants randomly; they associate them in sets which have recognized socio-regional connotations: 'lower middle class south side', 'coastal fishing village' and so on. But it is characteristic of many societies that their speakers learn two or more dialects, both switching between them and mixing them with varying degrees of social meaning.

2. A register is a variety 'according to use'. It is what a person is speaking (at a given moment), determined by what he is doing at the time. What he is doing means the socially recognized type of activity in which he is engaging, and in which speech is playing some part. In principle, registers are ways of saying different things.

All that we have said about dialects and registers applies equally to written language. We have used the words *speech*, *speaking*, and so on, because there is no convenient terminology that is neutral between the two media, the spoken and the written. But both register and dialect are matters of reading and writing as well as of listening and speaking.

207

Both dialects and registers reflect the social order. The existence of dialectal variety reflects the social structure, and the specific phenomenon of social dialects reflects the hierarchical form of the social structure. The existence of registers reflects the variety of human roles and actions, and in particular the social division of labour.

An individual has a 'register range' related to his social roles (Ellis 1965). At the same time, since the division of labour in society is a function of the social structure, there is a systematic association between registers and dialects: certain types of social action typically take place in the 'standard' dialect, others in the 'regional' and others again in the 'local' dialect. The appropriate dialectal choices are learnt along with the register.

The same processes are at work in a multilingual community, except that here we replace 'choice of dialect' (in part, at least) by choice of language. For a bilingual or multilingual speaker, the decision which language to use is a matter of register. This does not mean that there is no individual discretion; as with the choice of dialect, there always is – but in the typical instance there is one 'unmarked' choice, representing the social norm, and any departure from this carries its own special meaning. Of course, there may be conflicting social norms adopted by different groups within the community; but that does not affect the general account.

1.5. Components of the social context

The notion of social context will serve as an explicit determinant of register. The register is the configuration of meanings that are typically associated with a given social context; and of the words and structures (or "wordings", as we have called them) that express these meanings. In order to show the social context as a determinant of register, we can use Labov's two vectors, in a more generalized form, and add a third:

(a) Field. The nature of the social action: what is going on, that has recognizable meaning in the social system, typically a complex of acts in some ordered configuration. What we call "subject matter" is a special aspect of the "field".

(b) Tenor. The role structure: the cluster of socially meaningful participant relationships, both permanent attributes of the participants and role relationships specific to the situation. The "tenor" includes also speech roles, the social roles that come into being as a function of the exchange of meanings: speaker, questioner, respondent and so on.

(c) Mode. The symbolic organization: the particular status that is accorded to the verbal action, and its function in the situation. The "mode" includes the choice of medium (speech or writing), and the rhetorical channel or generic form.

Field, tenor and mode are the generalized components of the social context, similar at a more abstract level to the schemes proposed by Firth and Hymes. They serve to relate a particular context of situation to the social system on the one hand and the linguistic system on the other. We might specify one type of context in which this Symposium is particularly interested briefly as follows:

Field: formal education in school; mathematics
Tenor: teacher (adult) and pupils (children, adolescents); teacher as speaker
Mode: spoken instruction in class

For any speech community, this will identify the register – the typical configurations of meanings, and their lexicogrammatical realizations; and also, by the conventional relation between register and dialect already discussed, the dialect or language in which these meanings are typically encoded. A change on any one of these dimensions may lead to significant variation; for example, if we replace 'mathematics' by 'civics', or 'teacher as speaker' by 'pupil as speaker', or 'spoken' by 'written', or 'instruction' by 'test', we can expect certain systematic differences to appear in each case.

Types of register:
closed   restricted languages (e.g. verbal routines in games)
         languages for special purposes (e.g. weather reporting)
         technical, institutional and other
         'strategized' forms of interaction
            (e.g. classroom discourse)
open   'free' interaction (e.g. gossip)

2. Language and the social order

2.1. *Language and the construction of reality*

It is clear from what preceded that there is no natural boundary between 'language and social context' and 'language and the social order'. Consideration of the one leads into the other, and points in the direction of a sociological theory that will have language as an essential ingredient.

Some of the relevant background may be found in the work of Mead, and subsequently of Goffman and Garfinkel, all of whom have taken account of the place of language in the social definition and maintenance of individual identity. Although none of these three is concerned primarily with language, Mead's treatment of self-identification (1934), Goffman's of self-management (1967) and Garfinkel's of self-explanation (1967) (to characterize them in vastly oversimplified terms) all contain explicit reference to the role of speech in the various forms and sequences of interaction through which the individual achieves his identity.

Coming closer to our present concern is Berger and Luckmann's account of the social construction of reality (1966). Again these authors are not primarily concerned with language, but their work (subtitled "A treatise in the sociology of knowledge") contains important insights into how an individual, largely through verbal interaction, constructs, maintains and manipulates a model of the world in which he lives. The foundations of his reality are laid in the course of primary socialization within the family, however the family is defined in the particular culture in question. These foundations may be strengthened, modified, undermined or even shattered in the course of further socialization, most critically in the family, the children's peer group and the school.

Much more directly concerned with language, and of considerable theoretical significance, is the work of Sacks and Moerman (1964) and Schegloff (1968) on the nature of verbal interaction. Their work shows how ordinary everyday conversational encounters have meaning on many levels at once, in the way that we normally associate with a poem or a novel – indeed Sacks' method of *'explication de texte'* is not unlike an exercise in literary interpretation. This not only reveals a great deal about the nature of social intercourse, and the individual's ability to survive it; it also enables us to see how the innumerable small exchanges that take place in daily life can convey the deeper meanings that lie at the heart of the culture – as they must, since these meanings are not as a rule transmitted through overt instruction.

The fact that people understand each other at all is due to this "reality-generating power of conversation" (Berger & Luckmann 1966): since we have learnt to share the same reality, we can take much of it for granted, and fill in what is left unsaid. What is 'left unsaid' is not omitted so much as condensed, or highly coded; and we know how to unscramble the code.

The educational significance of these observations is reasonably clear. To reduce it to its simplest terms: in our own language, in our own culture, we know most of what the other person is going to say – or rather what he is going to mean, whether or not and in whatever way he says it. The significance of an incoming message lies not in the fact that we do not know what it contains, as in a mathematical model of communication, but in the fact that we do know. The sociolinguistic concept of information is very far removed from that of information theory. If a pupil cannot predict about 90 per cent of what a teacher is going to say, he is unlikely to learn very much. One of the main problems of multilingual education is to create conditions in which at any one moment the pupil knows most of the meanings that are coming at him next, so that those which are unknown are kept down to learnable proportions.

2.2. Sociolinguistic coding orientations

Our understanding of the 'sociolinguistic order' and its educational implications is due above all to the work of Bernstein (1971, 1973). In the course of a long series of brilliantly designed and carefully executed experimental studies in London, Bernstein has shown that different social groups within a complex society may be characterized by different "socio-linguistic coding orientations". For any given social context, they will tend to select different semantic configurations, or registers. The individual's freedom to mean what he likes is constrained by his membership of a social group.

This goes a long way towards explaining the differential response to educational opportunity that is a notable feature of urban life in Western Europe and North America. It is clear that the processes of education – as at present constituted, whether or not they could be constituted otherwise – demand certain particular types of orientation: certain forms of the exchange of meanings are associated with structured learning situations. Different types of family – differing, that is, in terms of their family role systems and socialization practices – differ in the extent to which the sociolinguistic coding orientations achieved by their children correspond with the expectations of the school. And since family type is linked to social class, children from certain social classes tend to experience a sharp discontinuity between ways of meaning in the home and ways of meaning in the school. The school has to compensate by making explicit the principles on which meanings are exchanged in classroom situations.

Thus learning to learn in school is not just a matter of learning technical registers. It is also a matter of learning to exchange meanings in new social contexts; this is still to do with register, but register in the broader sense. In the multilingual context, Hymes has remarked that "the role of language may differ from community to community" (1964). The differences are within limits, no doubt; but limits that are broad enough to generate educationally significant variation. It is not impossible to find within a single classroom children who are culturally, or sub–culturally, predisposed to very different ways of learning through language; all of them in turn being different from the assumptions present in the teacher's training and in the culture from which the language of instruction is derived.

2.3. Learning the mother tongue

Studies of how a child learns his mother tongue, for a time largely confined to the acquisition of grammar and vocabulary, have recently come to emphasize the construction of the semantic system; and this in turn has come to be interpreted as a cognitive process and as a social process. A child learns by listening and talking, especially with "significant others" in "critical socializing contexts". Having built up in infancy an initial picture of the social functions of language, of what language has in it for him, so to speak, he seems to adopt a strategy of distinguishing between language as doing and language as learning, or between action and reflection; and on this basis he constructs a semantic system embodying the Lévi-Straussian characterization of the two-fold role of the environment in all human cultures – as material to be quarried, and as terrain to be explored.

In the interactive process, the learning of language and the learning of the culture through the language take place simultaneously. The child finds the environment reflected in the linguistic structure; but not in any direct way. Language does not 'reflect reality'. What it reflects, in its semantic structure (and therefore, but still more

212

indirectly, in its lexicogrammatical structure), is the social interpretation of reality in the culture in which the child is growing up. In some aspects there is little difference from one culture to another; we all live on the same planet and share the same perceptual apparatus and brain structure. But 'things' (objects, processes, qualities, etc.) are encoded into meanings by virtue of their significance in human interaction; they are the bearers of social value. Hence even such apparently 'objective' notions as transitivity, natural taxonomy, countability and the like are filtered through interpretative processes which may differ from one society to another and which may leave their mark on the language. This is, of course, even more true of the interpersonal areas of the semantic system.

At the same time a child – or even an adult – is not the prisoner of his language. He can always learn to penetrate another sociolinguistic universe; but it requires some kind of a positive act of semiotic reconstruction for him to do so. No doubt some consideration of this kind lay behind the recommendation of the UNESCO meeting of experts in 1951, that whenever possible the mother tongue should be used as the medium of fundamental education (1953).

Hymes' concept of "communicative competence" has been developed by Susan Ervin-Tripp, under the name of "sociolinguistic competence", to refer to the child's developing mastery of a register range (1973). This suggests itself as a measure of individual differences in the command of language. But while no one would deny that individuals do differ in their command of language, there has been little investigation of this from a sociolinguistic point of view, probably because where educationally critical differences in verbal ability have been systematically studied they have always turned out to be determined by social factors.

3. Problems and applications

3.1. Language distance

It is often assumed that genetically related languages are more alike than others; but this is not necessarily true. English is in many respects more closely resembled by Chinese, which is not related to it, than by Russian, which is.

There are indefinitely many ways in which languages can resemble each other; and none of these can be satisfactorily quantified, let alone all of them together, duly weighted. Hence language distance remains an impressionistic concept. Nevertheless it is on the whole a valid and useful one (Neustupný 1971).

The reason is that languages from the same general culture area tend to resemble each other in significant ways, whether they are related or not. This phenomenon, known as "areal affinity", is attested in many areas, for example Western Europe, East Africa, East Asia, South Asia, the South Pacific. An extreme instance has been documented from the Kannada–Marathi border area in South India; these two languages are quite unrelated, but in this particular region they share what is for all practical purposes a common semantics and a common phonology (Gumperz & Wilson 1971).

The mechanisms by which this sort of areal resemblance arises are not at all well understood. But its consequences are important. In general, it is likely to be easier to function effectively in a second language that is from the same culture area than in one that is geographically and culturally remote.

Of the many respects in which one language may differ from another, some are likely to have no great significance for mathematical education, or for education generally. Other kinds of difference, though not necessarily very fundamental in terms of the semantic systems of the languages concerned, may nevertheless turn out to have a considerable effect on how children learn certain general concepts; and if so they might be relevant to questions of pedagogical design.

An example could be drawn from lexical taxonomy, the representation of classes in the vocabulary. In some instances, classification is explicit in the form of the words, while in others it is not. Contrast the names of vehicles in Chinese and in English:

(a)	(b)
chē	vehicle
mǎchē	cart
diànchē	tram (streetcar)
huǒchē	train
qìchē	car (automobile)
zìxíngchē	bicycle

In the former, the general term chē 'vehicle' is present as an element in the make-up of all the specific terms; in the latter it is not. English has sets of the former type, but they are both less regular and less typical than they are in Chinese.* Moreover, the existence of a morphological series like that in (a) is in itself no guarantee of class membership; consider the following words in Malay:

(c)

mata	'eye'	
mata hari	'sun'	(hari = 'day')
mata ayer	'spring'	(ayer = 'water')
mata katu	'knot'	(katu = 'wood')
mata susu	'nipple'	(susu = 'breast')
mata kuching	(kind of fruit)	(kuching = 'cat')

Whereas car, train, tram, etc. are all kinds of vehicle, sun, spring, knot, etc. are not kinds of eye; the Malay series illustrates metaphorical compounding, by contrast with the taxonomic compounding of the Chinese. Frequently both types occur within the same series: an oaktree is a kind of tree, but a shoetree is not.

Here we have illustrated (a) a class which is expressed by a morphological series, (b) a class which is not a morphological series, and (c) a morphological series which is not a class. Probably most languages, perhaps all, display all these patterns; but they display them in different measure (and in different parts of the vocabulary).

The relevance of this phenomenon not only to the creation of terminology but also to the teaching of mathematical concepts seems fairly clear. But there is a caution to be added. It would be easy to use these examples to demonstrate that English was a very inefficient language for mathematics and science; and a whole lot of other arguments could be used to 'prove' the superiority of Chinese in this respect. Now Chinese of course functions very effectively in these contexts; but so do Russian, English, Hungarian, Japanese and a number of other very diverse languages. Appropriateness is often a matter of people's attitude, and attitudes reflect **socio**linguistic distance, not linguistic distance: a language with a very different set of cultural functions (different from some implicit norm, such as English) tends to be regarded as exotic, and as representing a distinct mode of logical thought, even when in terms of its internal structure it is not strikingly different.

---

* A further difference is that in Chinese the general term chē is an ordinary colloquial word along with the rest, used in contexts where it is not necessary to be more specific. If the tram stops in front of you, you say 'hurry up and get on the vehicle' (kuài shàng chē), not 'get on the tram'. The English word *vehicle* belongs to a different register.

A major problem, then, is to identify the two kinds of linguistic distance that may be of significance in the present context:

(i) non-semantic differences which affect the forms of expression of key concepts (see the example of lexical taxonomy, above)

(ii) semantic differences, those which affect the system of meanings (and may suggest different interpretations of reality).

and to separate both of these from sociolinguistic distance, specifically

(iii) differences of register, such as the presence or absence of a register of mathematics, or mathematics teaching.

It is the last of these which calls for a measure of language planning.

3.2. Language planning

Language planning has two aspects to it, the linguistic and the sociolinguistic. The first is concerned with the development of language as a system (i.e. with the language itself), the second with the development of language as an institution (i.e. with the relation of the language to its speakers).

1. The development of language as a system is chiefly interpreted in practice as the addition of new vocabulary. Planning may take the form of creating a commission on terminology charged with the codification of new terms – typically, technical terms from the sciences, law, administration and the like.

In some instances the specialists concerned, perhaps responding to expressions of feeling among the public, have rejected as undesirable the practice of "borrowing" words from a foreign language, in favour of creating matching terms out of elements of the native vocabulary (in the way that German *fernsprechen* matches the international form *telephone*, being made up of 'distant' and 'speak'). In some languages this process of borrowing via translation, known in linguistics as "calquing", is entirely natural; Chinese is an example of a language which nearly always imports new terms in this way. In other languages, however, it is very unnatural. Both Japanese and English are 'borrowing' languages and do not take readily to calques (there have been unsuccessful attempts to introduce them into English from time to time).

The development of vocabulary is really a semantic process, one of adding new 'thing-meanings' – names of objects, processes, institutions and so on. It can take place in a number of ways: not only by

216

importation from outside, in the form of borrowing or calquing, but also by creating new compounds from inside (like Chinese *huŏchē* 'fire vehicle', a popular nineteenth-century creation for 'steam train' which then came into general use); by extending the meaning of existing words (like English *train*, from the expression 'a train of coaches'), often with very picturesque analogies; and sometimes by inventing entirely new words, like *gas* in the eighteenth century, or modern *laser* (from *light maser*, *maser* being an acronym of 'microwave amplification by stimulated emission of radiation').

There have been some studies of the development of technical and industrial terminology in European languages, but information on the natural processes of lexical development in other languages is very scarce. Yet this kind of planning would benefit very much from studies of how people in different language communities create their own new terms when faced with new techniques and new artifacts. No language is fully consistent; every language is a mixture of types, and it would be wrong to suggest that there can be no typological innovations in the creation of new terms. In the last resort, only the speakers of a language have a feeling for what transplants will 'take' and what will not.

The issue of grammatical structure is more problematical. Many linguists would question the assumptions made in Appendix I to the Short Description of the Symposium, to the effect that "the logical structure of the world languages corresponds closely to the needs in mathematics for systematization, precision and reasoning", whereas the logical structure of a vernacular language may not. They would argue that all languages have essentially the same logical structure and that the differences are merely superficial. Others who would not go so far as this would nevertheless maintain that, while languages do differ in their essential structure, none is intrinsically more or less well suited to mathematical reasoning and systematization than any other; it was impossible to do modern mathematics in Chaucerian English, and what is needed is that the process of introducing new semantic configurations, which in English took four or five centuries, should somehow be speeded up. It is important to add, incidentally, that there is no consensus as to what the "logical" structure of a natural language really means.

2. The development of language as an institution usually involves (a) the adoption of one or more than one national language (also perhaps 'official', 'regional', etc. languages), and/or, for any language, the adoption of one (occasionally more than one) standard dialect; (b)

decisions about the use of these tongues in specified social contexts, including their place in the educational process.

(a) Adopting national, official or regional languages means, in effect, codifying the respective status of the different languages of the community. This is not so much an 'all-or-nothing' matter as a matter of the assignment of different roles. A country may have, say, two national languages each with one standard dialect; an international or official language; and a number of recognized regional languages – all of these having their defined functions, often overlapping but still recognizably distinct. Experience suggests that planning of this kind can be effective provided it is aimed at assisting, and perhaps speeding up, tendencies that are taking place naturally. It is generally not effective if it seeks to run counter to such tendencies.

(b) Decisions may be taken about the use of these languages in particular fields of social action – ranging from administration and the laws of the country to family names and street signs. The successful implementation of such decisions depends on the extent to which they are matched by effective educational language planning. The latter determines what languages are taught in school, and when; and what languages are the media of instruction, and when.

Clearly there is a close relation between the choice of a language as a medium of instruction and the development of that language as a system. If a language has not previously been used in mathematical contexts it cannot serve as a medium of mathematical education without some preparation. The translation of textbooks is probably as quick and practical a way as any of extending a language into a new educational field.

Finally it is perhaps relevant to note that, in addition to the language of instruction, there is also the language of interaction, the language in which the teacher and pupils actually talk to each other in situations other than those of formal teaching. In many instances this differs from the official educational medium, and it would be interesting to find out to what extent, for really difficult and critical steps in the learning process, teachers switch away from the official medium and into a vernacular – even if this is not an accredited language for the specialized topic concerned.

PART THREE

LANGUAGE AND SOCIAL CLASS

EDITOR'S INTRODUCTION

The two papers in this section, ' "Foreword" to Basil Bernstein's *Class, Codes and Control* vol. 2' (1973) and 'Language and the theory of codes' (1994) underscore the centrality of language in Bernstein's theory. Professor Halliday credits Basil Bernstein with having given linguists "a richer view of the processes of meaning", and likens his influence to that of such leading figures from outside the discipline of linguistics as Bühler and Malinowski.

Prompted by his experience teaching in inner London in the late 1950s, Bernstein sought to find out why educational failure was particularly prevalent among children from the lower working class. As for the role played by language in educational failure, Bernstein's work clearly showed it was neither about language as a system (the deficit version) nor language as an institution (the difference version). Rather, the reason why "not all children have equal access to the mysteries of educational discourse" has more to do with "differences in the relative orientation of different social groups towards the various functions of language in given contexts and towards the different areas of meaning that may be explored within a given function". While some children enjoy "a continuity of culture between home and school", others are disadvantaged by differences in values, communication patterns and learning styles between their sub-culture and those built into the educational process.

Bernstein developed his theory of *codes* to explain this sub-cultural variation in patterns or habits of speech adopted by speakers who speak the same language. From a linguistic perspective, codes may be interpreted as the "differences in orientation within the total semiotic potential". Or as in Bernstein's own words, "a code is a regulative

221

principle, tacitly acquired, which selects and integrates relevant meanings, forms of realizations, and evoking contexts" (Bernstein 1990: 101); the codes "essentially transmit the culture and constrain behaviour" (Bernstein 1971: 122).

As reported in Chapter 8, in the years between when the two papers in this section were written, during the mid-1980s, Professor Ruqaiya Hasan assembled a database of authentic speech comprising 100 hours of mother-child interaction as the basis for an evaluative study of Bernstein's findings. The outcome of her investigation, which drew on recent advances in theory and methodology for conducting large-scale quantitative studies of language, confirmed Bernstein's results.

Emerging from Bernstein's work are real concerns about social equality and social justice. The problem, as summed up by Professor Halliday, is this: if attaining social equality depends on being educated, and in order to be educated you have to operate with a particular code, then those without access to that code, for whatever reason, are being denied social justice: either their access to it must be opened up, or the processes of education must be changed.

Chapter Seven

FOREWORD TO BASIL BERNSTEIN'S *CLASS, CODES AND CONTROL VOL. 2: APPLIED STUDIES TOWARDS A SOCIOLOGY OF LANGUAGE* (1973)

The work of Professor Basil Bernstein has sometimes been referred to as 'a theory of educational failure'. This seems to me misleading; the truth is both more, and less, than this implies. More, because Bernstein's theory is a theory about society, how a society persists and how it changes; it is a theory of the nature and processes of cultural transmission, and of the essential part that is played by language therein. Education is one of the forms taken by the transmission process, and must inevitably be a major channel for persistence and change; but there are other channels – and the education system itself is shaped by the social structure. Less, because Bernstein does not claim to be providing a total explanation of the causes of educational failure; he is offering an interpretation of one aspect of it, the fact that the distribution of failure is not random but follows certain known and sadly predictable patterns – by and large, it is a problem which faces children of the lower working class in large urban areas. Even here Bernstein is not trying to tell the whole story; what he is doing is to supply the essential link that was missing from the chain of relevant factors.

Nevertheless, it is perhaps inevitable that Bernstein's work should be best known through its application to educational problems, since these are the most striking and the most public of the issues with which he is concerned. After the relative confidence of 15 post-war years, the 1960s were marked by growing awareness of a crisis in education, a realization that it was not enough to ensure that all children were

'Foreword', from Basil Bernstein (ed.), *Class, Codes and Control Vol. II: Applied Studies towards a Sociology of Lanugage,* London: Routledge and Kegan Paul, 1973, pp.ix–xvi. Copyright © Taylor and Francis Ltd.

adequately nourished and spent a certain number of years receiving formal education in school. The 'crisis' consists in the discovery that large numbers of children of normal intelligence, who have always had enough to eat, pass through the school system and come out as failures. We say, 'society has given them the opportunity, and they have failed to respond to it'; we feel hurt, and we want to know the reason why. (The formulation is not intended to imply a lack of genuine concern.)

Many people are aware of the existence of a hypothesis that educational failure is in some sense to be explained as linguistic failure. Something has gone wrong, it is suggested, with the language. This notion is in the air, so to speak; and the source of it is to be found in Bernstein's work – even though the various forms in which it is mooted often bear little relation to Bernstein's ideas. The terms that have become most widely current are Bernstein's "elaborated code" and "restricted code"; and in spite of the care which Bernstein has taken to emphasize that neither is more highly valued than the other, and that the hypothesis is that both are necessary for successful living – though the processes of formal education may demand the elaborated code – there is a widespread impression that Bernstein is saying (1) that some children speak elaborated code and some children speak restricted code and (2) that the latter is an inferior form of speech, and therefore children who speak it are likely to fail. With these is sometimes compounded a further distortion according to which elaborated code is somehow equated with standard language and restricted code with non-standard. And the confusion is complete.

But if there is confusion, it is because there is something to be confused about. The difficulty is a very real one, and it is this. If language is the key factor, the primary channel, in socialization, and if the form taken by the socialization process is (in part) responsible for educational failure, then language is to blame; there must be something wrong about the language of the children who fail in school. So the reasoning goes. Either their language is deficient in some way, or, if not, then it is so different from the 'received' language of the school (and, by implication, of the community) that it is **as if** it was deficient – it acts as a barrier to successful learning and teaching. So we find two main versions of the 'language failure' theory, a "deficit" version and a "difference" version; and these have been discussed at length in the context of 'Black English' in the United States, where the problem of educational failure tends to be posed in ethnic rather than in social class terms. The language failure theory is sometimes referred to Bernstein's work, and he has even been held responsible for the deficit version of the theory, although nothing

224

could be further removed from his own thinking. The fact that language failure is offered both as an interpretation of Bernstein's theories and as an alternative to them shows how complex the issues are and how easily they become clouded.

Let us consider the notion of language failure. According to the deficit version of the theory, the child who fails in school fails because he has not got enough language. It then becomes necessary to say where, in his language, the deficiency lies; and according to linguistic theory there are four possibilities, although these are combinable – the deficiency might lie in more than one: sounds, words, constructions and meanings.

Probably few people nowadays would diagnose the trouble as deficiency in sounds, although the 'our job is to teach them to talk properly' view of education is still with us, and might be taken to imply some such judgement of the case. If we leave this aside, there are two, and possibly a third, variants of the theory: not enough vocabulary, not enough grammar (or "structures", in contemporary jargon), and a rarer and rather sophisticated alternative, not enough meanings. (Perhaps we should recognize another variant, according to which the child has no language at all. This cannot seriously be called a theory; but some people who would vigorously deny it if it was put to them in that form behave as if they held this view – 'they have been exposed to good English, so obviously they have not the resources with which to absorb it'.) We have to take these views seriously; they are held by serious-minded people of good faith who have thought about the problem and are anxious to find a solution. At the same time it needs to be said quite firmly that they are wrong.

There is no convincing evidence that children who fail in school have a smaller available vocabulary, or a less rich grammatical system, than those who succeed. Studies measuring the extent of the vocabulary used by children in the performance of specific tasks, though very valuable, do not tell us about their total resources; and formulations of the overall size of a child's vocabulary tend to conceal some doubtful assumptions about the nature of language. In the first place, one cannot really separate vocabulary from grammar; the two form a single component in the linguistic system, and measuring one without the other is misleading. It may well be that one individual extends his potential more by enlarging his grammatical resources, while another, or the same individual at a different time, does so by building up a larger vocabulary; and different varieties of a language, for example its spoken and written forms, tend to exploit these resources differentially. Second, there are so many problems in counting – how do we decide what a person **could** have said, or whether two things he **did** say were the same or different? – that it is hardly possible to assess an individual's linguistic resources accurately in quantitative terms. Finally, even if we could do so, it would tell us very little about his linguistic potential, which depends only in the last resort on the size of inventory. One does not count the gestures in order to evaluate the qualities of an actor, or judge a composer by the number of different chords and phrases he uses; it is only necessary to think of the immense variation, among writers, in the extent of the linguistic resources they typically deploy. In other words, there is no reliable way of saying 'this child has a smaller linguistic inventory (than that one, or than some presumed standard)'; and it would not help us much if we could.

But there are more serious weaknesses in the deficit theory. If there is a deficit, we have to ask: is it that the child has not got enough language, or that he does not know how to use what he has? But this question is meaningless. There is no sense in which we can maintain that he knows a linguistic form but cannot use it. (Of course one may get the meaning of a word or a construction wrong, but that is not what the question is about; in that case one does not know it.) The fact that we are led to pose the question in this way is an indication of the basic fallacy in the theory, a fallacy the nature of which we can see even more clearly when we pose another awkward question: is the presumed deficit an individual matter, or is it subcultural? Here we must assume the second, since the former would not offer any explanation of the pattern of educational failure. In other words the supposition is that there are groups of people – social class groups, ethnic groups, family types or some other – whose language is deficient; in linguistic terms, that there are deficient social dialects. As soon as we put it like that, the fallacy becomes obvious. Unfortunately, as Joan Baratz pointed out in a similar context, the idea of a deficient dialect is so patently self-contradictory and absurd that no linguist has ever taken the trouble to deny it. Perhaps the time has come to make an explicit denial.

We are left with the "difference" version of the theory. This holds that some children's language is different from others'; this is undeniable, so the question is whether it is relevant. If one child's language differs from another's, but neither is deficient relative to the other, why is one of the children at a disadvantage?

The answer comes in two forms, one being a stronger variant of the other. We assume that the difference is that between a dialect and the standard language (in linguistic terms, between non-standard and standard dialects). Then, in the weaker variant, the child who speaks the non-standard dialect is at a disadvantage because certain factors demand the use of the standard. Many such factors could be cited, but they tend to fall under three headings: the teacher, the subject matter and the system. The child who speaks non-standard may be penalized by the teacher for doing so; he has to handle material presented in the standard language, for example in textbooks; and he has to adjust to an educational process and a way of life that is largely or entirely conducted in the standard language. This already raises the odds against him; and they are raised still higher if we now take the stronger variant of the difference theory, which adds the further explanation that non-standard dialects are discriminated against by society. In other words, the standard language is required not only by specific factors in the child's education but also by social pressures and prejudices, which have the effect that the child's own mother tongue is downgraded and he is stereotyped as likely to fail.

Now all this is certainly true. Moreover, as Frederick Williams found in testing the "stereotype hypothesis" in the United States, the teacher's expectations of a pupil's performance tend to correspond rather closely to the extent to which that pupil's dialect diverges from the standard – and children, like adults, tend to act out their stereotypes: if you have decided in advance that a child will fail, he probably will. Many of the assumptions of the difference theory are justified, and these undoubtedly play some part in educational failure.

But there is still one question unanswered. If children are suffering because of their dialect, why do they not learn another one? Children have no difficulty in doing this; in many parts of the world it is quite common for a child to learn three or even four varieties of his mother tongue. Rural dialects in Britain differ from the standard much more widely than the urban dialects do, either in Britain or in America; yet rural children do not have the problem, which is well known to be an urban one. Moreover there is considerable evidence that these children who, it is claimed, are failing because they cannot handle the standard language can imitate it perfectly well outside the classroom, and often do. Perhaps then the problem lies in the written language: has the dialect-speaking child a special difficulty in learning to read in the standard? But here we are on even weaker ground, because the English writing system is splendidly neutral with regard to dialect. It is as well adapted to Glaswegian or Harlem speech as it is to standard British or American; that is its great strength. There are no special **linguistic**

227

problems involved in learning to read just because one happens to speak a non-standard variety of English.

In other words, the 'difference' version of the language failure theory does not explain why dialect-speaking children come off badly – for the very good reason that the child who speaks a non-standard dialect is not under any linguistic disadvantage at all. His disadvantage is a social one. This does not mean that it is not real; but it means that it is misleading to treat it as if it was linguistic and to seek to apply linguistic remedies. Part of the social disadvantage lies in society's attitudes to language and to dialect – including those of the teacher, who may interpose false notions about language which **create** problems of a linguistic nature. But these are only manifestations of patterns in the social structure; they do not add up to a linguistic explanation of the facts.

So the language failure theory, in both versions, stands rejected. We have removed all linguistic content from the hypothesis about educational failure. The fault rests neither with language as a system (the deficit version) nor with language as an institution (the difference version); the explanation is a social one (and, in Bernstein's words, "education cannot compensate for society"). And here, in my own thinking, the matter rested, for a considerable time; I did not accept that there was any essentially linguistic element in the situation.

But, reconsidering in the light of Bernstein's work, especially his more recent thinking, we can see that the question 'deficit or difference?' is the wrong question. It is not what the issue is about. If we look at the results of investigations carried out by Bernstein and his colleagues, as reported in the present volume, and in other monographs in the series, we find that these studies reveal certain differences which correlate significantly with social class; these differences are there, and they are in some sense linguistic – they have to do with language. But the differences do not usually appear undisguised in the linguistic forms, the grammar and vocabulary, of the children's speech. They are, rather, differences of interpretation, evaluation, orientation, on the part of the children and of their mothers. Even where the primary data are drawn from samples of children's spontaneous speech, and this is analysed in linguistic terms, the focus of attention is always on the principles of the social functioning of language. Two features of the research stand out in this connection. One is the emphasis on "critical social contexts", as Bernstein has defined and identified them: generalized situation types which have greatest significance for the child's socialization and for his interpretation of experience. The other is the focus on the variable **function** of language within these contexts, and on the functional

228

meaning potential that is available to, and typically exhibited by, the child who is participating.

What Bernstein's work suggests is that there may be differences in the relative orientation of different social groups towards the various functions of language in given contexts and towards the different areas of meaning that may be explored within a given function. Now if this is so, then when these differences manifest themselves in the contexts that are critical for the socialization process they may have a profound effect on the child's social learning; and therefore on his response to education, because built in to the educational process are a number of assumptions and practices that reflect differentially not only the values but also the communication patterns and learning styles of different sub-cultures. As Bernstein has pointed out, not only does this tend to favour certain modes of learning over others, but it also creates for some children a continuity of culture between home and school which it largely denies to others.

This puts the question of the role of language in a different light. We can interpret the codes, from a linguistic point of view, as differences of orientation within the total semiotic potential. There is evidence in Bernstein's work that different social groups or sub-cultures place a high value on different orders of meaning. Hence differences arise in the prominence accorded to one or another socio-semantic 'set', or meaning potential within a given context. For any particular sub-culture, certain functions of language, or areas of meaning within a given function, may receive relatively greater emphasis; these will often reflect values which are implicit and submerged, but in other instances the values might be explicitly recognized – such different concepts as 'fellowship', 'soul', 'blarney', 'brow' (highbrow, lowbrow), suggest certain functional orientations which might well be examined from this standpoint. And there will be other orders of meaning, and other functions of language, that are relatively less highly valued and receive less emphasis. In general this does not matter. But let us now suppose that the semiotic modes that are relatively stressed by one group are **positive** with respect to the school – they are favoured and extended in the educational process, either inherently or because this is how education has come to be actualized – while those that are relatively stressed by another group are largely irrelevant, or even **negative**, in the educational context. We then have a plausible interpretation of the role of language in educational failure. It is, certainly, much over-simplified, as we have stated it here. But it places language in a perspective that is relevant to education – namely as the key factor in cultural transmission – instead of isolating it as something on its own.

This is somewhat removed from the notion of 'language failure', in either the deficit or the difference versions. We have had to direct attention beyond the forms of language, beyond accent and dialect and the morphological and syntactic particulars of this or that variety of English, on to meaning and social function. Of course, there are myths and misconceptions about, and attitudes towards, the forms of language, and these enter into and complicate the picture. It is important to make it clear that speakers of English who have no initial *h* or no postvocalic *r*, no verbal substitute or no definite article or no –*s* on the third person singular present tense, are not verbal defectives (if they are, then we all are, since any such list could always be made up – as this one was – of standard as well as non-standard features); nor is the underlying logic of one group any different from that of another. But just as the language element in educational failure cannot be reduced to a question of linguistic forms, so also it cannot be wholly reduced to one of attitudes to those forms and the stereotypes that result from them. It cannot be reduced to a concept of linguistic failure at all.

However, if we reject the equation 'educational failure = linguistic failure', this does not mean that we reject any interpretation of the problem in linguistic terms. Language is central to Bernstein's theory; but in order to understand the place that it occupies, it is necessary to think of language as meaning rather than of language as structure. The problem can then be seen to be one of linguistic success rather than linguistic failure. Every normal child has a fully functional linguistic system; the difficulty is that of reconciling one functional orientation with another. The remedy will not lie in the administration of concentrated doses of linguistic structure. It **may** lie, in part, in the broadening of the functional perspective – that of the school, as much as that of the individual pupil. This, in turn, demands a broadening of our own conceptions, especially our conceptions of meaning and of language. Not the least of Bernstein's contributions is the part that his work, and that of his colleagues, has played in bringing this about.

230

Chapter Eight

LANGUAGE AND THE THEORY OF CODES
(1994)

Given that (1) native wit is not determined by social class, and (2) all children now receive equivalent basic schooling, why are those children who **fail** to become educated almost all from the lower working class? This was the question that Bernstein set out to answer, when teaching in inner London in the late 1950s. He began by explaining it in terms of perception: working-class children learn to be sensitive to content, and to perceive phenomena in terms of the boundaries between them, whereas middle-class children learn to be sensitive to structure, and to perceive phenomena in terms of the relationships of one to another. But early on in his work he came to see that the differences were essentially semiotic: differences in the way the children learn to **mean**. The sources therefore had to be found in language.

What first brought language into the explanatory model was Bernstein's sense that language mediated more strongly in middle-class than in working-class forms of interaction. Where the working-class attitude to things, and to social relationships, was non-instrumental, with present activities having greater value than future goals, the middle-class attitude was one of orientation to distant ends; hence both personal experience and interpersonal relations were more highly verbalized, and "the word mediates between the expression of feeling and its approved social recognition" (CCC1: 25).[1] To give a prototypical example, any parent will tell a child *Shut up!*, where the authority, while arbitrary, is made explicit; but the verbally elaborated

'Language and the Theory of Codes', from Alan Sadovnik (ed.), *Knowledge and Pedagogy: The Sociology of Basil Bernstein,* Westport: Greenwood Publishing Group, 1995. Copyright © 1995 by Alan Sadovnik and contributors. Reproduced with permission of Greenwood Publishing Group, Inc., Westport, CT.

alternative *I'd rather you made less noise with your whistle, darling* is much more likely to be heard in a middle-class context. In the latter, the child is being oriented to certain values, but at the same time he or she is being identified as an individual; the authority is implicit, while the child, and the child's personal experience, are being explicitly differentiated in the wording.

What differed significantly here, according to Bernstein, was not the formal properties of the language, such as extent of vocabulary, but the "mode of language use": the middle class' personal qualifications and differentiation of experience, contrasted with the working class' immediacy of communication, an expressive symbolism with few personal qualifications. Bernstein referred to the two modes as "formal language" and "public language". The public language was character-ized by "fragmentation and logical simplicity", few causal connections, and referencing in the here-and-now; whereas in the formal language relations of causality were foregrounded and space, time and social relationships "regulated" in explicit terms. (CCC1: 30). Typically, a middle-class child controls both forms of language, while a working-class child may be restricted to participation in the "public" mode.

Since the school demands a formal language, middle-class children come prepared; they can enter into personal relationship with the teacher and give meaning to their new experience within the context of the old. Working-class children face a discontinuity; their new experiences cannot be referred back to existing principles and generalizations, and hence teacher and pupil tend to disvalue one another. Thus "a great deal of potential ability is being lost" (CCC1: 31); and this was borne out by current measures of "intelligence": while there was no difference between the class populations in non-verbal intelligence scores, there was in the scores for tests of "verbal intelligence". Not only did the working-class children show a greater discrepancy between the two, but the higher the level of non verbal intelligence the greater the discrepancy appeared.

Bernstein then tried to make the difference between public language and formal language explicit in linguistic terms. He listed the following as features of public language (CCC1: 42–3): short, grammatically simple, often unfinished sentences; simple repetitive use of conjunc-tions; frequent use of short commands and questions; rigid and limited use of adjectives and adverbs; infrequent use of impersonal pronouns as subject; statements formulated as implicit questions which set up a "sympathetic circularity" (e.g. *You wouldn't believe it!*); reason and conclusion confounded to produce a categoric statement (e.g. *You're not going out!*); frequent selection from a group of idiomatic phrases; symbolism of a low order of generality; and individual qualification left implicit in the sentence structure. This last point is glossed "therefore it is a language of implicit meaning. *It is believed that this fact determines the form of the language*" (Bernstein's italics). As they stand, such formulations are difficult to interpret; but they are expanded in the discussion which follows, and explicitly contrasted with the characteristics of a formal language. Bernstein concludes that "A public language contains its own aesthetic, a simplicity and directness of expression, emotionally virile, pithy and powerful, and a metaphoric range of considerable force and appropriateness. ... The problem would seem to be to preserve *public* language usage but also to create for the individual the possibility of utilizing a *formal* language" (CCC1: 54).

By this time, however, Bernstein was moving towards a more general theory of language and cultural transmission. As early as 1959 he was pointing out, with acknowledgement to Sapir, that "*the semantic function of a language is the social structure*" (Bernstein's italics); and by 1962 this had become the point of departure for a "theory of social learning" in which "the social structure transforms language possibility into a specific code which elicits, generalizes and reinforces those relationships necessary for its continuance" (CCC1: 76). At this point, Bernstein introduced the concept of linguistic codes:

> Two general types of code can be distinguished: *elaborated* and *restricted*. They can be defined, on a linguistic level, in terms of the probability of predicting for any one speaker which syntactic elements will be used to organize meaning.
>
> (CCC1: 76)

In the elaborated code, the speaker selects from a wider range of alternatives, and therefore the "pattern of organizing elements" is less easy to predict.

The codes have thus replaced the formal and public languages. The restricted code is fluent, well organized and unplanned – that is, not under attention as the speaker goes along; its major function is "to reinforce the *form* of the social relationship (a warm and inclusive relationship) by restricting the verbal signalling of individuated responses" (CCC1: 78). The elaborated code is explicit and individuated; there is a high degree of verbal planning, and the listener's intent is not taken for granted. The elaborated code thus construes meanings in terms of general principles, whereas in the restricted code meanings are "less conventionalized through language" and hence are prototypically specific. By the same token, the meanings of the restricted code are accessible to all; whereas those of the elaborated code are accessible only to those having a decision-making role in social processes. Bernstein makes this appear paradoxical by using the terms "universalistic/particularistic" to label both oppositions – both general versus specific meanings, and open versus limited access; but the paradox is only apparent. It is clear that semantic generalization = knowledge = authority = power, and power in the social structure is by definition available to some members but not all.

Once again Bernstein sought to characterize the opposition in concrete, linguistic terms, this time using speech samples from recorded discussions among two groups of secondary school pupils. He found that the middle-class group used more (1) subordinations, (2) verbal group complexes, (3) passives, (4) adjectives, (5) uncommon adjectives, adverbs and conjunctions, (6) first person pronouns and (7) subjective modalities (like *I think*); the working-class group used more (8) personal pronouns, (9) third person pronouns, (10) second person pronouns and (11) question tags (and other elements grouped together as "sympathetic circularity"). These differences were interpreted as follows: middle-class speakers make their intent more verbally explicit and differentiated (1–5), and structure the discourse by referring to their individuated selves (6–7); working-class speakers assume "implicit agreement about the referent", alternating between the highly specific and the highly general (8–9), and structure the discourse by reinforcing their shared intent (10–11).

"The particular form a social relation takes acts selectively on what is said, when it is said and how it is said. The form of the social relation regulates the options which speakers take up at both syntactic and lexical levels" (CCC1: 123–4). Hence "as the child learns his speech or, in the terms used here, learns specific codes which regulate his verbal acts, he learns the requirements of his social structure". Speech is "the process by which a child comes to acquire a specific social identity", the "constellation of shared learned meanings through which he enters into interaction with others" (*ibid.*). Language is unequivocally being assigned a critical role in the social construction of reality; and Bernstein cites Mead, Sapir and Whorf, and Malinowski and Firth, as predecessors who have adopted this view. His theory of "codes" explains the mechanism by which language comes to function in this way, constructing a 'reality' that is based on social class. The codes *"essentially transmit the culture and constrain behaviour"* (CCC1: 122; Bernstein's italics).

The problem was to locate the concept of "code" within the framework of a general theory of language. Linguists were familiar with two kinds of linguistic variation: dialectal and diatypic (see Gregory 1967; Halliday 1970*a*). Dialectal variation is regional and social: your dialect, or dialect repertory, is determined by where you come from, geographically and/or social-hierarchically, and dialects differ in form and expression rather than in meaning: prototypically, they are different ways of saying the same things. Diatypic variation is functional: your register range is determined by what you do, in the division of labour, and registers prototypically differ in meaning: they are ways of saying different things. Where do codes belong in the overall scheme?

That code differed both from register and from social dialect was clearly brought out by Hasan (1973; in CCC2: Chapter 10), who was a member of Bernstein's Sociological Research Unit at the time of writing. Hasan pointed out that codes differed from dialects in that their distinctive properties are semantic, not formal and expressive, and that their link to extra-linguistic factors is causal not incidental (CCC2: 258). They differed from registers in that their semantic properties correlate with generalized role systems rather than with specific factors of a particular context of situation (CCC2: 282); hence they are transmitted through more general situation **types**, especially Bernstein's "critical socializing contexts", the regulative, instructional, imaginative (or innovating) and interpersonal. Hasan observes that "code is thus a much more global concept than register" (CCC2: 286).

Bernstein was concerned to avoid any suggestion that the two codes he had identified should be thought of as different languages. At this time a sharp distinction was being drawn, in the dominant American school of linguistics following Chomsky, between "competence" and "performance": a reworking of Saussure's "*langue/parole*" dichotomy in terms of Chomsky's conception of language as a litany of rules. Bernstein tried to adapt this distinction to the task of explaining the codes (CCC1: 173–4). In doing so, he located the codes squarely within performance. Using the terminological opposition of "language" and "speech", he referred to the codes as "speech codes" or "speech forms":

> But if we are to study speech, *la parole*, we are inevitably involved in a study of a rather different rule system [sc. from that of the formal properties of the grammar]; we are involved in a study of rules, formal and informal, which regulate the options we take up in various contexts in which we find ourselves. This second rule system

is the cultural system. . . . On this argument, language is a set of rules to which all speech codes must comply, but which speech codes are realized is a function of the culture acting through social relationships in specific contexts. . . .

It should be clear from these opening remarks that I am not concerned with language, but with speech, and concerned more specifically with the contextual constraints upon speech.

(CCC1: 173–4)

In other words the codes are different patterns or habits of **speech** (in one place Bernstein had used the formulation "speech systems", CCC1: 131) adopted by speakers of the same **language** as a result of sub-cultural variation. (I shall come back to "difference versus deficit" below; but this formulation clearly seems to rule out any interpretation of code in terms of deficit.) Interestingly, Hymes, who faced a similar problem of trying to formulate his ideas in Chomskyan terms, came up at about the same time with the opposite solution; he coined the term "communicative competence" to account for sociolinguistic norms and their attainment in patterns of speech (Hymes, 1971).

But the real problem lies in the nature of the dichotomy itself, no matter what it is called. We are talking here about a general property of all semiotic systems, with language being the prototype: language (or "competence") is the **potential** of the system, as a resource for making meaning; speech (or "performance") is its **instantiation** in text. But system and text, however we may reify them with terminological oppositions like *"langue/parole"* or "language" and "speech", are not two different orders of phenomena. They are the same thing, seen from different ends. There is only one phenomenon here, the social activity of making meaning through language; but this phenomenon can be **viewed** from opposite perspectives – either as potential, or as (sets of) instances. What we call "language" and "speech" represent different standpoints of the observer. They are very much like "climate" and "weather". Faced with the prolonged drought in southern Africa, we ask: is this a perturbation in the weather patterns, or is it a change in the climate? But what this means is: from what depth in time should we be viewing it? where should we locate ourselves along the cline of instantiation?

The difficulty we have with the concept of "code" in Bernstein's model, as I have suggested elsewhere (Halliday 1992: 71–3, 88), is that – very much as with the concept of global warming – we need to position ourselves at some midpoint along the scale. In order to be able to do this, we have to view "code" simultaneously from both perspectives, seeing it both as **variation in the system** (in the semiotic climate, or meaning potential) and as **different patterns in the text** (in the semiotic weather, the way this potential is instantiated). The regularities that Bernstein is observing and accounting for lie just at this intermediate depth.

This is not a matter of verbal juggling. On the contrary; our choice of perspective will determine not only how we interpret the situation but also whether, and if so how, we intervene. Bernstein's point of departure was that "clearly, one code is not better than another; each possesses its own aesthetic, its own possibilities. Society, however, may place different values on the orders of experience elicited ... through the different coding systems" (CCC1: 135). As a weatherman – an instance observer – he saw that the more highly valued coding system, the one demanded by the school, could be learnt by children of any background; it could therefore be taught, as appropriate canons of "performance". In this way one could intervene in the educational process. But as a climatologist – a system observer – he also saw that the codes played the major role in transmitting culture (and Bernstein's theory of socialization showed how these processes took place);[2] hence they were relatively stable and self-perpetuating. Codes were a feature of a class society, refracting, symbolizing, transmitting and ongoingly recreating the social order. From this perspective it becomes clear that "education cannot compensate for society" (see CCC1: Chapter 10). The only way to intervene is to bring about "changes in the social structure of educational institutions" (CCC1: 136): that is, changes in "competence".

Bernstein therefore gave up his attempt to define the codes exclusively in terms of performance. Since this perspective, especially in its Chomskyan formulation, was so obviously one-sided, and in conflict with his own deeper insights, we need to ask why he had embarked on this detour in the first place. But there were reasons. In part, he naturally wanted to relate his work to the dominant trend within linguistics. More pointedly, however, he was by this time being subjected to vicious attacks by (mainly American, but with some fellow-travellers from elsewhere) sociolinguists and educators, for (as they alleged) putting forward a "deficit" theory of linguistic variation. His concept of "restricted code" was denounced as imputing inferior intelligence to the working classes, and an entire mythology was built up around the issue of "deficit versus difference" in which Bernstein's assigned role was as a whipping-boy for the deficit cause. So consigning the codes to the realm of performance was a way of saying that they had nothing to do with the underlying potential of the system.

To those of us interacting closely with Bernstein at the time, listening to him and reading what he wrote, the idea of associating him with this kind of "deficit" hypothesis was so bizarre that we could not see how to respond. (The first such accusation that I came across I actually took to be a misprint.) For one thing, as Mary Douglas had made clear, it was very obvious that Bernstein's personal sympathies were strongly aligned with the children of the working class; as she expressed it at the time, "[Bernstein's] analysis cuts us, the middle class parents, down to size. Our verbosity and insincerity and fundamental uncertainty are revealed. ... The elaborated code is far from glorious when the hidden implications of the central system that generates it are laid bare" (Douglas 1972). But this itself is not the major point. The issue of deficit versus difference was an emotive issue brought up by those (mainly white) liberals in the United States who were fighting for recognition of Black English. Since some of their opponents were ultra-conservatives who really believed that blacks were intellectually inferior, they had to engage in polemic proclaiming that the dialect spoken by blacks was not deficient; it was as valid a form of speech as any other. But this had nothing to do with what Bernstein was trying to explain, which, as he made explicit in various places, was not a matter of anyone's social dialect. In relation to the general theory of codes, the slogan "deficit or difference" is entirely beside the point (for my own view of this at the time, see CCC2: Foreword; also this volume, Chapters 3 and 4). If attaining social equality depends on being educated, and in order to be educated you have to operate with elaborated code, then anyone who has no access to elaborated code, for whatever reason, is being denied social justice: either their access to it must be opened up, or the processes of education must be changed. What Bernstein had done was to show up the mechanism by which access to elaborated code was a function of social class. In the United States, where the class structure, although not significantly different from that of Britain, tends always to be masked by ethnicity, explicit discussion of class was still regulated by taboo; so Bernstein's open manner of discourse was felt as particularly threatening, and the relentless attack on his standing was essentially a panic response.

Meanwhile the linguists in Bernstein's Sociological Research Unit – Ruqaiya Hasan, Peter Hawkins, Bernard Mohan, Geoffrey Turner – were sharpening the tools for linguistic analysis of the data. It was clear that what was needed was a function-oriented semantically based grammar, and the "systemic" grammar being developed by my colleagues and myself at University College London seemed to be heading in the right direction. It was located within the mainstream European functional tradition, but had the specifically Firthian characteristic of being paradigmatic: it represented the grammar as a network of semantically motivated options – that is, as choices in meaning. This made it possible to use it for quantitative comparison of different samples of text; and although it was still at a fairly crude stage of development the linguists in the Unit were able to refine it and adapt it to their own research needs (see Turner and Mohan 1970).

By this time the codes were no longer conceptualized in terms of overt lexicogrammatical variation. Rather, the code was a "principle which regulates the selection and organization of speech events" (CCC1: 145), a "basic organizing concept" transmitted through the speech patterns of the culture or sub-culture (CCC1: 164). Bernstein now preferred the term "sociolinguistic coding orientation", intending by this formulation to suggest regular and systematic variation in the way the meaning potential is deployed in given social situations. On the basis of the four "critical socializing contexts" referred to above (see CCC1: 181), a number of key studies were carried out, using a variety of experimental designs yielding different bodies of data; and the linguistic analysis consistently showed up moderate but statistically significant differences in the meanings chosen by middle-class and working-class subjects (see CCC2, *passim*).

But there were problems with this very demanding programme of research, with its focus directed primarily on to language. One was that the linguistic theory was not yet really able to cope with the cryptotypic features of grammar that were now beginning to be recognized as critical. My own work on transitivity and theme had been published in 1967/68 (q.v.), and the essential "metafunctional" principle behind the grammar was in place and being worked out (*ibid.*; also Halliday 1970); but only a partial study of cohesion was available (Hasan 1968), and there was little or no work in the key areas of the clause complex, and other "complex" structures, or in grammatical metaphor (Halliday 1985: Chapters 7 and 10). The second problem was that the database was **linguistically** weak. While the statistical sampling and question- naire methods used were entirely reliable, and the quantity and variety of the findings extremely rich, the data available **for linguistic analysis** consisted exclusively of secondary text: elicited children's narratives, adults' answers to interviewers' questions such as " what would you be likely to say if ... ?", children's responses to picture story verbalizing tasks and the like. But these are all contexts where the language being used is under the subject's own attention, closely self-monitored as it progresses, whereas (as Boas used to stress in relation to his ethnographic work a century ago) language is perhaps the most unconscious aspect of human behaviour, and may therefore be considerably displaced in being reflected on. There is a wide gulf between what people say and what they think they say – let alone what they think they ought to say; and sensitive investigations of this kind require a database of authentic, natural, unselfconscious speech.

For various reasons – not the least being that Bernstein continued to face a chorus of attacks on his personal integrity – the major research effort that began in the sixties was not followed up by another round of intensive data gathering which might have been extended to include spontaneous speech. But there was still a considerable scope for further investigations using data of the kind already assembled; and while in his own research work Bernstein now tended to focus more on the philosophy and sociology of education, his colleagues in the Unit continued to achieve significant results in the domain of language (see especially Cook-Gumperz 1973; Adlam 1977). A special feature of the work of this period was the emphasis on the relation of code to context, and the structuring of the investigations around the socializing contexts identified earlier (regulative in Cook-Gumperz 1973; instructional-descriptive in Adlam 1977), with the degree of dependency on context as a significant variable (see especially Adlam 1977: Chapter 4). It is worth quoting Bernstein's redefinition of codes formulated during this period.

> The general definition of codes which has been used since [Adlam 1977] ... emphasizes the relation between meanings, realizations and context. *Thus a code is a regulative principle, tacitly acquired, which selects and integrates relevant meanings, forms of realizations, and evoking contexts.*
> (CCC4: 101 Bernestein's italics)

In the paper from which this is taken (Bernstein 1987), Bernstein provides a sustained and reasoned exposition of the concept of code, dealing with many of the criticisms to which it had been subjected and using these in order to further to clarify his own position.

In the mid-1980s Ruqaiya Hasan, now at Macquarie University in Sydney, began assembling a database of authentic speech that could be used to evaluate Bernstein's findings and strengthen the linguistic foundations of research into language and social processes. She identified a sample population of 24 mother–child dyads, among

240

urban English-speaking Australian families in four areas within Sydney, where the child was of immediately pre-school age (between 3;6 and 4;0); the sample was structured by class and sex: the sex of the child, and the occupation of the main breadwinner (there were some single parents) – whether a lower autonomy profession ("LAP") or a higher autonomy profession ("HAP"). In inviting the mothers to participate in the research, Hasan explained that she and her colleagues were interested in the sort of things that children talked about in ordinary everyday life, which was something that teachers would find it useful to know; she asked the mother to leave the recorder on at odd times around the house, and simply pick up the natural conversation that went on between the child and herself as she got on with whatever she was doing. If there was any part that she was uneasy about, she could wipe it off (in the event, none of the mothers did expunge any of the discourse). In this way Hasan's team collected 100 hours of mother-child interaction; allowing for periods of silence this gave them about 60,000 clauses, of which they analysed a little over 22,000, or just under a thousand clauses from each of the 24 dyads.

In carrying out this research Hasan was able to take advantage of two developments that had taken place in linguistics in the intervening period. One was the development of systemic functional theory, and specifically the systemic analysis of the grammar of English (see Halliday and Hasan 1976; Halliday 1985; Butler 1985). Hasan constructed a grammar-based semantic network, having some 500 features organized in 185 systems; using this network, the researchers were able to assign a description (a "selection expression", in systemic terms) to each message unit, showing which features had been selected. A message unit corresponds prototypically to a non-embedded clause in the grammar; on average, each message was described in terms of some 40 or more semantic features. By reference to the network, the description also showed which features had **not** been selected: in other words, for each message unit the analysis reveals what particular options in meaning out of the total set of possibilities are and are not being taken up.

The other development was that of cluster analysis applied to large-scale quantitative studies of language, deriving from the work of Labov (Sankoff 1978). Hasan analysed the results in terms of "principal components": each principal component is a cluster of features which is identified by the program as accounting for a high percentage of variation in the data. The essential property of this analysis is that neither of the variables, social or semantic, is taken as given: neither the sex/class matrix of the original sample, nor the systemic relation among the semantic features in the network, is incorporated into the input. Thus the program could show up quite different patterns of socio-semantic variation, having nothing to do with sex or class and revealing no obvious underlying semantic motifs.

There are of course many ways within such a database of selecting subsets of the data for analysis. What Hasan and her colleagues did was to select discourse sequences that could be related to Bernstein's critical socializing contexts: for example, question-and-answer sequences, where they identified "children's questions + mothers' answers" and "mothers' questions + children's answers", or rationality sequences where mothers are presenting arguments for behavioural norms. They then input the results of the semantic analysis for every instance of the given sequence. The results reported so far have been remarkably unambiguous: every study has divided the population almost unequivo-cally along lines of class or sex, with clusters of semantic features that are readily interpretable in terms of some recognizable semantic motif. Thus for example in the case of mothers answering their children's questions, the first principal component, which accounted for some 30 per cent of variance, showed significant correlation with social class: the distinctive semantic motifs were the kinds of question asked by the children and the extent to which the mothers elaborated in their answers. With the mothers' questions both sex and class appear significant. In the "mothers' reasoning" sequences the first principal component was again correlated with class: the semantic variable here was the type of grounding favoured by the mothers in their explanations of rules of behaviour (logical or social; social grounding = LAP mothers). For details of this research, see Hasan 1988, 1989, 1991, 1992*a*, 1992*b*; Hasan and Cloran, 1990.

The key factor in this investigation, linking it with Bernstein's codes, is Hasan's development of the concept of semantic variation. Let us return for a moment to code, register and social dialect. What distinguishes register variation from dialect variation is that, prototypically, dialects are different ways of saying the same things, whereas registers are ways of saying different things. In other words, dialectal variation is phonological or lexicogrammatical, with a higher-level constant in the semantics (same meanings, different wordings and sounds). With register variation there is no higher-level constant: the meanings are different because they represent different spheres of activity. With code, on the other hand, there is semantic variation: the meanings are different – but there is a higher-level constant, namely the context of situation (which in systemic theory is modelled as another level in the stratal organization of language). Thus for example if the situation is one of a mother explaining a particular principle of behaviour, semantic variation refers to the fact that, in the same context and with the same semiotic function, different options in meaning may be taken up. Such variation might of course be random; but if it is systematic, such that it distinguishes statistically between one group within the population and another, this constitutes a difference of **code**. The variation present in Hasan's data turns out to be a manifestation of code.

Hasan's work confirms Bernstein's results – and with data from a culture which has a strongly egalitarian ideology. It thus complements Bernstein's later writings (e.g. 1987, 1990) by supplying the direct linguistic evidence for the discourse element in Bernstein's theory, through the analysis and interpretation of large quantities of natural speech. At the same time it demonstrates the validity of Bernstein's underlying conception of language itself, as the essential link in his explanatory chain. Bernstein saw clearly that language was not a passive reflection either of a (conceptual construction of) material reality or of a predetermined pattern of social relations; on the contrary, it was an active component in the construction both of the natural and of the social order. Therefore, the forms of discourse could not be neutral. They were an integral part of the dynamic of social process; and if the social process contained inequalities, in people's access to knowledge and power, then these inequalities must be present in the semiotic activities by which knowledge and power are construed.

If we look back at Bernstein's early attempts to characterize the difference between restricted and elaborated codes, the latter appears as 'elaborated' in two complementary senses. On the one hand, it is more explicit in its verbalization of experience, making fewer assumptions about what is shared. On the other hand, it is more concerned with enumerating general principles. But by the same token, it is more verbose – and also more oblique and indirect: that is, it employs forms of wording that are, given Bernstein's functional view of language, in some sense marked in the way that they construe the meanings in question. We can interpret this in terms of the stratal and metafunctional framework of systemic theory (Matthiessen 1989; Halliday and Martin 1993: Chapter 2). The elaborated code makes considerably greater use of grammatical metaphor: that is, grammatical constructions of meaning that are metaphorical in relation to the way the grammar works in its prototypical realizations (Halliday 1985: Chapter 10; Halliday and Martin 1993: *passim*).

Many of Bernstein's examples were of grammatical metaphor in the

interpersonal function (language as enactment of interpersonal, "social" relationships), like the *I'd rather you made less noise, darling* cited at the start: notably in the studies of children's perceptions of the language of control, and of modalities and other representations of the speaker's angle (see Turner 1973; Turner and Pickvance 1973; in CCC2: Chapters 7 and 5). The language used to construe educational knowledge in school is also loaded with grammatical metaphor; but this is metaphor in the **ideational** function (that of language as construal of human experience). This is the form of metaphor that turns properties and processes into things, using the grammar's resources of nominalization, as in the expressions like *large thicknesses of snow, the compression of the snow* taken from a school science text (contrast *the snow is thick, the snow gets compressed*).

In the present day it is impossible to become educated – or even to become literate, in any functional sense – without controlling the semiotic resources of this kind of grammatical metaphor. Two essential features of our current educational discourse depend on it: (1) technicality – creating systematic taxonomies of technical terms; and (2) consequentiality – constructing ongoing sequences of logical argument. Both of these may be illustrated from the following extract:

> ... diamond is energetically unstable ... The energetic instability of diamond leads to its transformation into worthless graphite.

Here, 'unstable' is technicalized as *instability*, which contrasts systematically with *stability*; within this, *energetic (in)stability* contrasts with *kinetic (in)stability* (e.g. in *nitrogen oxide is kinetically stable. The kinetic stability of nitrogen oxide shows ...*). This is then built into a logical (here causal) sequence *the energetic instability of diamond leads to its transformation into graphite*; compare the earlier example [*the snow*] *is compressed by its own weight and hardened. The compression of the snow can cause it to form into large bodies of ice.* The grammatical metaphor of nominalization technicalizes the concepts and construes them into logical sequences. In principle, it is always possible to take particular instances and **re**construe them in other ways; so, just as Bernstein raised the question of changing the **social** structure of education (see above), we could also raise the question of changing its **semiotic** structure, by removing or at least reducing these kinds of elaboration from its grammar. But at present all educational discourse is locked in to some version or other of this highly metaphorical mode.

Thus the elaborated code of the home, whatever may give rise to it (e.g. personal rather than positional family role systems, as Bernstein suggested in CCC1: Chapter 8, 152–3), is like the language of the school in that it already contains considerable amounts of grammatical metaphor. This may be primarily interpersonal metaphor, as in *I don't think that's a very nice way to behave*; but it may also include ideational (experiential/logical) metaphor, as in *large thicknesses of snow* – at one point Berstein distinguished two types of elaborated code along these lines, as "facilitating the verbal elaboration of relations between *persons* or between *objects*" (CCC1: 133). But whichever form it takes, the elaborated code opens up the way to the metaphoric construal of experience. A child accustomed to discourse of an elaborated kind in the home is *ipso facto* prepared for the semiotic formations in which educational knowledge is construed.

Two points seem to emerge. One is that Bernstein's basic insight into semiotic variation, that he called "code", is essentially valid. Although he labelled it in terms of two poles, "restricted" and "elaborated", he was well aware that a number of different dimensions of meaning were involved and that the overall pattern was one of gradience not discrete categories: what is at issue is the multidimensional semantic space that constitutes the meaning-making resources of a language. Considered from a linguistic viewpoint, the particular locus of such variation in the social structure, in any form of social hierarchy, is irrelevant; what matters is that not all children have equal access to the mysteries of educational discourse. The other point is that the entire issue of difference versus deficit is devoid of any substance; it is simply a meaningless question. Any linguistic differential (such as the fact that I don't speak Japanese) can be made to appear as either one or the other, just by the way it is expressed. That such a fiction was allowed for so long to obscure the fundamental issues – and to disfigure the reputation of one of the most potent thinkers of our time – is something that surely leads us to question the way 'knowledge' is ratified and compiled.

But it would be wrong to give the impression that Bernstein's work has been universally misrepresented. Among sociologists Grimshaw stands out as an informed and thoughtful commentator; while Atkinson provides a clear, balanced and perceptive account of Bernstein's overall achievements (see Grimshaw 1976; Atkinson 1985: especially Chapters 5 and 6). Seen from a linguistic viewpoint, Bernstein appears unique among sociologists in according language a central place in social processes, more especially in socialization and cultural transmissions. But in doing so, Bernstein was not merely supplying the critical component in his own theoretical model. He was also forcing us, as linguists, to answer the question: what must language be like, to be able to function in this way? If language disposes of such powerful resources in the way it construes experience and enacts interpersonal relationships, this tells us a great deal about its functional and stratal organization and about its systematic relation to context. In this respect Bernstein belongs with Bühler and Malinowski as one of the leading figures from outside the discipline of linguistics that have critically influenced our thinking about language. The codes set up a challenge to established concepts and models, which were not ready to absorb their full complexity. Linguists have a richer view of the processes of meaning as a result of Bernstein's work.

Notes

1. Throughout this chapter, Bernstein 1971, 1973, 1975 and 1990 are referred to as CCC1, CCC2, CCC3 and CCC4 respectively.
2. Socialization was defined as the process whereby the biological is transformed into a specific cultural being. The most formative influence on the procedures of socialization is social class. Class limits access to universalistic orders of meaning, those in which the principles and operations are made linguistically explicit (CCC1: Chapter 9, *passim*).

PART FOUR

LANGUAGE AND SOCIAL STRUCTURE

EDITOR'S INTRODUCTION

It is not just that linguistic structure reflects social structure but rather it is "the realization of social structure, actively symbolizing it in a process of mutual creativity". Variation in language, for example, is described, in 'An interpretation of the functional relationship between language and social structure' (1978), as "the symbolic expression of variation in society: it is created by society, and helps to create society in its turn".

Professor Halliday distinguishes between (i) language as system and (ii) language as institution. With the notion of system, he represents language as a resource, involving interconnected choices organized in terms of three functional components (ideational, interpersonal, textual). Using socio-semantic networks, these choices can also be related to recognizable and significant social contexts. Critical to the notion of language as institution is that it is variable, both according to user, i.e. dialect, and to use, i.e. register. Interaction between dialect and register in language "expresses" the interaction between social structure and social process. "Above and beyond 'language as system' and 'language as institution'", is what Professor Halliday refers to as "'language as social semiotic': language in the context of the culture as a semiotic system".

In Chapter 9, Professor Halliday briefly touches on the notion of 'anti-language', describing it as "a language of social conflict – of passive resistance or active opposition". He explores this topic in greater depth in the tenth and final chapter of this section, 'Anti-Languages' (1976). An anti-language is the language of an anti-society, constructed by those "striving to maintain a counter-reality that is under pressure from the established world". Professor Halliday explains his interest in studying this phenomenon by noting that "It has commonly been found with other aspects of the human condition – the social structure, or the individual psyche – that there is much to be learnt from pathological manifestations, which are seldom as clearly set off from the 'normal' as they at first appear. In the same way a study of sociolinguistic pathology may lead to additional insight into the social semiotic."

Chapter Nine

AN INTERPRETATION OF THE FUNCTIONAL RELATIONSHIP BETWEEN LANGUAGE AND SOCIAL STRUCTURE (1978)

In this chapter I shall summarize what has been said or implied earlier about how language expresses the social system. In the course of the discussion I shall move towards the view that the relation of language to the social system is not simply one of expression, but a more complex natural dialectic in which language actively symbolizes the social system, thus creating as well as being created by it. This, it is hoped, will clarify my interpretation of language within the framework of the culture as an information system, and give some indication of what I understand by the concept of 'language as social semiotic'.

As an underlying conceptual framework, I shall distinguish between (i) *language as system* and (ii) *language as institution*. The salient facts about language as system are (a) that it is *stratified* (it is a three-level coding system consisting of a semantics, a lexicogrammar and a phonology) and (b) that its semantic system is organized into *functional* components (ideational, including experiential and logical; interpersonal; textual). The salient fact about language as *institution* is that it is *variable*; there are two kinds of variation, (a) *dialect* (variation according to the *user*), and (b) *register* (variation according to the *use*). This is, of course, an idealized construct; there are no such clear-cut boundaries in the facts themselves.

'An Interpretation of the Functional Relationship between Language and Social Structure', from Uta Quasthoff (ed.), *Sprachstruktur – Sozialstruktur: Zur Linguistischen Theorienbildung*, 3-42. Copyright © Scriptor, Konigstein.

251

1. Language as institution

1.1 Dialect

Classical dialectology, as developed in Europe, rests on certain implicit assumptions about speakers and speech communities. A speech community is assumed to be a social unit whose members (i) communicate with each other, (ii) speak in a consistent way and (iii) all speak alike. This is obviously, again, an idealized picture; but in the type of settled rural community for which dialect studies were first developed, it is near enough reality to serve as a theoretical norm.

Dialectal variation, in such a model, is essentially variation between speech communities. We may recognize some variation also within the community – squire and parson, or landlord and priest, probably speak differently from other people – but this is at the most a minor theme; and we do not envisage variation as something that arises **within** the speech of an individual speaker.

When dialectology moved into an urban setting, with Labov's monumental New York city studies, variation took on a new meaning. Labov showed that, within a typical North American urban community, the speech varies (i) **between** the members according to social class (low to high), and (ii) **within** each member according to "style scale" (amount of monitoring or attention paid to one's own speech, casual to formal). The effect of each of these factors is quantitative (hence probabilistic in origin), but the picture is clear: when single dialect variables are isolated for intensive investigation, some of them turn out to be socially stratified. The forms of the variable ('variants') are **ranked** in an order such that the 'high' variant is associated with higher social status **or** a more formal context of speech, and the 'low' with lower social status **or** a more casual context of speech.

1.2 Social dialect

As long as dialect variation is geographically determined, it can be explained away: one group stays on this side of the mountain, the other group moves to the other side of the mountain, and they no longer talk to each other. But there are no mountains dividing social classes; the members of different social classes do talk to each other, at least transactionally. What is the explanation of this socially determined variation? How do "social dialects" arise?

One of the most significant of Labov's finding was the remarkable uniformity shown by people of all social groups in their attutudes towards variation in the speech of others. This uniformity of attitude means that the members are highly sensitive to the social meaning of dialectal variation, a form of sensitivity that is apparently achieved during the crucial years of adolescence, in the age range of about 13–18.

We acquire this sensitivity as a part of growing up in society, because dialect variation is functional with respect to the social structure. And this is why it does not disappear. It was confidently predicted in the period after World War II that, with the steadily increasing dominance of the mass media, dialects would disappear and we should soon all be speaking alike. Sure enough, the **regionally**-based dialects of rural areas **are** disappearing, as least in industrial societies. But with the urban dialects the opposite has happened: diversity is increasing. We can explain this by showing that the diversity is socially functional. It expresses the structure of society.

It would be a mistake to think of social structure simply in terms of some particular index of social class. The essential characteristic of social structure as we know it is that it is hierarchical; and linguistic variation is what expresses its hierarchical character, whether in terms of age, generation, sex, provenance or any other of its manifestations, including caste and class.

Let us postulate a perfectly homogeneous society, one without any of these forms of social hierarchy. The members of such a society would presumably speak a perfectly homogeneous language, one without any dialectal variation. Now consider the hypothetical antithesis of this: a society split into two conflicting groups, a society and an anti-society. Here we shall expect to find some form of matching linguistic order: two mutually opposed linguistic varieties, a language and an anti-language. These are, once again, idealized constructs; but phenomena approximating to them have arisen at various times and places. For example, the social conditions of sixteenth-century England generated an anti-society of 'vagabonds', who lived by extorting wealth from the established society; and this society had its anti-language, fragments of which are reported in contemporary documents. The anti-language is a language of social conflict – of passive resistance or active opposition; but at the same time, like any other language, it is a means of expressing and maintaining the social structure – in this case, the structure of the anti-society.

Most of the time what we find in real life are dialect hierarchies, patterns of dialectal variation in which a "standard" (representing the power base of society) is opposed by non-standard varieties (which the members refer to as "dialects"). The non-standard dialects may become languages of opposition and protest; periods of explicit class conflict tend to be characterized by the development of such protest languages, sometimes in the form of 'ghetto languages', which are coming closer to the anti-language end of the scale. Here dialect becomes a means of expression of class consciousness and political awareness. We can recognize a category of 'oppressed languages', languages of groups that are subjected to social or political oppression. It is characteristic of oppressed languages that their speakers tend to excel at verbal contest and verbal display. Meaning is often the most effective form of social action that is available to them.

1.3 Register

Dialects, in the usual sense of that term, are different ways of saying the same thing. In other words, the dialects of a language differ from each other phonologically and lexicogrammatically, but not, in principle, semantically.

In this respect, dialectal variation contrasts with variation of another kind, that of **register**. Registers are ways of saying different things.

Registers differ semantically. They also differ lexicogrammatically, because that is how meanings are **expressed**; but lexicogrammatical differences among registers are, by and large, the automatic consequence of semantic differences. In principle, registers are configurations of meanings that are typically exchanged   that are 'at risk', so to speak – under given conditions of use.

A dialect is 'what you speak' (habitually); this is determined by 'who you are', your regional and/or social place of origin and/or adoption. A register is 'what you are speaking' (at the given time), determined by 'what you are doing', the nature of the ongoing social activity. Whereas dialect variation reflects the social order in the special sense of *the hierarchy of social structure*, register variation also reflects the social order but in the special sense of *the diversity of social processes*. We are not doing the same things all the time; so we speak now in one register, now in another. But the total **range** of the social processes in which any member will typically engage is a function of the structure of society. We each have our own repertory of social actions, reflecting our place at the intersection of a whole complex of social hierarchies. There is a division of labour.

Since the division of labour is **social**, the two kinds of language variety, register and dialect, are closely interconnected. The structure of society determines who, in terms of the various social hierarchies of class, generation, age, sex, provenance and so on, will have access to which aspects of the social process – and hence, to which registers. (In most societies today there is considerable scope for individual discretion, though this has not always been the case.) This means, in turn, that a particular register tends to have a particular dialect associated with it: the registers of bureaucracy, for example, demand the "standard" (national) dialect, whereas fishing and farming demand rural (local) varieties. Hence the dialect comes to symbolize the register; when we hear a local dialect, we unconsciously switch off a large part of our register range.

In this way, in a typical hierarchical social structure, dialect becomes the means by which a member gains, or is denied, access to certain registers.

So if we say that linguistic structure "reflects" social structure, we are really assigning to language a role that is too passive. (I am formulating it in this way in order to keep the parallel between the two expressions "linguistic structure" and "social structure". In fact, what is meant is the linguistic *system*; elsewhere I have not used "structure" in this general sense of the organization of language, but have reserved it for the specialized sense of constituent structure.) Rather we should say that linguistic structure is the *realization of* social structure, actively symbolizing it in a process of mutual creativity. Because it stands as a metaphor for society, language has the property of not only transmitting the social order but also maintaining and potentially modifying it. (This is undoubtedly the explanation of the violent attitudes that under certain social conditions come to be held by one group towards the speech of others. A different set of **vowels** is perceived as the symbol of a different set of **values**, and hence takes on the character of a threat.) Variation in language is the symbolic expression of variation in society: it is created by society, and helps to create society in its turn. Of the two kinds of variation in language, that of dialect expresses the diversity of social structure, that of register expresses the diversity of social process. The interaction of dialect and register in language expresses the interaction of structure and process in society.

2. Language as system

2.1 Function

We have considered how variation in language is socially functional. We must now consider how the linguistic **system** is socially functional.

The most important fact about language as system is its organization into **functional components**.

It is obvious that language is used in a multitude of different ways for a multitude of different purposes. It is not possible to enumerate them; nor is it necessary to try: there would be no way of preferring one list over another. These various ways of using language are sometimes referred to as "functions of language". But to say language has many 'functions', in this sense, is to say no more than that people engage in a variety of social actions – that they do different things together.

We are considering 'functions' in a more fundamental sense, as a necessary element in the interpretation of the linguistic system. The linguistic system is orchestrated into different modes of meaning, and these represent its most general functional orientations. No doubt language has evolved in this way because of the ways in which it is used; the two concepts of function are certainly interrelated. But if we seek to explain the internal workings of language we are forced to take into consideration its external relation to the social context.

The point is a substantive one, and we can approach it from this angle. Considered in relation to the social order, language is a resource, a meaning potential. Formally, language has this property: that it is a coding system **on three levels**. Most coding systems are on two levels: a **content** and an **expression**: for example, traffic signals, with content 'stop/go' coded into expression 'red/green'. But language has evolved a third, abstract level of *form* intermediate between the two; it consists of content, form and expression, or, in linguistic terms, of semantics, lexicogrammar and phonology. Now, when we analyse the content side, the semantic system and its representation in the grammar, we find that it has an internal organization in which the social functions of language are clearly reflected.

2.2 Functional components

The semantic system is organized into a small number of components – three or four depending on how one looks at them – such that **within** one component there is a high degree of interdependence and mutual

256

constraint, whereas **between** components there is very little: each one is relatively independent of the others.

The components can be identified as follows:

1 ideational (language as reflection), comprising
    (a) experiential
    (b) logical
2 interpersonal (language as action)
3 textual (language as texture, in relation to the environment).

When we say that these components are relatively independent of one another, we mean that the choices that are made within any one component, while strongly affected by other choices within the same component, have no effect, or only a very weak effect, on choices made within the others. For example, given the meaning potential of the interpersonal component, out of the innumerable choices that are available to me I might choose (i) to offer a proposition, (ii) pitched in a particular key (e.g. contradictory-defensive), (iii) with a particular intent towards you (e.g. of convincing you), (iv) with a particular assessment of its probability (e.g. certain) and (v) with indication of particular attitude (e.g. regretful). Now, all these choices are strongly interdetermining; if we use a network mode of representation, as in systemic theory, they can be seen as complex patterns of internal constraint among the various sub-networks. But they have almost no effect on the ideational meanings, on the **content** of what you are to be convinced of, which may be that the earth is flat, that Mozart was a great musician, or that I am hungry. Similarly, the ideational meanings do not determine the interpersonal ones; but there is a high degree of interdetermination **within** the ideational component: the kind of process I choose to refer to, the participants in the process, the taxonomies of things and properties, the circumstances of time and space, and the natural logic that links all these together.

2.3 Functional components and grammatical structure

So far, I have been looking at the matter from a semantic point of view, taking as the problem the interpretation of the semantic system. Suppose now we take a second approach, from a lexicogrammatical point of view – 'from below', as it were. In the interpretation of the lexicogrammatical system we find ourselves faced with a different problem, namely that of explaining the different **kinds of structure** that are found at this level. Consideration of this problem is beyond our scope here; but when we look into it, we find that the various types of grammatical structure are related to these semantic components in a systematic way. Each kind of meaning tends to be realized as a particular kind of structure. Hence in the encoding of a text each component of meaning makes its contribution to the structural output; but it is a contribution which has on it the stamp of that particular mode of meaning. We would summarize this as follows (see Halliday 1977):

Semantic component	Type of grammatical structure by which typically realized
1 ideational:	
(a) experiential	constituent (segmental)
(b) logical	recursive
2 interpersonal	prosodic
3 textual	culminative

2.4 Functional components and social context

Thirdly, we may approach the question 'from above', from the perspective of language and the social order – at what I have called the **social semiotic** level. When we come to investigate the relation of language to social context we find that the functional components of the semantic system once again provide the key. We saw that they were related to the different types of grammatical structure. There is also a systematic relationship between them and the semiotic structure of the speech situation. It is this, in part, that validates the notion of a speech situation.

Let us assume that the social system (or the 'culture') can be represented as a construction of meanings – as a semiotic system. The meanings that constitute the social system are exchanged through a variety of modes or channels, of which language is one; but not, of course, the only one – there are many other semiotic modes besides. Given this social-semiotic perspective, a **social context** (or 'situation', in the terms of situation theory) is a temporary construct or instantiation of meanings from the social system. A social context is a semiotic structure which we may interpret in terms of three variables: a 'field' of social process (what is going on), a 'tenor' of social relationships (who are taking part) and a 'mode' of symbolic interaction (how are the meanings exchanged). If we are focusing on language, this last category

258

of 'mode' refers to what part the language is playing in the situation under consideration.

As said above, these components of the context are systematically related to the components of the semantic system; and once again, given that the context is a semiotic construct, this relation can be seen as one of realization. The meanings that constitute the social context are *realized* through selections in the meaning potential of language. To summarize:

Component of social context	Functional-semantic component through which typically realized
1 field (social process)	experiential
2 tenor (social relationship)	interpersonal
3 mode (symbolic mode)	textual

The linguistic system, in other words, is organized in such a way that the social context is predictive of the text. This is what makes it possible for a member to make the necessary predictions about the meanings that are being exchanged in any situation which he encounters. If we drop in on a gathering, we are able to tune in very quickly, because we size up the field, tenor and mode of the situation and at once form an idea of what is likely to be being meant. In this way we know what semantic configurations – what register – will probably be required if we are to take part. If we did not do this, there would be no communication, since only a part of the meanings we have to understand are explicitly realized in the wordings. The rest are unrealized; they are left out – or rather (a more satisfactory metaphor) they are out of focus. We succeed in the exchange of meanings because we have access to the semiotic structure of the situation from other sources.

3. Language as social semiotic

3.1 Variation and social meaning

The distinction between language as system and language as institution is an important one for the investigation of problems of language and society. But these are really two aspects of a more general set of phenomena, and in any interpretation of the 'sociolinguistic order' we need to bring them together again.

A significant step in this direction is taken by variation theory. We have said that a feature of language as *institution* is that it is variable: different groups of speakers, or the same speakers in different task-roles, use different dialects or registers. But this is not to imply that there is no variation in the *system*. Some linguists would deny this, and would explain all variation institutionally. Others (myself among them) would argue that this is to make too rigid a distinction between the system and the institution, and would contend that a major achievement of social dialectology has been to show that dialect-like variation is a normal feature of the speech of the individual, at least in some but possibly in all communities. At certain contexts in the language a speaker will select, with a certain probability, one among a small set of variants all of which are equivalent in the sense that they are alternative realizations of the same higher-level configuration. The conditions determining this probability may be linguistic or social or some combination of the two. To know the probability of a particular speaker pronouncing a certain variant (say [t], glottal stop or zero) at a certain point in the speech chain (say word-final), we take the product of the conditioning effects of a set of variables such as: is the word lexical or structural? does the following word begin with a vowel? is the phrase thematic? is the speaker angry? and is his father a member of the working class? (This is, of course, a caricature, but it gives a fair representation of the way these things are.)

So variation, which we first recognize as a property of language as institution (in the form of variation **between** speakers, of a dialectal kind), begins to appear as an extension of variation which is a property of the system. A 'dialect' is then just a sum of variants having a strong tendency to co-occur. In this perspective, dialectal variation is made out to be not so much a consequence of the social structure as an outcome of the inherent nature of language itself.

But this is one-sided. In the last analysis, the linguistic system is the product of the social system; and seen from that angle, dialect-like variation **within** an individual is a special case of variation **between** individuals, not the other way round. The significant point, however, is that there is no sharp line between this externally conditioned, so-called "sociolinguistic" variation that is found in the speech of an individual **because** it is a property of language as institution, and the purely internally conditioned variation that occurs within a particular part of the linguistic system (e.g. morphophonemic alternation). Conditioning environments may be of any kind; there is ultimately no discontinuity between such apparently diverse phenomena as (i) select [ʔ] not [t]

260

before a consonant and (ii) select [ʔ] not [t] before a king. This explains how it comes about that all variation is potentially meaningful; any set of alternants may (but need not) become the bearer of social information and social value.

3.2 Language and social reality

Above and beyond "language as system" and "language as institution" lies the more general, unifying concept that I have labelled "language as social semiotic": language in the context of the culture as a semiotic system.

Consider the way a child constructs his social reality. Through language as system – its organization into levels of coding and functional components – he builds up a model of the exchange of meanings, and learns to construe the interpersonal relationships, the experiential phenomena, the forms of natural logic and the modes of symbolic interaction into coherent patterns of social context. He does this very young; this is in fact what makes it possible for him to learn the language successfully – the two processes go hand in hand.

Through language as institution – its variation into dialects and registers – he builds up a model of the social system. This follows a little way behind his learning of grammar and semantics (compare the interesting suggestion by Sankoff (1974) that some patterns at first learnt as categorical are later modified to become variable), though it is essentially part of single unitary process of language development. In the broadest terms, from dialectal variation he learns to construe the patterns of social hierarchy, and from variation of the 'register' kind he gains an insight into the structure of knowledge.

So language, while it represents reality **referentially**, through its words and structures, also represents reality **metaphorically** through its own internal and external form. (1) The functional organization of the semantics symbolizes the structure of human interaction (the semiotics of social contexts, as we expressed it earlier). (2) Dialectal and "diatypic" (register) variation symbolize respectively the structure of society and the structure of human knowledge.

But as language becomes a metaphor of reality, so by the same process reality becomes a metaphor of language. Since reality is a social construct, it can be constructed only through an exchange of meanings. Hence meanings are seen as constitutive of reality. This, at least, is the natural conclusion for the present era, when the exchange of information tends to replace the exchange of goods-and-services as

261

the primary mode of social action. With a sociological linguistics we should be able to stand back from this perspective, and arrive at an interpretation of language through understanding its place in the long-term evolution of the social system.

3.3 Methodological considerations

It has been customary among linguists in recent years to represent language in terms of rules.

In investigating language and the social system, it is important to transcend this limitation and to interpret language not as a set of rules but as a **resource**. I have used the term *meaning potential* to characterize language in this way.

When we focus attention on the processes of human interaction, we are seeing this meaning potential at work. In the microsemiotic encounters of daily life, we find people making creative use of their resources of meaning, and continuously modifying these resources in the process.

Hence in the interpretation of language, the organizing concept that we need is not structure but **system**. Most recent linguistics has been structure-bound (since structure is what is described by rules). With the notion of system we can represent language as a resource, in terms of the choices that are available, the interconnection of these choices, and the conditions affecting their access. We can then relate these choices to recognizable and significant social contexts, using socio-semantic networks; and investigate questions such as the influence of various social factors on the meanings exchanged by parents and children. The data are the observed facts of 'text-in-situation': what people say in real life, not discounting what they think they might say and what they think they ought to say. (Or rather, what they **mean**, since saying is only one way of meaning.) In order to interpret what is observed, however, we have to relate it to the system: (i) to the linguistic system, which it then helps to explain, and (ii) to the social context, and through that to the social system.

After a period of intensive study of language as an idealized philosophical construct, linguists have come around to taking account of the fact that people talk to each other. In order to solve purely internal problems of its own history and structure, language has had to be taken out of its glass case, dusted, and put back in a living environment – into a "context of situation", in Malinowski's term. But it is one thing to have a 'socio-' (that is, real life) component in the explanation of the facts of language. It is quite another thing to seek explanations that relate the linguistic system to the social system, and so work towards some general theory of language and social structure.

Chapter Ten

ANTI-LANGUAGES (1976)

Of the various kinds of anti-word, such as antibiotic, antibody, antinovel, antimatter, and so on, the kind that is to be understood here is that represented by anti-society. An anti-society is a society that is set up within another society as a conscious alternative to it. It is a mode of resistance, resistance which may take the form either of passive symbiosis or of active hostility and even destruction.

An anti-language is not only parallel to an anti-society; it is in fact generated by it. We do not know much about either the process or its outcome, because most of the evidence we have is on the level of travellers' tales; but it is reasonable to suppose that, in the most general terms, an anti-language stands to an anti-society in much the same relation as does a language to a society. Either pair, a society and its language or an anti-society and its (anti-) language, is, equally, an instance of the prevailing sociolinguistic order. It has commonly been found with other aspects of the human condition – the social structure, or the individual psyche – that there is much to be learnt from pathological manifestations, which are seldom as clearly set off from the "normal" as they at first appear. In the same way a study of sociolinguistic pathology may lead to additional insight into the social semiotic.

In Elizabethan England, the counterculture of vagabonds, or "cursitors" in Thomas Harman's (1567) mock-stylish designation, a vast population of criminals who lived off the wealth of the established society, had their own tongue, or "pelting (= paltry) speech"; this is

---

'Anti-languages', from *American Anthropologist,* 78.3, 570-584, (1976). Copyright © 1976 by the American Anthropological Association.

frequently referred to in contemporary accounts, though rarely described or even illustrated with any detailed accuracy. The anti-society of modern Calcutta has a highly developed language of its own, substantially documented by Bhaktiprasad Mallik in 'Language of the Underworld of West Bengal' (1972). The "second life," the term used by Adam Podgórecki (1973) to describe the sub-culture of Polish prisons and reform schools, is accompanied by an elaborated anti-language called *grypserka*. We shall take these as our three cases for discussion.

What can be said about the characteristics of anti-languages? Like the early records of the languages of exotic cultures, the information usually comes to us in the form of word lists. These afford only very limited possibilities of interpretation, although they are perhaps slightly more revealing here than in other contexts because of the special relation that obtains between an anti-language and the language to which it is counterposed.

The simplest form taken by an anti-language is that of new words for old; it is a language relexicalized. It should not be assumed that it always arises by a process of fission, splitting off from an established language; but this is one possibility, and it is easier to talk about it in these terms. Typically this relexicalization is partial, not total: not all words in the language have their equivalents in the anti-language. (For an interesting case of total relexicalization, compare the Dyirbal mother-in-law language as described by Dixon [1970] − perhaps a related phenom-enon, since this is the language used by the adult male to his affinal kin, who constitute a kind of institutionalized anti society within society.) The principle is that of same grammar, different vocabulary; but different vocabulary only in certain areas, typically those that are central to the activities of the sub-culture and that set it off most sharply from the established society. So we expect to find new words for types of criminal act, and classes of criminal and of victim; for tools of the trade; for police and other representatives of the law enforcement structure of the society; for penalties, penal institutions and the like. The Elizabethan chroniclers of the pelting speech list upward of 20 terms for the main classes of members of the fraternity of vagabonds, such as *upright man, rogue, wild rogue, prigger of prancers* (= horse thief), *counterfeit crank, jarkman, bawdy basket, walking mort, kinchin mort, doxy* and *dell*; numerous terms for specific roles in their often highly elaborate villainies, and names for the strategies themselves, which are known collectively as *laws* − for example, *lifting law* (stealing packages) which involves a *lift*, a *marker* and a *santer* (the one who steals the package, the one to whom it is handed, and the one who waits outside to carry it off); names for the tools, e.g. *wresters* (for picking locks), and for the spoils, e.g. *snappings* or *garbage*; and names for various penalties that may be suffered, such as *dying the jerk* (being whipped) or *trining on the chats* (getting hanged).

Such features belong to our commonsense picture of an argot, or cant (to give it its Elizabethan name). By themselves, they are no more than the technical and semitechnical features of a special register; they amount to an anti-language only if we admit into this category something that is simply the professional jargon associated with the activities of a criminal counterculture.

It is noticeable, however, that even these purely technical elements seem to be somewhat larger than life. The language is not merely **re**lexicalized in these areas: it is **over**lexicalized. So in Mallik's account of the Calcutta underworld language we find not just one word for 'bomb' but 21; 41 words for 'police', and so on (1972: 22–3). A few of these are also technical expressions for specific subcategories; but most of them are not – they are by ordinary standards synonymous, and their proliferation would be explained by students of slang as the result of a neverending search for originality, either for the sake of liveliness and humour or, in some cases, for the sake of secrecy.

But there is more to it than that. If we consider underworld languages in terms of a general comparison with the languages of the overworld, we find in them a characteristic functional orientation, away from the experiential mode of meaning towards the interpersonal and the textual modes. Both the textual orientation (the "set" towards the message, in Jakobson's terms) and the interpersonal (the "set" towards addresser/ addressee, although as we shall suggest this is to be interpreted rather as a set towards the social structure) tend to produce this overlexicalization: the former because it takes the form of verbal competition and display, in which kennings of all kinds are at a premium; the latter because sets of words which are denotatively synonymous are clearly distinguished by their attitudinal components. Mallik's 24 synonyms for 'girl' include the whole range of predictable connotations – given that, as he remarks, "the language of the criminal world [with some exceptions] is essentially a males' language" (1972: 27).

Both of these are normal features of everyday language, in which textual and interpersonal meanings are interwoven with experiential meaning into a single fabric of discourse. What characterizes what we are calling anti-languages is their **relatively greater** orientation in this direction. In all languages, words, sounds and structures tend to become charged with social value; it is to be expected that, in the anti-language, the social values will be more clearly foregrounded. This is an instance of what Bernstein (1974) refers to as the "sociolinguistic coding orientation," the tendency to associate certain ways of meaning with certain social contexts. Any interpretation of the phenomenon of anti-languages involves some theory about what kinds of meaning are exchanged in different environments within a culture.

Let us try and answer more specifically the question why anti-languages are used. Mallik in fact put this question to "a large number of criminals and anti-social elements" – 400 in all; he got 385 replies (including only 26 "don't know"), of which 158 explained it as the need for secrecy, and 132 as communicative force or verbal art. In Podgórecki's account of the second life both these motifs figure prominently: one of the ways in which an inmate can be downgraded to the level of a "sucker" in the social hierarchy is by breaking the rules of verbal contest, and another is by "selling the secret language to the police" (1973: 9). But the fact that an anti-language is **used for** closed communication and for verbal art does not mean that these are what gave rise to it in the first place. It would be possible to create a language just for purposes of contest and display; but this hardly seems sufficient to account for the origin of the entire phenomenon. The theme of secrecy is a familiar one in what we might call "folk anti-linguistics" – in members' and outsiders' explanations of the use of an anti-language. No doubt it is a part of the truth: effective teamwork does depend, at times, on exchanging meanings that are inaccessible to the victim, and communication among prisoners must take place without the participation of the jailer. But while secrecy is a necessary strategic property of anti-languages, it is unlikely to be the major cause of their existence. Secrecy is a feature of the jargon rather than a determinant of the language.

What then lies behind the emergence of the anti-language? Yet another way of being "suckered down" is by "maliciously refusing to learn the grypserka"; and it is clear from Podgórecki's discussion that there is an inseparable connection between the "second life" and the anti-language that is associated with it. The *grypserka* is not just an optional extra, serving to adorn the second life with contest and display while keeping it successfully hidden from the prison authorities. It is a fundamental element in the existence of the "second life" phenomenon. Here is Podgórecki's initial summing up:

The essence of the second life consists in a secular stratification which can be reduced to the division of the inmates into "people" and "suckers" . . . The people are independent and they have power over the suckers. Everyday second life is strongly ritualized. The body of these rituals are called *grypserka* (from *grypa* – a slang word designating a letter smuggled secretly to or from a prison); S. Malkowski defined this as "the inmates' language and its grammar." In this language, certain . . . words . . . are insulting and noxious either to the speaker or to one to whom they are addressed.

(1973: 7)

The language comes to the investigator's attention in the context of the familiar twin themes of ritual insult and secrecy. But Podgórecki's discussion of the "second life" shows that it is much more than a way of passing the time. It is the acting out of a distinct social structure; and this social structure is, in turn, the bearer of an alternative social reality.

On closer scrutiny, the Polish investigators found that the division into people and suckers was only the principal division in a more elaborate social hierarchy. There were two classes of "people" and three of "suckers", with some degree of mobility among them, though anyone who had once reached the highest or lowest category stayed there. There were a number of other variables, based on age, provenance (urban/rural), type of offence and prison standing (first offender/old lag); and the place of an individual in the social structure was a function of his status in respect of each of these hierarchies. Account was also taken of his status in the free underworld, which, along with other factors, suggested that "second life" was not a product of the prison, or of prison conditions, but was imported from the criminal sub-culture outside. Nevertheless,

> . . . the incarcerated create in their own social system a unique stratification which is based on the caste principle. The caste adherence in the case of "second life" is based not on a given social background or physical features, but is predominantly determined by a unique link with magical rules which are not functional for the social system in which they operate. The only function which these rules have is to sustain the caste system.

(1973: 14)

Comparative data from American sources quoted by Podgórecki show the existence of a similar form of social organization in correctional institutions in the United States, differing mainly in that each of the two anti-societies appears as a distorted reflection of the structure of the particular society from which it derives.

Podgórecki cites explanations of the "second life" as resulting from conditions of isolation, or from the need to regulate sexual behaviour, and rejects them as inadequate. He suggests instead that it arises from the need to maintain inner solidarity under pressure, and that this is achieved through an accumulation of punishments and rewards:

> "Second life" is a system which transforms the universal reciprocity of punishments into a pattern of punishments and rewards, arranged by the principles of stratification. Some members of the community are in a position to transform the punishments into rewards. It might be said that this type of artificial social stratification possesses features of collective representation which transform the structure of existing needs into an operating fabric of social life which tries to satisfy these needs in a way which is viable in the given conditions.
>
> (1973: 20)

The formula is therefore:

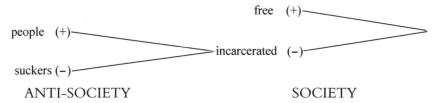

ANTI-SOCIETY   SOCIETY

which is the Lévi-Straussian proportion b1 : b2 :: a : b (see Bourdieu 1971). At the individual level, the "second life" provides the means of maintaining identity in the face of its threatened destruction:

> In a world in which there are no real things, a man is reduced to the status of a thing ... The establishment of a reverse world (in which reducing others to things becomes a source of gratification by transforming a punitive situation into a rewarding one) can also be seen as a desperate attempt to rescue and reintegrate the self in the face of the cumulative oppression which threatens to disintegrate it. Thus "second life". ... can be interpreted as a defence and a means of reconstruction, to which the self resorts just before total disruption by means of mutually enhancing oppressive forces.
>
> (1973: 24)

The "second life" is a reconstruction of the individual and society. It provides an alternative social structure, with its systems of values, of sanctions, of rewards and punishments; and this becomes the source of an alternative identity for its members, through the patterns of acceptance and gratification. In other words, the "second life" is an alternative reality.

It is in this light that we can best appreciate the function of the "second-life" anti-language, the *grypserka*. The *grypserka* serves to create and maintain this alternative reality. An anti-language is, in this respect, no different from a language 'proper': both are reality-generating systems. But because of the special character of the "second-life" reality – its status as an alternative, under constant pressure from the reality that is 'out there' (which is still a subjective reality, but nevertheless stands always ready to be reaffirmed as the norm) – the reality-generating force of the anti-language, and especially its power to create and maintain social hierarchy, is strongly foregrounded.

At this point we should quote at some length a critically relevant passage from Berger and Luckmann's *The Social Construction of Reality*:

> The most important vehicle of reality-maintenance is conversation. One may view the individual's everyday life in terms of the working away of a conversational apparatus that ongoingly maintains, modifies and reconstructs his subjective reality. Conversation means mainly, of course, that people speak with one another. This does not deny the rich aura of non-verbal communication that surrounds speech. Nevertheless speech retains a privileged position in the total conversational apparatus. It is important to stress, however, that the greater part of reality-maintenance in conversation is implicit, not explicit. Most conversation does not in so many words define the nature of the world. Rather, it takes place against the background of a world that is silently taken for granted. Thus an exchange such as, "Well, it's time for me to get to the station," and "Fine, darling, have a good day at the office," implies an entire world *within which* these apparently simple propositions make sense. By virtue of this implication the exchange confirms the subjective reality of this world.
>
> If this is understood, one will readily see that the great part, if not all, of everyday conversation maintains subjective reality. Indeed, its massivity is achieved by the accumulation and consistency of casual conversation – conversation that can *afford to be* casual precisely because it refers to the routine of a taken-for-granted world. The loss of casualness signals a break in the routines and, at least potentially, a threat to the taken-for-granted reality. Thus one may imagine the effect on casualness of an exchange like this: "Well, it's time for me to get to the station." "Fine, darling, don't forget to take along your gun."
>
> At the same time that the conversational apparatus ongoingly

maintains reality, it ongoingly modifies it. Items are dropped and added, weakening some sectors of what is still being taken for granted and reinforcing others. Thus the subjective reality of something that is never talked about comes to be shaky. It is one thing to engage in an embarrassing sexual act. It is quite another to talk about it beforehand or afterwards. Conversely, conversation gives firm contours to items previously apprehended in a fleeting and unclear manner. One may have doubts about one's religion: these doubts become real in a quite different way as one discusses them. One then "talks oneself into" these doubts: they are objectified as reality within one's own consciousness. Generally speaking, the conversational apparatus maintains reality by "talking through" various elements of experience and allocating them a definite place in the real world.

This reality-generating potency of conversation is already given in the fact of linguistic objectification. We have seen how language objectifies the world, transforming the *panta rhei* of experience into a cohesive order. In the establishment of this order language *realizes* a world, in the double sense of apprehending and producing it. Conversation is the actualizing of this realizing efficacy of language in the face-to-face situation of individual existence. In conversation the objectifications of language become objects of individual consciousness. Thus the fundamental reality-maintaining fact is the continuing use of the same language to objectify unfolding biographical experience. In the widest sense, all who employ this same language are reality-maintaining others. The significance of this can be further differentiated in terms of what is meant by a "common language" from the group-idiosyncratic language of primary groups to regional or class dialects to the national community that defines itself in terms of language.

(1966: 17–2)

An individual's subjective reality is created and maintained through interaction with others, who are 'significant others' precisely because they fill this role; and such interaction is, critically, verbal – it takes the form of conversation. Conversation is not, in general, didactic; the 'others' are not teachers, nor do they consciously 'know' the reality they are helping to construct. Conversation is, in Berger and Luckmann's term, casual. Berger and Luckmann do not ask the question, what must language be like for casual conversation to have this magic power. They are not concerned with the nature of the linguistic system. For linguistics, however, this is a central problem; and for linguistics in the perspective of a general social semiotic, it might be said to be **the** central problem: how can we interpret the linguistic system in such a way as to explain the magical powers of conversation?

Let us consider the anti-language in this light. As Berger and Luckmann point out, subjective reality can be transformed:

> To be in society already entails an ongoing process of modification of subjective reality. To talk about transformation, then, involves a discussion of different degrees of modification. We will concentrate here on the extreme case, in which there is a near-total transform-ation; that is, in which the individual "switches worlds." ... Typically, the transformation is subjectively apprehended as total. This, of course, is something of a misapprehension. Since subjective reality is never totally socialized, it cannot be totally transformed by social processes. At the very least the transformed individual will have the same body and live in the same physical universe. Nevertheless there are instances of transformation that appear total if compared with lesser modifications. Such transformations we will call alternations.
>
> Alternation requires processes of re-socialization.
>
> (1966: 176)

The anti-language is the vehicle of such resocialization. It creates an alternative reality: the process is one not of construction but of reconstruction. The success condition for such a reconstruction is, in Berger and Luckmann's words, "the availability of an effective plausibility structure, that is, a social base serving as the 'laboratory' of transformation. This plausibility structure will be mediated to the individual by means of significant others, with whom he must establish strongly affective identification" (1966: 177).

The processes of **re**socialization, in other words, make special kinds of demand on language. In particular, these processes must enable the individual to "establish strongly affective identification" with the significant others. Conversation in this context is likely to rely heavily on the foregrounding of interpersonal meanings, especially where, as in the case of the second life, the cornerstone of the new reality is a new social structure – although, by the same token, the interpersonal elements in the exchange of meanings are likely to be fairly highly ritualized.

But it is a characteristic of an anti-language that it is not just an ordinary language which happens to be for certain individuals a language of resocializing. Its conditions of use are different from the types of alternation considered by Berger and Luckmann, such as forms of religious conversion. In such instances an individual takes over what for others is **the** reality; for him it involves a transformation, but the reality itself is not inherently of this order. It is **somebody's** ordinary, everyday, unmarked reality, and its language is **somebody's** "mother tongue". An anti-language, however, is nobody's "mother tongue"; it exists solely in the context of **re**socialization, and the reality it creates is inherently an alternate reality, one that is constructed precisely in order to function in alternation. It is the language of an anti-society.

Of course, the boundary between the two is not hard and fast. The early Christian community was an anti-society, and its language was in this sense an anti-language. But nevertheless there are significant differences. Alternation does not of itself involve any kind of anti-language, merely the switch from one language to another. (It could be said that, in the perspective of the individual, the second is in fact functioning as an anti-language. Thus for example in Agnes' recon-struction of an identity, as described by Garfinkel [1967] in his famous case history, the language of femininity, or rather of femaleness, was for her an anti-language, since it was required to construct what was in the context a counteridentity. But a language is a social construct; Agnes did not, and could not by herself, create a linguistic system to serve as the medium for the reconstruction. Indeed to do so would have sabotaged the whole effort, since its success depended on the new identity appearing, and being accepted, as if it had been there from the start.) The anti-language arises when the alternative reality is a **counter**-reality, set up **in opposition to** some established norm.

It is thus not the **distance** between the two realities but the **tension** between them that is significant. The distance need not be very great; the one is, in fact, a metaphorical variant of the other (just as *grypserka* is clearly a variant of Polish and not some totally alien language). Moreover, unlike what happens in a transformation of the religious conversion kind, the individual may in fact switch back and forth between society and anti-society, with varying degrees of intermediate standing: the criminal sub-culture outside the prison is in that sense intermediate between the second life and the established society. Likewise Mallik identifies three distinct groups of people using the underworld language of Bengal: criminals, near-criminals, and students; and he notes significant differences among them, both in content and in expression: "while the criminals speak with a peculiar intonation, the students or other cultured people speak normally" (1972: 27). There is continuity between language and anti-language, just as there is continuity between society and anti-society. But there is also tension between them, reflecting the fact that they are variants of one and the same underlying semiotic. They may express different social structures; but they are part and parcel of the same social system.

An anti-language is the means of realization of a subjective reality: not merely expressing it, but actively creating and maintaining it. In this respect, it is just another language. But the reality is a counter-reality, and this has certain special implications. It implies the foregrounding of the social structure and social hierarchy. It implies a preoccupation with the definition and defence of identity through the ritual functioning of the social hierarchy. It implies a special conception of information and of knowledge. (This is where the secrecy comes in: the language is secret because the reality is secret. Again there is a counterpart in individual verbal behaviour, in the techniques of information control practised by individuals having something to hide, which they do not want divulged [see Goffman's (1963) study of stigma].) And it implies that social meanings will be seen as oppositions: values will be defined by what they are not, like time and space in the Looking-Glass world (where one lives backwards, and things get further away the more one walks towards them).

Let us enumerate here some of the features of the Calcutta underworld language described by Mallik. Mallik states that it is "a full and complete language, though mixed and artificial to some extent" (1972: 73); it is "primarily Bengali, in which strains of Hindi infiltration are discernible" (1972: 62). He considers that the language has its own phonology and morphology, which could and should be described in their own terms. But these can also be interpreted in terms of variation within Bengali, and Mallik relates the underworld forms to standard Bengali wherever he can.

In phonology, Mallik distinguishes some 30 different processes – for example, metathesis: e.g. kodān (shop) from dokān, karcā (servant) from cākar; back formation: e.g. khum (mouth), from mukh; consonantal change: e.g. konā (gold) from sonā; syllabic insertion: e.g. biṭuri (old woman) from buṛi; and variation involving single features, such as nasality, cerebral articulation or aspiration. Many words, naturally, have more than one such process in their derivation: e.g. chappi (buttock) from pāch; ãske (eyes) from akṣi; mākrā (joke) from maskarā.

In morphology also, Mallik identifies a number of derivational processes – for example, suffixing: e.g. koṭni (cotton bag) from English *cotton*; dharān (kidnapper) from dharā (hold); compounding: e.g. bilākhānā (brothel) from bilā (general derogatory term) + khānā (-orium, place for); simplifying; shift of word class; lexical borrowing:

275

e.g. khālās (murder) from Arabic xalās (end), replacing khun. Again, we find various combinations of these processes, and very many instances that are capable of more than one explanation.

All these examples are variants, in the sense in which the term is used in variation theory (Cedergren and D. Sankoff 1974; G. Sankoff 1974). Labov (1969) defines a set of variants as "alternative ways of 'saying the same thing'" (his quotation marks); and while the principle behind variation is much more complex than this innocent-sounding definition implies, it is true that, in the most general terms, we can interpret a variant as an alternative realization of an element on the next, or on some, higher stratum. So, for example, kodān and dokān are variants (alternative phonological realizations) of the same **word**, "shop." Similarly koṭni and its standard Bengali equivalent are variants (alternative lexicogrammatical realizations) of the same **meaning**, "cotton bag." Assuming the semantic stratum to be the highest stratum within the linguistic system, **all** sets of variants have the property of being identical semantically; **some** have the property of being identical lexicogrammatically as well:

Now the significant thing about the items that are phonologically or morphologically distinctive in the underworld language is that many of them are not, in fact, variants at all; they have no semantic equivalent in standard Bengali. This does not mean they cannot be **translated** into standard Bengali (or standard English, or standard anything else); they can. But they do not function as **coded** elements in the semantic system of the everyday language. Here are some examples from Mallik:

Item	Definition	Source
ghõṭ	to swallow a stolen thing to avoid detection	ḍhõk (swallow)
logām	theft in a moving goods train	māl gāṛi (goods train)

276

Item	Definition	Source
okhrān	one who helps the chief operator in stealing from a goods train	oprāno (uproot)
bhappar	outside disturbance at the time of a theft	bhir bhappar (crowd)
ulṭi	underworld language	ulaṭ (turn down)
cukru	kidnapper of sleeping child	curi (theft)
bilāhalat	serious condition of a victim in an assault	bilā (queer) and halat (condition–Hindi)
bidhobā	boy without girlfriend	bidhobā (widow)
ruṭihā	to share bread secretly with a convict detained in a prison	ruṭi (bread)
bastā	person promised employment but cheated	bastā (sack)
pancabāj	one who leaves victim at crossroads after a snatch	panca (five), bāj (expert)
paune-āṭṭā	boy prostitute	paune-āṭṭā (seven and three quarters)
khām	thigh of a girl	thām (pillar)
guanā	hidden cavity inside the throat to hide stolen goods	gahan (secret)
nicu-cākkā	pick pockets by standing on footboard of train or bus	nicu (low), cākā (wheel)

Intermediate between these and the straightforward variants are numerous metaphorical expressions of the type that would most readily be thought of as typical of inner city gangland speech, such as:

Item	Definition	Source
sāinbord-olā	married woman	(reference to vermilion mark on forehead of married woman) and olā (owner)
kā̃cā-kalā	young girl	(unripe, banana)
sardi-khāsi	notes and coins	(cold, cough – in reference to noises made)
cok-khāl	spectacles	(eye, pocket)

Item	Definition	Source
ātap	widow	(sunbaked) from ātap cāl (sunbaked rice, eaten by widows)
ṭhunkā	casual (client of prostitute)	portmanteau of ṭhunko (fragile) and thāuko (small-scale, retail)
ḍabal-ḍekār	plump woman	(English *double decker*)
chāmiā	girl	māch (fish) reversed to chām + suffix –i + suffix –ā
suṭā	cigarette	sukh (happiness) + ṭān (puff)
aeṛi-mārā	impotent	ãṛa (testicles) + mārā (strike; dead)
obhisār-āenā	seductive eyes	abhisār (tryst) + āynā (mirror)

Thomas Harman's account of the Elizabethan pelting speech contains many similar examples: *crashing-cheats* (teeth) (*cheat* = general element for 'thing which ...'), *smelling-cheat* (nose; also garden, orchard), *belly-cheat* (apron), *Rome-booze* (wine), *stalling-ken* (house that will receive stolen ware [*stall* = make or ordain, i.e. order + *ken* = house]), *queer-ken* (prison-house [*queer* = nought, i.e. general derogatory element, see Bengali bilā]), *darkmans* (night), *queer cuffin* (justice of the peace).

There is no way of deciding whether such metaphorical representations 'have the same meaning' as everyday forms or not, i.e. whether they are or are not variants in Labov's definition. (To say "same denotation, different connotation" is merely to avoid deciding; it means 'both yes and no'.) Nor is there any need to decide. We can call them all "metaphorical variants," since it is helpful to relate them to variation theory; what is most important is the fact that they are metaphorical. It is this metaphorical character that defines the anti-language. An anti-language is a metaphor for an everyday language; and this metaphorical quality appears all the way up and down the system. There are phonological metaphors, grammatical metaphors – morphological, lexical and perhaps syntactic – and semantic metaphors; for example, see Table 1 (**not** a complete list of types). As we have pointed out already, many instances can be interpreted in more than one way, and many are complex metaphors, involving variation at more than one level.

By interpreting the total phenomenon in terms of metaphor we can relate the semantic variants to the rest of the picture. The notion of a semantic variant is apparently contradictory: how can two things be variants ('have the same meaning') if their meanings are different? But this is the wrong way of looking at it. The anti-society is, in terms of Lévi-Strauss' distinction between metaphor and metonymy, metonymic to society – it is an extension of it, within the social system; while its realizations are (predictably) metaphorical, and this applies both to its realization in social structure and to its realization in language. The anti-society is, in its structure, a metaphor for the society; the two come together at the level of the social system. In the same way the anti-language is a metaphor for the language, and the two come together at the level of the social semiotic. So there is no great difficulty in assimilating the "second life" social hierarchy to existing internalized representations of social structure; nor in assimilating concepts like 'hidden cavity inside the throat to receive stolen goods,' or 'to share bread secretly with a convict', to the existing semiotic that is realized through the language. Semantic variants 'come together', i.e. are interpretable, at the higher level, that of the culture as an information system.

Table 1: Types of metaphor

phonological:		alternation	sonā ≡ konā 'gold'
		metathesis	khum ≡ mukh 'mouth'
grammatical	morphological:	suffixation	koṭni (koṭan 'cotton' + i) ≡ 'bag'
		compounding	bilākhānā ('queer' + 'house') ≡ 'brothel'
	lexical:	alternation	billi ('cat') ≡ 'prostitute'
	syntactic:	expansion	chappar khāoā ≡ lukāno 'hide' (Cf. Engl. bing a waste ≡ 'depart')
semantic:			ghōṭ ('swallow stolen object') ≡ ?
			nicu-cākkā ('pick pockets from footboard of tram') ≡ ?

The phenomenon of metaphor itself is, of course, not an "anti-linguistic" one; metaphor is a feature of **languages**, not just anti-languages (although one could express the same point another way by saying that metaphor constitutes the element of anti-language that is present in all languages). Much of everyday language is metaphorical in origin, though the origins are often forgotten, or unknown. What distinguishes an anti-language is that it is itself a metaphorical entity, and hence metaphorical modes of expression are the norm; we should **expect** metaphorical compounding, metatheses, rhyming alternations and the like to be among its regular patterns of realization.

We know much less about its modes of meaning, its semantic styles. Harman gives a dialogue in Elizabethan anti-language, but it is almost certainly one he has made up himself to illustrate the use of the words in his glossary (1567: 148–50). Mallik includes no dialogue, although he does quote a number of complete sentences, which are very helpful (1972: 83–4, 109–10). It is not at all easy to record spontaneous conversation (especially in an anti-language!). But, as Berger and Luckmann rightly point out, the reality-generating power of language lies in conversation; furthermore it is cumulative, and depends for its effectiveness on continuous reinforcement in interaction. To be able to interpret the real significance of an anti-language, we need to have access to its conversational patterns: texts will have to be collected, and edited, and subjected to an exegesis that relates them to the semantic system and the social context. Only in this way can we hope to gain insight into the characterology (to use a Prague School term) of an anti-language – the meaning styles and coding orientations that embody its characteristic counter-cultural version of the social system.

Meanwhile, the easiest way in to an anti-language is probably through another class of languages that we could call "music-hall languages" (or, in American, "vaudeville languages"). It is worth speculating (but speculation is no substitute for finding out) whether Gobbledygook – in its original sense as a "secret language" of Victorian working-class humour, not its metaphorical sense as the language of bureaucrats – is, in origin, a descendant of the Elizabethan anti-language, with its teeth drawn once the social conditions in which the anti-language emerged and flourished had ceased to exist. Gobbledygook has some distinctively anti-language features: one brief example, *erectify a luxurimole flackoblots* (erect a luxurious block of flats), contains metathesis, suffixation and compounding with a common morph – all totally vacuous, hence the comic effect. The banner of Gobbledygook was borne aloft (and raised to semantic heights) in England in the 1950s by Spike Milligan, who created an anti-language of his own – a "kind of mental slapstick," in the words of H. R. H. The

Prince of Wales – known as Goonery. Here is a specimen of conversation (Milligan 1973):

Quartermess:	Listen, someone's screaming in agony – fortunately I speak it fluently.
Willium:	Oh sir. Ohh me krills are plurned.
Quartermess:	Sergeant Fertangg, what's up? Your boots have gone grey with worry.
Willium:	I was inside the thing, pickin' up prehistoric fag-ends, when I spots a creature crawling up the wall. It was a weasel, suddenly it went ...
(sound effects)	POP
Quartermess:	What a strange and horrible death.
Willium:	Then I hears a 'issing sound and a voice say ... 'minardor'.
Quartermess:	Minardor? We must keep our ears, nose and throat open for anything that goes Minardor.
Henry:	Be forewarned Sir, the Minardor is an ancient word, that can be read in the West of Ministers Library.
Quartermess:	It so happens I have Westminster Library on me and, Gad, look there I am inside examining an occult dictionary.
(sound effects)	THUMBING PAGES

But when we reach this point, it is high time to ask: why the interest in anti-languages? They are entertaining; but have they any importance, or are they just collectors' pieces? I think if we take them seriously – though not solemnly! – there are two ways in which anti-languages are of significance for the understanding of the social semiotic.

(1) In the first place, the phenomenon of the anti-language throws light on the difficult concept of social dialect, by providing an opposite pole, the second of two idealized extremes to which we can relate the facts as we actually find them.

Let us postulate an ideally homogeneous society, with no division of labour, or at least no form of social hierarchy, whose members (therefore) speak an ideally homogeneous language, without dialectal variation. There probably never has been such a human group, but that does not matter; this is an ideal construct serving as a thesis for deductive argument. At the other end of the scale, we postulate an ideally dichotomized society, consisting of two distinct and mutually hostile groups, society and anti-society; the members of these speak two totally distinct tongues, a language and an anti-language. Again, there has probably never been such a thing – it reminds us of the Eloi and the Morlocks imagined by H. G. Wells in *The Time Machine*. But it serves as the antithesis, the idealized opposite pole.

What we do find in real life are types of sociolinguistic order that are interpretable as lying somewhere along this cline. The distinction between standard and non-standard dialects is one of language versus anti-language, although taking a relatively benign and moderate form. Popular usage opposes *dialect*, as "anti-" to (*standard*) *language*, as the established norm. A non-standard dialect that is consciously used for strategic purposes, defensively to maintain a particular social reality or offensively for resistance and protest, lies further in the direction of an anti-language; this is what we know as a "ghetto language" (see Kochman's [1972] account of Black English in the United States).

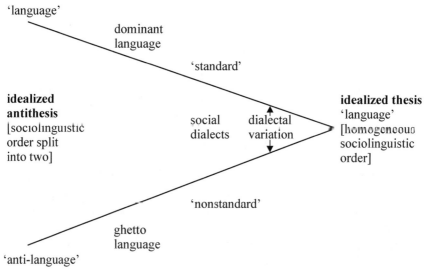

'language'

dominant
language

'standard'

idealized
antithesis
[sociolinguistic
order split
into two]

social
dialects

dialectal
variation

idealized thesis
'language'
[homogeneous
sociolinguistic
order]

'nonstandard'

ghetto
language

'anti-language'

Figure 1: Types of sociolinguistic order

Social dialects are not necessarily associated with caste or class; they may be religious, generational, sexual, economic (urban/rural), and perhaps other things too. What distinguishes them is their hierarchical character. The social function of dialect variation is to express, symbolize and maintain the social order; and the social order is an essentially hierarchic one. An anti-language is, at one and the same time, **both** the limiting case of a social dialect (and hence is the realization of one component in the hierarchy of a wider social order that includes both society and anti-society), **and** a language (and hence the realization of a social order that is constituted by the anti-society itself); in the latter role, it embodies its own hierarchy, and so displays internal variation of a systematic kind – Mallik, for example, refers to the different groups existing within the anti-society, each with its own social status and each having its own distinctive speech forms (1972: 28–9).

The perspective of the anti-language is one in which we can clearly see the meaning of variability in language: in brief, the function of alternative language is to create alternative reality. A social dialect is the embodiment of a mildly but distinctly different world view – one which is therefore potentially threatening, if it does not coincide with one's own. This is undoubtedly the explanation of the violent attitudes to non-standard speech commonly held by speakers of a standard dialect: the conscious motif of 'I don't like their vowels' symbolizes an underlying motif of 'I don't like their values'. The significance for the social semiotic, of the kind of variation **in the linguistic system** that we call social dialect, becomes very much clearer when we take into account the nature and functions of anti-languages.

(2) In the second place, there is anti-language as **text**. A central problem for linguistics is that of relating text to system, and of relating modes of text description that are applicable to conversation (Mitchell 1957; Sacks, Schegloff and Jefferson 1974) to a theory of the linguistic system. I have suggested elsewhere (Chapters 5 and 9) that this can be usefully approached through a functional interpretation of the semantic system, an interpretation in terms of its major functional components which are relatable (i) to the text, as an ongoing process of selection in meaning; (ii) to the linguistic system; and (iii) to the situation, as a semiotic construct derivable from the "social semiotic" (the culture considered as an information system). It is beyond the scope of this paper to develop this further here; but one point may be made which emerges specifically with reference to the description of anti-languages.

Conversation, as Berger and Luckmann point out, depends for its reality-generating power on being casual: that is to say, it **typically** makes use of **highly coded** areas of the **system** to produce **text** that is **congruent** – though once coding and congruence have been established as the norm, it can tolerate and indeed thrives on a reasonable quantity of matter that is incongruent or uncoded.

"Uncoded" means "not (yet) fully incorporated into the system"; "incongruent" means 'not expressed through the most typical (and highly coded) form of representation'; and both concepts are of a more or less kind, not all or nothing. Now, certain types of social context typically engender text in which the coding process, and the congruence relation, tend to be foregrounded and brought under attention. An example is the language of young children (and of others interacting with them), since children are simultaneously both interacting and constructing the system that underlies the text.

Other examples are provided by verbal contest and display. Here the foregrounding is not a sign of the system coming into being, but an effect of the particular functional orientation within the system, and the special features that arise in a context where a speaker is using language just in order to secure for himself the rewards that accrue to prowess in the use of language.

An anti-language has something of both these elements in it. Anti-languages are typically used for contest and display, with consequent foregrounding of interpersonal elements of all kinds. At the same time, the speakers of an anti-language are constantly striving to maintain a counter-reality that is under pressure from the established world. This is why the language is constantly renewing itself – to sustain the vitality that it needs if it is to function at all. Such is the most likely explanation of the rapid turnover of words and modes of expression that is always remarked on by commentators on underworld language. But there is more to it than that. Within the experiential mode of meaning, an anti-language may take into itself may encode at the semantic level – structures and collocations that are self-consciously opposed to the norms of the established language. This can be seen clearly in texts in the more intellectuated anti-languages such as those of mysticism (and see some of the Escher-like semantic sleights of Goonery, e.g. "I have Westminster Library on me and, Gad, look there I am inside"). But it is almost certainly present also in the typical conversation of the underworld and the "second life."

The result is that conversation in an anti-language is likely to display in sharper outline the systematic relations between the text and the linguistic system. The modes of expression of the anti-language, when seen from the standpoint of the established language, appear oblique, diffuse, metaphorical; and so they are, **from that angle**. But seen in their own terms, they appear directed, as powerful manifestations of the linguistic system in the service of the construction of reality. It is the reality that is oblique, since we see it as a metaphorical transformation of the "true" reality; but the function of the text with respect to that reality is a reinforcing one, all the more direct because it is a reality which needs more reinforcement.

An anti-language is not something that we shall always be able to recognize by inspection of a text. It is likely to be characterized by some or all of the various features mentioned, and hence to be recognizable by its phonological or lexicogrammatical shape as a metaphoric alternant to the everyday language. But in the last resort these features are not necessary to an anti-language. We have interpreted anti-language as the limiting case of social dialect, and this is a valid perspective; but it is an extreme, not a typical case because it is not primarily defined by variation – or, rather, the variation by which it could be defined would be variation in a special sense. A social dialect is a cluster of associated variants, that is, a systematic pattern of tendencies in the selection of values of phonological and lexicogrammatical variables under specified conditions. Attention is on variation rather than on the meanings that are exchanged. An anti-language, while it may display such variation, is to be defined, on the other hand, as a systematic pattern of tendencies in the selection of meanings to be exchanged. (We left open the question whether or not this could be brought under the rubric of variation.) In this respect, therefore, it is more like Bernstein's (1974) concept of a code, or coding orientation. A code may be defined just in this way: as a systematic pattern of tendencies in the selection of meanings to be exchanged under specified conditions. (Note that the "specified conditions" are in the socio-linguistic environment. They may be social or linguistic, the tendency being, naturally, that the higher the level of the variation, the more likely it is that the relevant context will be social rather than linguistic. Hence in the definition of code we could say "in specified social contexts".) So now we can interpret an anti-language as the limiting case of a code. Again it is an extreme, not a typical case, but this time for a different reason: because the subjective reality that is realized by it is a conscious counter-reality, not just a subcultural variant of, or angle on, a reality that is accepted by all. Still this is a relative matter: an anti-language is not a clearly distinct category – it is a category to which any given instance approximates more or less.

An anti-language of the kind presented at the start brings into sharp relief the role of language as a realization of the power structure of society. The anti-languages of prison and criminal countercultures are the most clearly defined because they have specific reference to alternative social structures, as well as the additional attributes of secret

285

languages and professional jargons; and hence they are full of overt markers of their anti-language status. The obliqueness of meaning and form that makes them so effective as bearers of an alternative reality also makes them inherently comic – so reflecting another aspect of the same reality, as seen by its speakers. In any case not all anti-languages are languages of social resistance and protest. The "arcane languages" of sorcery and mysticism are of the same order (hence some of Castaneda's [1971] difficulties in understanding Don Juan). An anti-language may be "high" as well as "low" on the diglossic spectrum. The languages of literature are in a certain sense anti-languages – or rather, literature is both language and anti-language at the same time. It is typical of a poetic genre that one or other mode of meaning is foregrounded. At times the effect comes close to that of an anti-language in the social sense, for example in competitive genres such as the Elizabethan sonnet; at other times the generic mode has little or nothing of the anti-language about it, leaving the individual poet free to impart his own subjective reality, if he so wishes, by creating an anti-language of his own. (And the listener, or reader, is free to **interpret** the text as anti-language if **he** so wishes.) The anti-linguistic aspect of literature is sometimes well to the fore; at other times and places it recedes into insignificance. A work of literature is its author's contribution to the reality-generating conversation of society – irrespective of whether it offers an alternative reality or reinforces the received model – and its language reflects this status that it has in the socio-semiotic scheme. But that is another topic.

AFTERWORD

I hope to have acknowledged, throughout these papers, my great debt to the very many colleagues and other scholars whose work has informed and inspired me across the past half century. There will inevitably have been lapses, and I take this chance to apologize to those that I have omitted to identify, or that I have in any way misrepresented.

But I owe a special debt to those who have made the present venture come alive. The one who set it all in motion was Robin Fawcett. He first suggested, more than ten years ago now, that I should put together a collection of some of my papers, many of which had always been hard to find. Robin was editor of the "Open Linguistics" series, then being published by Frances Pinter (Later Cassell, later still Continuum); he put the proposal of their publisher, Janet Joyce, and she accepted it.

Both Robin and Janet continue to support the idea and regularly pressed me to produce and submit a plan. Over five years I made several attempts to draw up the contents for a volume, or (with some misgiving) two volumes; but despite their constant encouragement I never succeeded. Whatever selection I tried out on one day always seemed pointless when I looked at it on the next.

Then on a visit to Singapore I was talking with Edwin Thumboo, and he asked me how the project was progressing. I was surprised that he knew about it; but I admitted I was making no headway. Edwin said, why don't you ask Jonathan Webster to help?

I protested that Jonathan was a busy man, with projects and problems of his own; but Edwin urged me, so rather diffidently I sought Jonathan's advice. I'd be very happy to help, he said. I showed him my failed attempts; but he set to work straightaway on the whole inventory of my publications and came out with a master plan – not for one, or two, volumes but for ten. If Continuum accepts these, I said, you will need to be the editor. Much to my surprise, they did.

Jonathan has spent a vast amount of time and energy selecting and organizing these materials and preparing them for publication. Meanwhile Janet had left Continuum, to set up a publishing house on her own; and Jenny Lovel was taking over as their editor with responsibility for linguistics. Jenny has been unceasingly positive and energetic in carrying the project ahead, maintaining the impetus and keeping pretty close to the original, rather tight schedule she set out for the entire series of ten volumes.

My warmest thanks go to all these folks who have collectively brought the enterprise to its realization. Watching over it all has been Ruqaiya, always in her dual persona as wife and as colleague. She helped with the selection and ordering of the contents, as well as the ongoing comment and advice; but most of all she has consistently encouraged me and reassured me that the whole project was worth while – something I was always inclined to question and to doubt. The best news is that now, thanks again to our valued friend Jonathan Webster, Ruqaiya's own collected works are in turn beginning to appear.

Urunga, N.S.W   M.A.K. Halliday
November 2006

BIBLIOGRAPHY

Abdulaziz, M. H. (1971) 'Tanzania's national language policy and the rise of Swahili political culture', in Whiteley (ed.) 1971.

Abercrombie, David (1965) *Studies in Phonetics and Linguistics*, London: Oxford University Press (*Language and Language Learning* 10).

Adlam, Diana S. (1977) *Codes in Context*, London and Boston: Routledge and Kegan Paul (Primary Socialization, Language and Education).

Atkinson, Paul (1985) *Language, Structure and Reproduction: An Introduction to the Sociology of Basil Bernstein*, London: Methuen.

Bailey, Charles-James N. (1974) *Variation and Linguistic Theory*, Washington, DC: Center for Applied Linguistics.

Baratz, Joan C. and Shuy, Roger W. (eds) (1969) *Teaching Black Children to Read*, Washington, DC: Center for Applied Linguistics.

Barnes, Douglas; Britton, James; Rosen, Harold and London Association for the Teaching of English (1969) *Language, the Learner and the School*, Harmondsworth: Penguin Books.

Barthes, Roland (1970) 'L'ancienne rhétorique', *Communications* 16.

Basso, Keith H. (1967) 'Semantic aspects of linguistic acculturation', *American Anthropologist* 69.

Berger, Peter L. and Kellner, Hansfried (1970) 'Marriage and the construction of reality', in Hans Peter Dreitzel (ed.), *Recent Sociology 2: Patterns of Communicative Behavior*, New York: Macmillan.

Berger, Peter L. and Luckmann, Thomas (1967) *The Social Construction of Reality: A Treatise in the Sociology of Knowledge*, New York: Doubleday; London: Allen Lane (The Penguin Press).

Bernstein, B. (1967) 'The role of speech in the development and transmission of culture', in G. J. Klopf and W. A. Hohman (eds.) *Perspectives on Learning*, New York: Mental Health Materials Center.

— (1970) 'A socio-linguistic approach to socialization; with some reference to educability', in J. J. Gumperz and D. H. Hymes (eds.) *Directions in Sociolinguistics*, New York: Holt, Rinehart and Winston.

— (1971) *Class, Codes and Control, Volume 1: Theoretical Studies Towards a Sociology of Language*, London: Routledge and Kegan Paul (Primary Socialization, Language and Education).

— (ed.) (1973) *Class, Codes and Control, Volume 2: Applied Studies Towards a Sociology of Language*, London: Routledge and Kegan Paul (Primary Socialization, Language and Education).

— (1975) 'Introduction' to *Class, Codes and Control, Volume 3: Towards a Theory of Educational Transmissions*, London: Routledge and Kegan Paul (Primary Socialization, Language and Education).

— (1986) 'On pedagogic discourse', in J. G. Richardson (ed.) *Handbook of Theory and Research for the Sociology of Education*, New York: Greenwood Press. Reprinted in Bernstein 1990: Chapter 5, 'The social construction of pedagogic discourse'.

— (1987) 'Class, codes and communication', in Ulrich Ammon, Norbert Dittmar and Klaus Mattheier (eds.) *Sociolinguistics: an International Handbook of the Science of Language and Society, Volume 1*

— (1990) *The Structuring of Pedagogic Discourse: Class, Codes and Control, Volume 4*, London and New York: Routledge.

Bernstein, Basil and Henderson, Dorothy (1969) 'Social class differences in the relevance of language to socialization', *Sociology*, 3:1–20.

Bickerton, Derek (1971) 'Inherent variability and variable rules', *Foundations of Language* 7.

— (1973) 'On the nature of a creole continuum', *Language* 49 .

Bloom, Lois (1973) *One Word at a Time*, The Hague: Mouton.

Bourdieu, Pierre (1971) 'The Berber house, or the world reversed', in J. Pouillon and P. Maranda, (eds.) *Echanges et Communications: Mélanges offerts à Claude Lévi-Strauss á l'occasion de son 60ᵉ Anniversaire*, The Hague: Mouton.

Brandis, Walter and Henderson, Dorothy (1970) *Social Class, Language and Communication*, London: Routledge and Kegan Paul (Primary Socialization, Language and Education).

Bright, William (ed.) (1966) *Sociolinguistics: proceedings of the UCLA*

Sociolinguistics Conference, 1964, The Hague: Mouton (Janua Linguarum Series Major 20).

Britton, James N. (1970) *Language and Learning*, London: Allen Lane (The Penguin Press).

Brown, Roger (1973) *A First Language: the Early Stages*, Cambridge, Mass: Harvard University Press.

Brown, Roger and Gilman, Albert (1960) 'The pronouns of power and solidarity', in Thomas A. Sebeok (ed.) *Style in Language*, Cambridge, Mass. and New York: MIT Press and Wiley. Reprinted in Fishman (ed.) 1968 and Giglioli (ed.) 1972.

Bühler, Karl (1934) *Sprachtheorie: die Darstellungsfunktion der Sprache*, Jena: Fischer.

Butler, Christopher S. (1985) *Systemic Linguistics: Theory and Applications*, London: Batsford Academic and Educational.

Castaneda, Carlos (1971) *A Separate Reality: Further Conversations with Don Juan*, New York: Simon and Schuster.

Cazden, C., John, V. P. and Hymes, Dell (eds.) (1972) *Functions of Language in the Classroom*, New York: Teachers College Press, Columbia University.

Cedergren, Henrietta and Sankoff, David (1974) 'Variable rules: performance as a statistical reflection of competence', *Language* 50.

Cedergren, Henrietta and Sankoff, Gillian (1971) 'Some results of a sociolinguistic study of Montreal French', in R. Darnell (ed.) *Linguistic Diversity in Canadian Society*, Edmonton, Alberta: Linguistic Research, Inc.

Cicourel, Aaron V. (1969) 'Generative semantics and the structure of social interaction', in *International Days of Sociolinguistics,* Rome: Bulzoni.

Clark, Eve V. (1973) 'What's in a word? on the child's acquisition of semantics in his first language', in T. E. Moore (ed.) *Cognitive Development and the Acquisition of Language*, New York: Academic Press.

Conklin, Harold C. (1962) 'Lexicographical treatment of folk taxonomies', in Fred W. Householder and Sol Saporta (eds) *Problems of Lexicography*, Supplement to *International Journal of American Linguistics* 28.2.

Cook-Gumperz, Jenny (1973) *Social Control and Socialization: a study of class difference in the language of maternal control*, London and Boston: Routledge and Kegan Paul (Primary Socialization, Language and Education).

Coulthard, R. M., Sinclair, J. McH., Forsyth, I. J. and Ashby, M. C.

(1972) *Discourse in the Classroom*, London: Centre for Information on Language Teaching and Research (mimeographed).

Daneš F. (1964) 'A three-level approach to syntax', *Travaux Linguistiques de Prague I*.

Daneš, František (ed.) (1974) *Papers on Functional Sentence Perspective*, Prague: Academia (Czechoslovak Academy of Sciences).

Dixon, Robert M. W. (1965) *What is Language? A New Approach to Linguistic Description*, London: Longman (Longman's Linguistics Library).

— (1970) *The Dyirbal Language of North Queensland*, Cambridge: Cambridge University Press.

Doughty, Peter; Pearce, John and Thornton, Geoffrey (1971) *Language in Use*, London: Edward Arnold.

— (1972) *Exploring Language*, London: Edward Arnold.

Douglas, Mary (1971) 'Do dogs laugh? a cross-cultural approach to body symbolism', *Journal of Psychosomatic Research* 15.

— (1972) 'Speech, class and Basil Bernstein', *The Listener* no. 2241, London: BBC (9 March).

— (1973) *Rules and Meanings: The Anthropology of Everyday Knowledge*, Harmondsworth: Penguin Books.

Dumont, Louis (1970) *Homo Hierarchicus: the Caste System and its Implications*. London: Weidenfeld & Nicolson.

Ellis, Jeffrey (1965) 'Linguistic sociology and institutional linguistics', *Linguistics* 19.

— (1966) 'On contextual meaning', in C. E. Bazell *et al.* (eds.) *In Memory of J. R. Firth*, London: Longman

Enkvist, Nils Erik; Spencer, John and Gregory, Michael (1964) *Linguistics and Style*, London: Oxford University Press (*Language and Language Learning* 6).

Ervin-Tripp, Susan M. (1969) 'Sociolinguistics', *Advances in Experimental Social Psychology* 4. Also in Fishman (ed.) 1971.

— (1972) 'Children's sociolinguistic competence and dialect diversity', in *Early Childhood Education*, Chicago: National Society for the Study of Education (Seventy-first Yearbook).

— (1973) *Language Acquisition and Communicative Choice: Essays Selected and Introduced by Anwar S. Dil*, Stanford, California: Stanford University Press.

Ferguson, Charles A. (1959). 'Diglossia', *Word* 15.

— (1968) 'Language development', in Joshua Fishman, J. Das Gupta and Charles A. Ferguson (eds) *Language Problems of Developing Nations*, New York: Wiley.

— (1971) *Language Structure and Language Use: Essays Selected and Introduced by Anwar S. Dil*, Stanford, California: Stanford University Press.

Firth, J. R. (1935) 'The Technique of Semantics', *Transactions of the Philological Society*. Reprinted in Firth, J. R. (1957) *Papers in Linguistics 1934–1951*. London: Oxford University Press.

— (1950) 'Personality and Language in Society', *The Sociological Review* 42. Reprinted in Firth 1957.

— (1968) 'Linguistic Analysis as a Study of Meaning', in Palmer, F. R. (ed.) *Selected Papers of J. R. Firth 1952–59*, London: Longman (Longman's Linguistics Library).

Fishman, Joshua A. (ed.) (1968) *Readings in the Sociology of Language*, The Hague: Mouton.

— (1971) 'The sociology of language: an interdisciplinary social science approach to language in society', in Fishman (ed.) 1971.

— (ed.) (1971) *Advances in the Sociology of Language, Vol. 1*. The Hague: Mouton.

Frake, Charles O. (1961) 'The diagnosis of disease among the Subanun of Mindanao', *American Anthropologist* 63. Reprinted in Hymes (ed.) 1964.

Friedrich, Paul (1966) 'Structural implications of Russian pronominal usage', in Bright (ed.) 1966.

Gahagan, D. M. and Gahagan, G. A. (1971) *Talk Reform: Explorations in Language for Infant School Children*, London: Routledge and Kegan Paul (Primary Socialization, Language and Education).

Garfinkel, Harold (1967) *Studies in Ethnomethodology*, Englewood Cliffs: Prentice-Hall.

Geach, Peter (1969) 'Should traditional grammar be ended or mended? – II', *The State of Language* (*Educational Review*, 22. 1, University of Birmingham School of Education).

Geertz, Clifford (1960) *The Religion of Java*, Glencoe, Illinois: Free Press.

Giglioli, Pier Paolo, (ed.) (1972) *Language and Social Context*, Harmondsworth: Penguin Books (Penguin Modern Sociology Readings).

Goffman, Erving (1963) *Stigma: Notes on the Management of Spoiled Identity*, Englewood Cliffs: Prentice-Hall.

— (1967) *Interaction Ritual: Essays on Face-to-Face Behavior*, New York: Doubleday (Anchor Books).

Gorman, T. P. (1971) in Whiteley (ed.) 1971.

Greenberg, Joseph (1963) *Essays in Linguistics*, Chicago and London: University of Chicago Press (Phonenix Books).

Gregory, Michael J. (1967) 'Aspects of varieties differentiation', *Journal of Linguistics* 3.2.

Greimas, A. J. (1969) 'Des modèles théoriques en sociolinguistique', in *International Days of Sociolinguistics*.

— (1971) 'Narrative grammar: units and levels', *Modern Language Notes* 86.6.

Grimshaw, Allen (1971) 'Sociolinguistics', in Fishman (ed.) 1971.

— (1976) 'Polity, class, school and talk: the sociology of Basil Bernstein', *Theory and Society* 3.4.

Gumperz, John J. (1968) 'The speech community', in *International Encyclopedia of the Social Sciences*, New York: Macmillan.

— (1971) *Language in Social Groups: Essays Selected and Introduced by Anwar S. Dil*, Stanford, California: Stanford University Press.

— (1972) Introducton to Gumperz and Hymes (eds) 1972.

Gumperz, John J. and Hymes, Dell H. (eds.) (1972) *Directions in Sociolinguistics: the Ethnography of Communication*. New York: Holt, Rinehart and Winston.

Gumperz, John J. and Wilson, Robert (1971) 'Convergence and creolization: a case from the Indo-Aryan/Dravidian border', in Hymes (ed.) 1971.

Halliday, M. A. K. (1967) *Intonation and Grammar in British English*. The Hague: Mouton (Janua Linguarum Series Practica 48), in Collected Works, Vol. 6, Chapters 8, 9, 2005.

— (1967–1968) 'Notes on transitivity and theme in English', parts 1–3, *Journal of Linguistics* 3.1, 3.2, 4.2, in Collected Works, Vol. 7, Chapters 1–3, 2005.

— (1969a) 'Functional diversity in language, as seen from a consideration of modality and mood in English', *Foundations of Language* 6, in Collected Works, Vol. 6, Chapter 5, 2005.

— (1969b) 'Relevant models of language', *The State of Language* (*Educational Review*, 22. 1, University of Birmingham School of Education), in Collected Works, Vol. 4, Chapter 12, 2003.

— (1970a) *Language and Social Man*, London: Longman (Papers of the Schools Council Programme in Linguistics and English Teaching, Second Series 3). Reprinted in Halliday 1978: Chapters 1 and 13. This volume, Chapter 3.

— (1970b) 'Language structure and language function', John Lyons (ed.) *New Horizons in Linguistics*, Harmondsworth: Penguin Books, in Collected Works, Vol. 1, Chapter 7, 2002.

— (1970c) 'On functional grammars', paper read to seminar *The Construction of Complex Grammars*, Boston, Mass. (mimeographed).

— (1972) *Towards a Sociological Semantics*, Urbino: Centro Internazionale di Semiotica e Linguistica (Working Papers and Prepublications 14/c), in Collected Works, Vol. 3, Chapter 15, 2003.

— (1973) *Explorations in the Functions of Language*, London: Edward Arnold (Explorations in Language Study).

— (1975a) 'Sociological aspects of semantic change', in Luigi Heilmann and Carlo Mastrelli (eds.) *Proceedings of the Eleventh International Congress of Linguists*, Bologna: Il Mulino. This volume, Chapter 4.

— (1975b) 'Language as social semiotic: towards a general socio-linguistic theory', in Adam Makkai and Valerie Becker Makkai, (eds), *The First LACUS Forum*, Columbia, South Carolina: Hornbeam Press. This volume, Chapter 5.

— (1975c) *Learning How to Mean: Explorations in the Development of Language*, London: Edward Arnold (Explorations in Language Study) in *Collected Works* Vol. 4, Chapters 2–4, 7, 2004.

— (1975d) 'Learning how to mean', in Eric and Elizabeth Lenneberg (eds).

Halliday, M. A. K. (1975e) 'Talking one's way in: a sociolinguistic perspective on language and learning'. In Alan Davies (ed.) *Problems of language and learning*. London: Heinemann, in association with the SSRC and SsRE.

— (1977) 'Text as semantic choice in social contexts', in T. A. van Dijk and J. Petöfi (eds). *Grammars and Descriptions*, Berlin: de Gruyter, in Collected Works, Vol. 2, Chapter 2, 2002.

— (1978) *Language as Social Semiotic: the Social Interpretation of Language and Meaning*, London: Edward Arnold.

— (1985) *An Introduction to Functional Grammar*, London: Edward Arnold; 3rd edn, revised by Christian Matthiessen, 2004.

— (1990) 'New ways of meaning: a challenge to applied linguistics', *Journal of Applied Linguistics* (Greek Applied Linguistics Association) 6. Reprinted in Martin Putz (ed.) *Thirty Years of Linguistic Evolution*, Amsterdam and Philadelphia: John Benjamins, in Collected Works, Vol. 3, Chapter 6, 2003.

Halliday, M. A. K., McIntosh, Angus and Strevens, Peter (1964) *The Linguistic Sciences and Language Teaching*, London: Longman (Longman's Linguistics Library); Bloomington, Indiana: Indiana University Press 1966.

Halliday, M. A. K. and Ruqaiya Hasan (1976) *Cohesion in English*, London: Longman (English Language Series 9).

Halliday, M. A. K. and J. R. Martin (1993) *Writing Science: Literacy and Discursive Power*, London and New York: Falmer Press.

Harman, Thomas (1567) *A Caveat or Warening for Commen Cursetories vulgarely called Vagabones*. London: Wylliam Gryffith ('A caveat for common cursitors', in Salgādo (ed.) 1972).

Hasan, Ruqaiya (1968) *Grammatical Cohesion in Spoken and Written English, Part 1*, London: Longman (Programme in Linguistics and English Teaching, Paper 7).

— (1971) 'Syntax and semantics', in Morton, J. (ed.) *Biological and Social Factors in Psycholinguistics*, London: Logos Press.

— (1973) 'Code, register and social dialect', in Bernstein (ed.) (1973).

— (1986) 'The ontogenesis of ideology: an interpretation of mother-child talk', in Terry Threadgold *et al.* (eds.) *Semiotics, Ideology, Language*, Sydney: Sydney Association for Studies in Society and Culture.

— (1988) 'Language in the processes of socialization: home and school', in Linda Gerot, Jane Oldenburg and Theo van Leeuwen (eds.) *Language and Socialization: Home and School*, North Ryde, NSW: Macquarie University.

— (1989) 'Semantic variation and sociolinguistics', *Australian Journal of Linguistics* 9.2.

— (1991) 'Questions as a mode of learning in everyday talk', in Thao Lê and Mike McCausland (eds) *Language Education: Interaction and Development*, Launceston, Tasmania: University of Tasmania.

— (1992a) 'Rationality in everyday talk: from process to system', in Jan Svartvik (ed.) *Directions in Corpus Linguistics*, Berlin and New York: Mouton de Gruyter.

— (1992b) 'Meaning in sociolinguistic theory', in Kingsley Bolton and Helen Kwok (eds) *Sociolinguistics Today: International Perspectives*, London and New York: Routledge.

Hasan, Ruqaiya and Carmel Cloran (1990) 'A sociolinguistic interpretation of everyday talk between mothers and children', in M. A. K. Halliday, John Gibbons and Howard Nicholas (eds) *Learning, Keeping and Using Language*, Amsterdam and Philadelphia: John Benjamins.

Haugen, Einar (1966) 'Dialect, language, nation', *American Anthropologist* 68. Reprinted in Anwar S. Dil (ed.) *The Ecology of Language: Essays by Einar Haugen*, Stanford, California: Stanford University Press 1972.

Hill, Trevor (1958) 'Institutional linguistics', *Orbis* 7.

Hoenigswald, Henry (1971) 'Language history and creole studies', in Hymes (ed.) 1971.

Hymes, Dell H. (1966) 'Two types of linguistic relativity (with examples from Amerindian ethnography)', in Bright (ed.) 1966.

— (1967) 'Models of the interaction of language and social setting', *Journal of Social Issues* 23.

— (1969) 'Linguistic theory and the functions of speech', in *International Days of Sociolinguistics*.

— (1971) 'Competence and performance in linguistic theory', in Renira Huxley and Elisabeth Ingram (eds) *Language Acquisition: models and methods*, London and New York: Academic Press.

— (1972) 'On communicative competence', in Gumperz and Hymes (eds).

Hymes, Dell H. (ed.) (1964) *Language in Culture and Society: a Reader in Linguistics and Anthropology*, New York: Harper and Row.

— (1971) *Pidginization and Creolization of Languages*, Cambridge: Cambridge University Press.

International Days of Sociolinguistics (1969), Rome: Luigi Sturzo Institute.

Joos, Martin (1967) *The Five Clocks*, New York: Harcourt, Brace and World.

Katz, J. J. and Fodor, J. A. (1963) 'The structure of a semantic theory', *Language* 39.

Kochman, Thomas (1972) *Rappin' and Stylin' Out: Communication in Urban Black America*, Urbana: University of Illinois Press.

Labov, William (1966) *The Social Stratification of English in New York City*, Washington, DC: Center for Applied Linguistics.

— (1968) 'The reflection of social processes in linguistic structures', in Fishman (ed.) 1968.

— (1969) 'Contraction, deletion and inherent variability of the English copula', *Language* 45: 715–62.

— (1970a). 'The study of language in its social context', *Studium Generale* 23. Reprinted in Fishman (ed.) 1971 and in Giglioli (ed.) 1972.

— (1970b) 'The logic of Non-standard English', *Georgetown University Monographs on Languages and Linguistics* 22. Reprinted in Williams (ed.) 1970.

— (1971) 'The notion of "system" in creole languages', in Hymes (ed.) 1971.

Labov, William and Waletzky, Joshua (1967) 'Narrative analysis: oral versions of personal experience', in June Helm (ed.) *Essays on the Verbal and Visual Arts*, Seattle: University of Washington Press.

Lamb, Sydney M. (1966) *Outline of Stratificational Grammar*, Washington, DC: Georgetown University Press.

— (1971) 'Linguistic and cognitive networks', in Paul Garvin (ed.) *Cognition: A Multiple View*, New York: Spartan Books.

— (1974) Discussion, in H. Parret, *Discussing Language*, The Hague: Mouton.

Leech, Geoffrey N. (1966) *English in Advertising*, London: Longman.

Lenneberg, Eric H. (1967) *Biological Foundations of Language*, New York: Wiley.

Lenneberg, Eric and Lenneberg, Elizabeth (eds) (1975) *Foundations of Language Development: a Multidisciplinary Approach*, Paris: UNESCO; and New York: Academic Press.

Levi-Strauss, Claude (1966) *The Savage Mind*, London: Weidenfeld and Nicholson.

Loflin, Marvin D. (1969) 'Negro nonstandard and standard English: same or different deep structure?', *Orbis* 18.

Lyons, John (ed.) (1970) *New Horizons in Linguistics*, Harmondsworth: Penguin Books.

Mackay, David, Thompson, Brian and Schaub, Pamela (1970) *Breakthrough to Literacy*, London: Longman (see especially Teacher's Manual).

Malinowski, B. (1923) 'The Problem of Meaning in Primitive Languages', Supplement 1 to C. K. Ogden and I. A. Richards *The Meaning of Meaning*, London: Kegan Paul (International Library of Psychology, Philosophy and Scientific Method).

— (1935) *Coral Gardens and their Magic, Volume II*, London: Allen and Unwin; New York: American Book Co.

Mallik, Bhaktiprasad (1972) *Language of the Underworld of West Bengal*, Calcutta: Sanskrit College (Research Series No. 76).

Martin, J. R. (1992) *English Text: System and Structure*, Amsterdam and Philadelphia: John Benjamins.

Matthiessen, Christian (1989) '[review of] M. A. K. Halliday: An Introduction to Functional Grammar' *Language* 65.3.

Mead, George Herbert (1934/1962) *Mind, Self and Society: From the Standpoint of a Social Behaviorist* (edited and with introduction by Charles W. Morris), Chicago: University of Chicago Press.

McIntosh, Angus (1963) '*As You Like It*: a grammatical clue to character', *A Review of English Literature* 4. Reprinted in Angus McIntosh and M. A. K. Halliday, *Patterns of Language: Essays in*

Theoretical, Descriptive and Applied Linguistics, London: Longman (Longman's Linguistics Library); Bloomington, Ind. : Indiana University Press 1966.

Milligan, Spike (1973) *More Goon Show Scripts: Written and Selected by Spike Milligan, with a Foreword by H. R. H. The Prince of Wales*, London: Sphere Books.

Mitchell, T. F. (1957) The language of buying and selling in Cyrenaica: a situational statement, *Hesperis* 26.

Mittins, W. H. (1970) *Attitudes to English Usage*, London: Oxford University Press (Language and Language Learning).

Mohan, B. A. (1969) *An Investigation of the Relationship between Language and Situational Factors in a Card Game, with Specific Attention to the Language of Instructions*, University of London Ph.D. thesis.

Molnos, Angela (1969) *Language Problems in Africa: a Bibliography and Summary*, Nairobi: East African Research Information Centre.

Morris, Desmond (1967) *The Naked Ape*, London: Jonathan Cape.

Nelson, Katherine (1971) 'Pre-syntactical strategies for learning to talk' (mimeographed).

Neustupný, Jiří V. (1971) 'Toward a model of linguistic distance', *Linguistic Communications* (Monash University) 5.

Opie, Iona and Opie, Peter (1959; 1967) *The Lore and Language of School Children*, Oxford: Clarendon Press.

Philp, Andrew (1968) *Attitudes to Correctness in English: a Linguistic View of Language in Use*, London: Longman (papers of the Programme in Linguistics and English Teaching, 6).

Pike, K. L. (1967) *Language in Relation to a Unified Theory of the Structure of Human Behaviour*. 2nd edn, revised, The Hague: Mouton (Janua Linguarum Series Major 24).

Podgórecki, Adam (1973) *"Second Life" and Its Implications* (mimeographed).

Priestley, J. B. (1934) *English Journey*, London: Heinemann in association with Gollancz.

Reid, T. B. W. (1956) 'Linguistics, structuralism, philology', *Archivum Linguisticum* 8.

Rubin, Joan (1968) 'Bilingual usage in Paraguay', in Fishman (ed.) 1968.

Sacks, Harvey, Schegloff, Emanuel and Jefferson, Gail (1974) 'A simplest systematics for the organization of turn-taking in conversation', *Language* 50.

—— (1964) 'On the analysis of natural conversation', in Dell H. Hymes (ed.) *Language in Culture and Society*, New York: Harper and Row.

Sacks, Harvey and Moerman, Michael (1988) 'On "understanding" in the analysis of natural conversation', in M. Moerman *Talking Culture: Ethnography and Conversation Analysis*, University of Pennsylvania Press, pp. 180–6.

Salgādo, Gāmini (ed.) (1972) *Cony-catchers and Bawdy Baskets: an Anthology of Elizabethan Low Life*, Harmondsworth: Penguin Books.

Sankoff, David (ed.) (1978) *Linguistic Variation: Models and Methods*, New York: Academic Press.

Sankoff, Gillian (1974) 'A quantitative paradigm for the study of communicative competence', in Richard Bauman and Joel Sherzer (eds) *Explorations in the Ethnography of Speaking*, Cambridge: Cambridge University Press.

Schegloff, Emanuel A (1968) 'Sequencing in conversational openings', *American Anthropologist*.

— (1971) 'Notes on a conversational practice: formulating place', in D. Sudnow (ed.) *Studies in Social Interaction*, Glencoe, Ill.: Free Press. Reprinted in Giglioli (ed.) 1972.

Schools Council (1968) *Programme in Linguistics and English Teaching 1–10 and Reading Lists*, London: Longman.

Shuy, Roger (ed.) (1971) *Sociolinguistics: a cross-disciplinary perspective*, Washington, DC: Center for Applied Linguistics.

Shuy, Roger, Wolfram, Walter A. and Riley, William K. (1967) *A Study of Social Dialects in Detroit*, Washington, DC: US Office of Education.

Sinclair, J. McH., Forsyth, I. J., Coulthard, R. M. and Ashby, M. (1972). *The English Used by Teachers and Pupils*, University of Birmingham, Department of English Language and Literature.

Spencer, John and Gregory, Michael J. (1964) 'An approach to the study of style', In Nils Erik Enkvist, John Spencer and Michael J. Gregory *Linguistics and Style*, London: Oxford University Press (*Language and Language Learning* 6).

Sykes-Davies, Hugh (1951) *Grammar Without Tears*, London: The Bodley Head.

Thornton, Geoffrey (1972) 'The language we acquire', in Doughty *et al.*, 1972.

Turner, Geoffrey (1973) 'Social class and children's language of control at age 5 and age 7', in Bernstein (ed.) 1973.

Turner, Geoffrey J. and Mohan, Bernard A. (1970) *A Linguistic Description and Computer Program for Children's Speech*, London:

Routledge and Kegan Paul (Primary Socialization, Language and Education).

Turner, G. J. and Pickvance, R. E. (1969) 'Social class differences in the expression of uncertainty in five-year-old children', *Language and Speech*. Reprinted in Bernstein (ed.) 1973.

Turner, Geoffrey J. 'Social class differences in the behaviour of mothers in regulative (social control) situations', University of London Institute of Education, Sociological Research Unit.

UNESCO (1953) *The Use of Vernacular Languages in Education*, Paris: UNESCO (Monographs on Fundamental Education 8).

Ure, Jean N. (1969) 'Practical registers: language in action' and 'Practical registers: collecting, describing, teaching', *English Language Teaching* 23.2, 3.

— (1971) 'Lexical density and register differentiation', in George Perren and J. L. M. Trim (eds) *Applications of Linguistics: selected papers of the Second International Congress of Applied Linguistics*, Cambridge: Cambridge University Press.

Ure, Jean N. and Ellis, Jeffrey (1972) 'Register in descriptive linguistics and linguistic sociology', in Oscar Uribe Villegas (ed.) *Las concepciones y problemas actuales de la sociolinguistica*, Mexico: University of Mexico Press.

Van Dijk, Teun A. (1972) *Some Aspects of Text Grammars: A Study in Theoretical Linguistics and Poetics*, The Hague: Mouton.

Wallwork, Jean F. (1969) *Language and Linguistics: an Introduction to the Study of Language*, London: Heinemann Educational.

Wegener, Philipp (1885) *Untersuchungen über die Grundfragen des Sprachlebens*, Halle: Niemeyer.

Weinreich, Uriel, Labov, William and Herzog, Marvin J. (1968) 'Empirical foundations for a theory of language change', in W. P. Lehmann and Y. Malkiel (eds) *Directions for Historical Linguistics: a Symposium*, Austin: University of Texas Press, 97–195.

Wexler, Peter (1955) *Etude sur la formation du vocabulaire des chemins-de-fer en français*, Genéve/Lille: Société de Publications Romanes et Françaises.

Whiteley, Wilfred H. (1969) *Swahili: the Rise of a National Language*, London: Methuen (Studies in African History 3).

Whiteley, Wilfred H. (ed.) (1971) *Language Use and Social Change: Problems of Multilingualism with Special Reference to Eastern Africa*, London: Oxford University Press (for International African Institute).

Whorf, Benjamin Lee (1956) *Language, Thought and Reality*, ed. J. B. Carroll, Cambridge, Mass.: MIT Press.

Wilkins, D. A., (1972) *Linguistics in Language Teaching*, London: Edward Arnold.

Wilkinson, A. (ed.) (1969) *The State of Language* (*Educational Review*, 22.1, University of Birmingham School of Education).

Wilkinson, Andrew (1971) *The Foundations of Language: Talking and Reading in Young Children*, London: Oxford University Press.

Williams, Frederick (ed.) (1970) *Language and Poverty: Perspectives on a Theme*, Chicago: Markham Press.

Wolfram, Walt (1971) 'Social dialects from a linguistic perspective', in *Sociolinguistics: a crossdisciplinary perspective*, Washington, DC: Center for Applied Linguistics.

Zumthor, Paul (1972) *Poétique médiévale*, Paris: Seuil.

INDEX

accent(s) 13-16, 30-34, 87, 109, 124-6, 230

adjectives 232, 234

adverb 232, 234

Africa 214, 236

ambilingual 7-8

anti-language(s) 249, 253-4, 265-9, 271, 273-5, 277, 279-86

anti-society 249, 253, 265-6, 274, 278, 281-2

attitude(s) 5, 7, 26-7, 30-7, 82, 96, 98, 123-6, 138, 160, 176, 184, 205, 207, 215, 228, 230, 255, 283

Bernstein, B. 43, 47, 49, 53, 56, 58, 62-4, 85-8, 91-2, 97, 101, 103, 129-30, 139-40, 142, 153, 160-4, 166-8, 176-80, 185-6, 211, 221-5, 228-40, 242-6, 268, 285

Bickerton, D. 175, 206

bilingual 7-8, 10, 208

Bourdieu, P. 270, 290

Britain 22, 26, 29, 32, 35-6, 87, 142, 161, 177, 227, 238

Cantonese 6, 11-13, 31

Chinese 6, 10, 12, 20, 22, 28, 31-2, 36, 213-17

Chomsky, N. 47-9, 76, 205-6, 235-7, 47-9, 76, 89, 205-6, 235-7

clause 17, 34, 51-2, 61, 113, 143, 155, 184, 239, 241

code 24, 58-9, 85-7, 92, 129-30, 134, 137-8, 140, 142, 160-3, 166, 168, 171-2, 177, 179, 181-3, 186, 197, 199-200, 211, 221-4, 225, 227, 229, 231, 233-46, 285

  elaborated 233-4, 238, 243-5

  restricted 60, 162, 224, 233-4

code-switching 132, 137, 175

cognitive 76, 153, 178, 183, 212

cohesion 190, 192, 239

collocation(s) 17-18, 196, 284

colloquial 21, 137, 204, 215

competence 8, 47-9, 62-3, 94, 134, 159, 167, 178, 213, 236

conversation(al) 17, 20, 22, 29, 45, 77, 110, 137, 143, 158, 210-11, 241, 271-3, 280, 283-4, 286

creole(s) 9-10, 29

creolization 132, 152, 171, 206

culture 44-5, 47, 66-7, 78, 82-5, 87-8, 97, 100-3, 106, 108, 117-18, 129, 137, 149, 151-2, 166-8, 170-2, 176-7, 179-80, 182-4, 193, 197-9, 201, 203, 207, 210-14, 221-2, 229, 234,

socialization 43, 45, 47, 52-3, 57-8, 64, 86-8, 91-2, 97-8, 100-3, 110, 117, 130, 132, 140, 162, 170-1, 176, 185, 198, 210, 212, 224, 228-9, 237, 245-6
  socializing 102, 140, 142, 155, 162, 164, 166, 177, 182, 196, 199, 212, 235, 239-40, 242
sociolinguistics 44, 59, 70, 131-2, 135, 143, 170-1, 174, 178
sociolinguistic
  competence 178
  context 143, 174, 183
  distance 215-16
  interpretation 144
  order 265, 282
  theory 41, 143, 177, 180, 185, 195
  universe 41, 146, 178, 195, 200, 213
sociology 49, 67, 70, 131-2, 137, 158, 167, 170, 210, 223, 231, 240
  sociological 46, 49, 51, 62, 64, 77, 97, 131, 133, 135-7, 139, 143, 145, 147, 149, 151, 153, 155, 157, 159, 161, 163, 165, 167, 170, 185-6, 210, 235, 238, 262
speech 14-15, 22-4, 27, 32-6, 46, 48, 51, 59-62, 74, 77-8, 81-2, 84, 86-7, 90, 93-5, 98, 104-8, 113-14, 119, 121-2, 125-6, 128-9, 132, 134-9, 142, 144, 146-7, 160-1, 163-6, 170-7, 179, 181, 191, 203-10, 221-2, 224, 227-8, 234-6, 238-40, 243, 252-3, 255, 258, 260, 265-6, 271, 276, 283
symbolic 57-9, 81-2, 86-8, 93, 132, 142, 153, 158, 164, 166, 171, 181-2, 185, 193, 196-7, 209, 249, 255, 258-9, 261
systemic 50, 241-3, 257

tenor 95, 105, 112-16, 118-9, 121, 123, 127, 134-6, 140, 181-2, 187, 192-3, 196-7, 199, 208-9, 259

tense 20, 52, 55, 148, 154, 158, 188, 230
terminology(-ies) 28, 75, 81, 150, 195, 207, 215-17
text 23, 42, 44-5, 61, 63, 93-5, 108, 113, 115, 119, 132-6, 140, 143-4, 146, 163, 171-4, 178-83, 185, 187-96, 198-200, 236-7, 239, 244, 258-9, 283-4, 286
  textual 18, 60-1, 88, 136, 143, 174, 183-4, 189, 192-3, 196, 199, 249, 251, 257-9, 267
  texture 184, 193, 199, 257

utterance(s) 20-1, 23-4, 29-30, 55-6, 61-2, 64, 80, 89, 90-1, 145-6, 170, 191, 194

variation
  dialect(al) 87, 109, 235, 242, 251-4, 260-1, 281-2
  linguistic 116, 139, 235, 237, 253
  register 93-4, 96, 105, 116, 242, 251, 254, 261
  sub-cultural 88, 200, 221, 236
verbal 55, 87, 103, 114, 120, 132, 134, 137, 142, 145, 161, 170-3, 175, 184, 194, 203-4, 209-10, 213, 230, 233-4, 237, 245, 254, 267-8, 272, 275, 284
vernacular 137, 217-18
vocabulary 55, 59, 80-1, 87, 94, 104, 106, 109, 112-13, 125-6, 133, 145, 149-50, 171, 178, 182, 212, 214-16, 225, 228, 232, 266
voice quality 17, 24, 33, 59, 114

Whorf, B.L. 129, 149, 234, 302
wording(s) 81, 98, 109-10, 115, 129, 199, 206, 232, 242-3, 259
written 5, 7, 12-3, 19-21, 25-6, 34-5, 37, 41, 90, 94-6, 100, 111-13, 116, 127, 130, 179-81, 184, 201, 207, 222, 225, 227